1996

REALISM

AND THE BIRTH OF
THE MODERN UNITED STATES

REALISM

AND THE BIRTH OF

THE MODERN UNITED STATES

Cinema, Literature, and Culture

STANLEY CORKIN

The University of Georgia Press

Athens and London

© 1996 by the University of Georgia Press
Athens, Georgia 30602
All rights reserved
Designed by Betty Palmer McDaniel
Set in 10/13 Galliard
by Tseng Information Systems, Inc.
Printed and bound by Braun-Brumfield
The paper in this book meets the guidelines for
permanence and durability of the Committee on
Production Guidelines for Book Longevity of the
Council on Library Resources.

Printed in the United States of America

oo   99   98   97   96   C   5   4   3   2   1

Library of Congress Cataloging in Publication Data

Corkin, Stanley.
Realism and the birth of the modern United States :
cinema, literature, and culture / Stanley Corkin.
p.   cm.
Revision of the author's thesis.
Includes bibliographical references and index.
ISBN 0-8203-1730-6 (alk. paper)
1. American fiction—20th century—History and
criticism.   2. Motion pictures—United States—History
and criticism.   3. Literature and motion pictures—
United States.   4. United States—Civilization—20th
century.   5. Realism in motion pictures.   6. Realism in
literature.   I. Title.
PS374.R37C67   1996
813'.520912—dc20   94-23968

British Library Cataloging in Publication Data available

For Joan

CONTENTS

ACKNOWLEDGMENTS

As I readily admit in my introduction, this book has been a long time in the making. Since I began it, I have relocated over several thousand miles, become the father of two children, lost several thousand hairs from my head, and, I like to think, grown significantly as a teacher and scholar. This study also has within it, though not visible to the naked eye, a remarkable story of the world of academic publishing. But I reserve the explicit details of that tale for other times and places.

The good things I have learned are of loyalty, selflessness, and good faith. Over the time I have written and rewritten this work I have been aided immeasurably by scholars in the field, all of whom have considerable responsibilities of their own but have been willing to read my work and discuss it at length. I do not necessarily know why this is, but I am thankful that it is. I have also been assisted by friends and family who, through the various ups and downs of this project, and of my work life in general, have offered their unflagging support. I have learned that if your confidence in yourself and your project is shaken, it is very difficult to write. This group of supporters has made the project's ultimate completion possible.

This study began as a dissertation, directed by Robert Sklar, ably assisted by David Reimers and Kenneth Silverman. Their guidance helped me to see the challenges of interdisciplinary scholarship and the directions I would need to take. Over the years, I have benefited from the encouragement and advice of Carol Flynn, Michael Kreyling, Eric Sundquist, Marjorie Roemer, Les Chard, Russel Durst, Tom LeClair, Jim Wilson, and Cynthia Lewiecki-Wilson. Dan LaBotz has assisted me to no end with his grasp of historiography and his extensive, and readily available, library. Other friends have helped me take necessary breaks to consider other vital matters (such as the fortunes of the Celtics and Red Sox, the state of the American cinema, the prospect of further athletics for men over forty): Charles O'Neill, John Lamb, Jeffrey Wolf, Elliot Glazer, Jonathan Neuhaus, Junior Backinoff, Nice Shot Herrmann, Bruce Bernard, and Dan Zins. My siblings, Susan Kalish, Michael Corkin, and Jonathan Corkin, have helped in untold ways. I would also like to acknowledge virtually all of

my colleagues at the University of Cincinnati for giving me a job and helping me to keep it, and I would like to single out my department chair, Jim
Hall, for his support. In the world of academia in the eighties and nineties,
these are no small matters. The Taft Memorial Fund at the University of
Cincinnati provided grants in the summers of 1988, 1990, and 1992, which
freed me from additional teaching.

As I revised this book, the acute readings and advice of Scott Simmon,
Michael Sprinker, Alan Trachtenberg, and the anonymous readers from the
University of Georgia Press have made my job easier and the manuscript
better. I would also like particularly to thank Walter Benn Michaels for his
interest in the project and his advice on the introduction. At Georgia, Gene
Adair's initial interest, Molly Thompson's assistance, and Malcolm Call's
ongoing commitment to this study were vital to its ultimate publication.

Back when this was barely an idea for a dissertation, Phyllis Frus and I
began trading ideas, then drafts. Over a decade later, she continued to read
drafts and discuss strategies for revision—with enthusiasm. I have benefited immeasurably from her encouragement and from her ability to read
the same chapters repeatedly and still find something likeable in them and
something significant to say about them.

I would like to express my appreciation to my parents, Marilyn and
Henry Corkin, who have provided invaluable moral and, at times, financial
support along the way. I also salute my children, Roxanne and Jesse, for
coming along and making life much more interesting and fun.

Above all, I wish to thank my wife, Joan Lichtman, who has been with
this project since before it was a project. Her unflagging belief, her good
humor, and her reminders that there is life outside the academy have made
possible whatever I have accomplished.

I acknowledge the permission of Praeger Publishers for allowing me to
reprint, in altered form, material that initially appeared in *A Moving Picture
Feast: A Filmgoers Hemingway,* edited by Charles Oliver, and that now appears in chapters 6 and 7; *Modern Fiction Studies,* which published an earlier
version of chapter 4; and *ETC.,* which published an earlier version of a
portion of chapter 3.

REALISM

AND THE BIRTH OF
THE MODERN UNITED STATES

ONE

Introduction

When I began this study some ten years ago, the field of cultural studies of the United States in the last part of the nineteenth and the first decades of the twentieth centuries looked quite different from the way it currently appears. In works that dealt primarily with the predominant objects of academic literary study from this period—realist and naturalist texts—the still reigning interpretations were the literary-historical works by Everett Carter, Edwin Cady, Warner Berthoff, Donald Pizer, and Larzer Ziff.[1] In general, these studies treated largely canonical works within a self-contained narrative of literary history. History was assumptive and unproblematic, and the goal of the critic was largely to define a body of works and determine their worth within a narrow context of other literary works. In the instances where a broader historical frame was noted, works of fiction were considered as expressions of the general impulse toward the democratization of American letters and, implicitly, as analogous to the broader cultural disposition toward democratic reform marked by Progressivism. This conception of the political reform movement was based in a historiography that preceded the new social history of the seventies and eighties and that largely ignored the various leftist revisions of this period that began to be published in the sixties. This interpretive stance was defined by a vision of the history of the United States as a series of crises and corrections that extended and refined the nation's democratic system, under the direction of a body—but not a class—of wise stewards of the common weal. This approach was exemplified by Daniel Aaron, Richard Hofstadter, George Mowry, and John Morton Blum.[2]

As I have written and rewritten my manuscript, this field of study has changed dramatically. In the eighties, the incidence of historical criticism in this area of literary studies became, if not dominant, then certainly commonplace. Scholars became disposed to consider texts—primarily works that had been valorized by the earlier literary historians and critics as "literary"—in relation to "history." Notably, studies by Christopher Wilson (*The Labor of Words*, 1985), Daniel Borus (*Writing Realism*, 1989), Walter Benn Michaels (*The Gold Standard and the Logic of Naturalism*, 1987), June Howard (*Form and History in American Literary Naturalism*, 1985), Amy Kaplan (*The Social Construction of American Realism*, 1988), Cecelia Tichi (*Shifting Gears*, 1987), and Miles Orvell (*The Real Thing*, 1989), posed historical questions to literary texts and, in the last two instances, to other types of aesthetic production.[3] Indeed, as historical criticism became fashionable within the academy, American literary realism and naturalism became focal subjects for reinterpretation. This strikes me as logical: because of their authors' relatively unproblematic idea of the relationship between the text and the world, the genres named as "realism" and "naturalism" by their practitioners and subsequent critics and scholars clearly had some distinct basis for being connected to contemporary historical practices. In this regard my study, in its consideration of textual productions in historical terms, begins with assumptions that can be found in a range of works written in the eighties. Yet, though all those works relate the literary text to larger historical occurrences of the period, they do so by substantially incorporating those events within the broad methodologies traditional to their discipline or area: in the case of those concerned with literary texts, it is textual analysis (Michaels, Howard, Kaplan) or literary history (Wilson and Borus); for those working within the methodologies of American studies, it is the cultural history of aesthetic forms (Tichi and Orvell).

What I have tried to do is somewhat different in method and result from any of these works. Rather than incorporating historical concerns within what methodologically remain studies of the aesthetic, I have studied imaginative works within a framework that employs disciplinary conventions of historical study. By this I mean my central question is not, as it largely is for the five textual analyses (Michaels, Howard, Kaplan, Tichi, and Orvell), What can we make of these writings by connecting them with the text of history through the methods of poststructuralism? This approach results in cases of extreme presentism. The concerns of my study are focally contextual: my central question is, What pieces of the historical puzzle did, and do, these texts constitute?

While recognizing that by now the act of posing historical questions to texts of this period has been done, and frequently, I insist upon the power of my method to redraw this period in a distinctive manner. As I wrote and rewrote this study, I added dimensions of historical explanation during each revision. What I found by delving deeper into histories of the period was that these imaginative texts did not create a world of their own.

The narrative defined by the literary canon of this period *really was* one of complicity in the broader social reorganization of American life from the top down. The best way to understand these texts in their history and as history is not to subject them to anachronistic reading strategies culled from poststructural insights, but to read *along* with them within the currents suggested by the most salient and convincing historical accounts of the period. Such a strategy seeks a sense of what these works looked like to those encountering them in the years before and after the turn of the twentieth century.

Since I am asserting the efficacy of the materialist narrative in which I embed my chosen texts, I note my debt to those who have been so prominent in recasting this period historiographically: Gabriel Kolko, James Weinstein, and, most saliently for the purposes of this study, Martin Sklar. This does not mean that I accept either their theses or their arguments in support of those theses in their entirety. My discussion locates—in the specific terms of these texts—a cultural process that complements the one detailed in Kolko's *The Triumph of Conservatism,* Weinstein's *The Corporate Ideal in the Liberal State,* and, most recently, Martin Sklar's *The Corporate Reconstruction of American Capitalism, 1890–1916.* In the general narrative of these historians, reform impulses were employed to create an entrenched bureaucracy in the attempt to regulate the vagaries of the marketplace so as to ensure the dominance of prevailing economic interests. Weinstein describes the social means by which dissent was contained, while Kolko characterizes the expressly political but ultimately economic means. Sklar details with precision the specific corporate decisions that informed this larger process. Indeed, Sklar's work is most persuasive in the way his broad conception is able to explain the logic of a number of specific corporate and political actions. James Livingston's study, *The Origins of the Federal Reserve System,* also lends weight to Sklar's view of this period with insightful and detailed analysis of banking reform from 1890 to 1913. In these analyses, the Progressive idea of reform helped create a class of experts, drawn from the business community or upper classes, who exercised political power to effect a "rational" economic and social order. The ideal of the movement was efficiency, which these historians reveal as a distinctly antidemocratic impulse. This view is at odds with those who see Progressivism as embodying a benign desire for the greatest good for the most people. Rather, Kolko, Weinstein, and Sklar argue that the ideal of efficiency was a means of minimizing the effect of those who posed a threat to corporate capitalism, while attempting seamlessly to offer a system that secured a "neutral" bureaucracy; this created an order that "worked." Progressivism invoked itself as inevitable, like progress itself, and thereby repressed alternative modes of economic and cultural reorganization. Since its system of structuring the workplace depended on high-level managers being ensconced as "experts," Progressive reform largely occurred from the top down. This strategy allows only for adjustments within its hierarchical methods, but resists questions of their basis. Indeed, to invest physical and metaphysical authority in a class named "expert" tends to mystify relations of production and resulting striations of class.[4]

I believe that the reigning impulses of Progressivism, as I have characterized them, are behind the prevailing worldview of the realist text, both literary and cinematic. I argue that realism and its derivative, naturalism, and naturalism's derivative, modernism, all aimed intrinsically at furthering a definition of being generalized from the same assumptions and intentions that produced Progressivism.

Thus, I would argue that the politics, and therefore the historiography, and therefore the method of my study are quite different from any of the recent historicist-literary works mentioned (though this is a more significant assertion in regard to those whose studies focus primarily on texts). I also believe—and perhaps this is a rather obvious point—that the historical dimension of my study, while certainly not the only one acceptable, paints a more compelling picture of the cultural expressions considered and their contemporary and subsequent reception than any of those noted. Indeed, because it is insistently historical in its constant attention to extratextual matters, quite precise in its readings, and not subject to rigid and illogical periodization, my work synthesizes the best of these three approaches: textual analysis, literary history, and the cultural history of aesthetic objects. I employ the first group's textual specificity, the second's historicity, and the third's chronological sweep. Though I could easily argue that the works of cinema and literature I discuss are *both* hegemonic and utopian in their impulses, I feel such discussion begs the historical question of what these works meant *within* a culture where specific activities to reorder social and economic activity from the top down were coalescing in business, politics, and social life.[5] I willingly follow the cautions of Robert Darnton, who points out, "By paying heed to history, literary critics may avoid the danger of anachronism; for they sometimes seem to assume that seventeenth-century Englishmen read Milton and Bunyan as if they were twentieth-century college professors" (181). Indeed, if we are to rewrite history with the intention of altering our hierarchies, then it is necessary to bring to light implicit aspects of prevailing cultural explanations. That is, we ought to question the manner by which we have arrived at these explanations through a close consideration of the material conditions that these explanations elevate or suppress.

Logically, the most historically minded of the studies named are those that employ the traditions of literary history. When literary history became a viable method of scholarship in the American academy in the twenties and thirties, it was developed as a means of providing rigor and rational method to the discipline of "English." As such, its narratives mirrored historical narratives in method and conclusion, but it maintained the separateness of its enterprise by defining the story of aesthetic movements in fairly narrow disciplinary terms.[6] Unlike those working in textual analysis, Christopher Wilson in *The Labor of Words* and Daniel Borus in *Reading Realism* employ a material conception of history and base their discussion on documents—texts, papers, letters—that are usual to historical methodology. Borus and Wilson engage in a specificity of reference but a relative narrowness of cause and effect. This is not to say that broad cultural conceptions of this period do not inform these studies. But both scholars primarily show how the predominant historical metaphors of the period work as a means of defining the relatively circumscribed activities of writers. That is, the somewhat narrow focus of both discussions on specific writers and writings limits treatment of their broader activities, on the one hand, and, on the other, restricts consideration of other textual expressions that resonate with the same themes. These studies, then, tend to locate the writer's enterprise within the literary culture of the day, as opposed to considering the larger ramifications of the writer and his or her writings. I am not, however, minimizing the value of these works. I found them informative and relevant to my discussion of publishing markets and the reading public. They are, however, distinct from my study in their method and focus.[7]

Howard, Michaels, and Kaplan all consider key writers and texts with an eye toward broader historical context. In this way, their works are in the same vein as my own study. Yet, in a vital and finally reorienting way, my concept of the period and my objects of study differ from theirs. Rather than invoking history only as a text and thus subject to the poststructuralist methods of reading common to many disciplines in the eighties and nineties, I believe in the materiality of historical actions and, correspondingly, find the cycle of cause and effect that defines the dynamic relationship between theory and practice rooted in practice, and in economic practice at that.

In *The Gold Standard and the Logic of Naturalism,* Walter Benn Michaels brought together a body of essays that he had begun publishing in 1980. To a large degree, as they first appeared his essays were instrumental in reconfiguring the study of late-nineteenth- and early-twentieth-century American literature. Michaels professes no political agenda, nor does he consider the terms of composition or reception of the works he discusses. Indeed, for Michaels history is a given, always already there and always assuming a comprehensible outline defined by its dominant strain. As a shrewd and insightful reader of texts and a masterful delineator of complex forms of argumentation, Michaels shows the nuanced agreements and distinctions among texts by figures from Dreiser to Karl Marx to David Ricardo to Adam Smith to Thorstein Veblen; from Frank Norris to Josiah Royce to Ignatius Donnelly to Tom Watson to Henry Lloyd. For example, Michaels astutely locates Dreiser's concept of the individual as similar to the definitions espoused by Adam Smith and David Ricardo in their formative theories of the mechanisms of market economies (31–58). In a later discussion, he shows how Frank Norris's extrahuman personification of the modern corporation disavows the populist tenets of Tom Watson and Ignatius Donnelly as it embraces the terms put forth in various legal decisions of the day that declared, "The man is not the company and the company is not the man, because the company, 'by fiction of law' is another man" (198). Yet, missing from his discussion is a detailing of material occurrence. Indeed, specific events are largely subsumed under the overarching concept of the system, capitalism, that provides his outline for history. Michaels's definition of context, then, is a broad sense of epoch and a precise reading of certain eminent nonliterary intellectual figures who write at the time of a particular novel's publication. As a history of ideas, then, this work is provocative and exemplary, but missing is an idea of causality that includes a precise construction of the material context in which those ideas either flourished or foundered.[8]

Amy Kaplan, in *The Social Construction of American Realism,* reads through her primary materials, novels, with an eye toward the manner in which they inscribe and disrupt social hierarchies. Realism in this case is a mediate form negotiating between high culture and the marketplace of mass culture. In this reading, realism becomes a mode of expression concerned distinctly with these abstract terms and therefore remote from the range of concrete referents that they address. This stance allows Kaplan to focus on the ways in which texts employ their apparently representational strategies to devise a decidedly nonreferential organization of their narratives.

One may then ask how she conceives of history and how she incorporates that conception within her study. Writes Kaplan, "This study attempts to recuperate realism's relation to social change not as a static background which novels either naively record or heroically evade, but as a foreground of the narrative structure of each novel" (9). In such a formulation social change becomes a rather broad description of a range of historical events. Indeed, such a term leads the study away from actual occurrence. Events contemporary with her study become the circumstances that prefigure the text but not circumstances to which the text refers. Thus, from a materialist point of view, her analysis leaves behind the historicity of the realist text. For example, Howells's New York in *A Hazard of New Fortunes* becomes, substantially, *only* his New York, with no further relationship to the real. History, then, as a body of things that happened, remains remote from the texts she considers and from the text she writes.

In June Howard's *Form and History in American Literary Naturalism*, history is far more central. She writes, "It is my hope that this study will bring my readers, as it has me, to a recognition of the irrevocable openness of any historical moment and an apprehension of naturalism not as an example in a gallery of literary types but as a dynamic solution to the problem of generating narrative out of the particular historical and cultural materials that offered themselves to these writers" (xi). Indeed, of these three scholars, I do find her use of historical materials the most compelling, and I broadly agree with her analysis of the cultural role of naturalism. But I would argue that the questions she asks are primarily questions of interpretation that remain textual, questions that privilege the literary text as an object of analysis. While Howard attempts to write "a new literary history" (182), my own study attempts to reincorporate literary studies within an interdisciplinary study of culture. This distinction is vital. Howard's method leaves her somewhat distanced from her historical object as it develops that object through a consideration of literary works. The result is a dynamic view of Frank Norris and Jack London but a somewhat static view of the period. Fittingly, because such a method subordinates its details to more abstract discussion, her historical sources are generally synthesizers with broad overviews of the period (Wiebe, Boorstin, Mowry) and largely within the liberal consensus tradition. This tendency toward overview and abstraction is most apparent, it seems to me, in her discussion of the reader. In these instances, she considers the reader implied by the formal properties of the text and not the reader in a given historical circumstance (24–25, 104–6).

Notable in these three works is a disposition by each writer to approach the period through a single and narrow illustrative term. That is, Kaplan substantially restricts her discussion to "realism," while Michaels and Howard stick primarily to "naturalism." This narrowness seems illogical in works that profess historicity. Realism and naturalism, in an historical sense, are closely related. Indeed, if one employs these terms as part of an historical project, it seems necessary to include *both*. Only by insisting on the juxtaposition of these terms can we locate the specific transitions that are crucial to historical narratives. In this case, considered together, realism and naturalism reveal a broader range of continuity and a lesser proportion of change. In these studies, however, the various apparatuses of textual analysis are not suited to defining historical movements, because of an excessively idealist conception of history. When history is viewed with an overemphasis on its textuality, nuanced distinctions may be lost in a maze comprised of interpretive devices. Such methodologies diminish the prominence of their material objects of scrutiny. In their emphasis on the literary, then, these three studies cannot account for the material changes that are focal to understanding a period historically. Indeed, if such material considerations did occur in these works, the type of discussion offered in each would necessarily undergo substantial alteration.

If these literary studies eschew considerations of history as a body of events that actually happened and therefore invoke contextual occurrences only as a kind of remote cause, the studies of this period that attempt to develop a broad cultural framework for considering works of literature in conjunction with art, photography, and other aesthetic objects glaringly reveal the limitations of the traditional American Studies approach to historical analysis. In their interdisciplinary scope, these works are perhaps most like my own. In their analytical assumptions, however, they are possibly the most at odds. Within these studies looms the ghost of myth and symbol criticism. That is, they employ a method, traditional to a type of American Studies scholarship, that defines a period by locating recurring aesthetic figures within a body of cultural works. The recurrence of these figures apparently, as Steven Watts notes, "unif[ies] a genuinely American culture" (625). This method became central during the fifties and results from the Cold War basis and mission of this area of study. It is strongly identified with scholars such as Henry Nash Smith, Leo Marx, and R. W. B. Lewis, among others.[9] By drawing on this tradition, Cecelia Tichi's *Shifting Gears* (1987) and Miles Orvell's *The Real Thing* (1989) reproduce its tendency to make history the procession of forms, which, as they invoke them, are immediately reduced from three dimensions to two. That is, concrete historical objects are aestheticized and replotted within a formalizing narrative.

Tichi's study celebrates the onset of "the modern" in the early years of the twentieth century. This movement is defined formally: she argues "that a technological revolution is a revolution not only of science and technology but of language, of fiction, and ultimately of poetry" (16). In this idealist construction of "culture," Tichi begs vital material questions. Thus, she can discuss Taylorism not as a means of reorganizing the shop floor to ensconce managers as the sole voice of authority, but as an inspiration for William Carlos Williams's poetry, providing "[an] entry to the poetry of the gear and girder world" (262). Orvell, not as celebratory of modernist aesthetics (wherever encountered) as Tichi, finds Taylor an inspiration for modern design, though he does note briefly "the effects of Taylorization on factory organization" (192–93). Despite this aside, however, Orvell by his own admission studies the succession of aesthetic (and aestheticized) forms "where the art work has the power to define reality by altering our consciousness, but sets it in the context of a cultural dynamic that it is the critic's business, in turn, to elucidate" (xx). His study is organized around questions of authenticity, which use as their point of departure not industrial growth and its social effects but Walt Whitman's poetry, as an expression of "art appropriate to the conditions of the country" (3). I subordinate the role of art and consider particular imaginative expressions as initially responsive to material conditions and then, conceivably, as instrumental in the reproduction of related conditions. Thus, for me the role of the railroad in the American economy—a fact—is far more central than Whitman's reproduction of its image in poetry. Indeed, in both of these works, to quote that great modernist Gertrude Stein, there is no there there. That is, change is reduced to its formalized expression in aesthetic objects within a vision of history that is itself largely aesthetic. Thus, we lose sight of the consequences of specific shifts in material practice, such as Taylorization. In this context, machines can become virtual poems. This method not only neglects materialist considerations but also actually dematerializes concrete objects. Indeed, Jackson Lears's comment in a review of *The Real Thing* aptly describes Tichi's work as well:

Posing the questions in this narrow framework allows one to overlook the darker dimensions of industrialization: the creation of new organizational hierarchies in political and economic life, of new forms of inequality, far more thoroughly elaborated in government and business than those of Whitman's time had been. By divorcing the machine from its institutional expression in the modern corporation and the bureaucratic state, Orvell can endorse [Gustav] Stickley's preposterous claim that the 20th century would be "the Age of the people"—a statement made in 1907, at precisely the same historical moment when regulatory and corporate elites began to insulate public policy from popular influence. (37–38)

Though my study is not one of primary historical investigation, I draw on a significant body of historians who broadly agree on the material outlines of the period; this list includes economic, social, labor, and intellectual historians where appropriate. My study grew from the double insight that some central cultural figures and texts from around the turn of the century exhibited and expressed similar worldviews, and that these figures and expressions all may be viewed as determined by and determining their material historical circumstances. My conception of the period allows me to see the range of organized and less organized activities of both a residual and an emerging upper class and the various effects of these activities. Because I largely accept certain historical explanations of "what happened" at this juncture in American history, my study is clearly not designed to reformulate the period materially. However, I do situate key aesthetic movements of this period in a way that allows us to reconceive their cultural role and legacy.

I will not argue for the primacy of the imaginative forms I consider. Indeed, their specific qualities, as I encounter them in my study, suggest the degree to which the imagination of a certain class and of those identifying with that class may be circumscribed by real conditions. Those working with uncritical liberal assumptions may view such a perspective as reductive, but this judgment seems predicated on the imagination of a world where such class relations do not exist and therefore all forms of thought and expression are always equally possible. It also maintains the conventional privileging of the aesthetic object in positing that object beyond its context and asserting its greater value. In each instance, this liberal critique exhibits the myopia of its own unexamined worldview.[10]

My study begins with a close consideration of William Dean Howells as an historical figure and of his highly influential critical writings. I examine his role in effecting an historical transition toward increasingly narrow and reified conceptions of the world. My reason for such a view stems from my reading of his politics, which we may now call liberal in their employment on the spectrum of U.S. politics, but which I generally refer to as conservative in my study. My use of the word *conservative* in this case locates his desire for order, his basic impulse to conserve to the degree possible that element of the older organizing hierarchy and systems of United States life. By paying attention to Howells the historical figure and not simply to the Howellsian text, I have located his wide sphere of influence in literature and politics. This has helped me to avoid being misled by such features of his career as his involvement in the discussion of the fate of the Haymarket defendants or his Christian Socialism that, if viewed without sufficient attention to the history of the period, might be interpreted as more radical than they were.

By beginning with Howells and locating him in this manner, I develop a different conception of literary realism than any of the textual explication group. By noting this specific distinction between my understanding of literary realism and these others', I mean to illuminate broader methodological contrasts. Thus, by avoiding the specific historical role of Howells in postbellum literature and politics, Michaels can declare him an anticapitalist, Howard can all but ignore him and move on to naturalism, while Tichi can ignore him and move on to modernism. Orvell, while aptly describing Howells's literary goals, limits his broader cultural role, his personal and public politics, and his specific interventions in the literary marketplace. Kaplan well discusses Howells's centrality and the social issues—class conflict, uprootedness—that concern him. However, since I am concerned with material change and the implications of these literary movements for and within that change, I read Howells the man *and* his writings with an eye toward broad historical occurrence, that is, the reorganization of American business and politics.

Again, this type of materialist reading is enabled by my attention to and belief in material context. I take Howells and his writings beyond a role that is simply mediating and show his class interests and their textual consequences. In doing so, I have found that the politics of literary realism were nominally progressive, but only in the limited terms of the political movement named Progressivism. By noting Howells's various roles in the political, economic, and literary culture of the day, we can see that realism is not simply a matter of textuality but also a means of naming a body of social interventions.

In part I of my study, "The Real," I look at Howells and Thomas Edison as key figures. I assert that these men acted somewhat alike and that these similarities not only reveal an affinity with a range of other activities defining the period, but influence those activities as well. This makes sense when we consider these individuals contextually. Indeed, how would we define a person's centrality if we could not plot an area of activities and individuals that he influenced or note a body of expressions among his contemporaries that reveal similar views of the world? To join these two figures in this section is to assert that these men, defined as central, co-incide to some notable degree in thought and actions. By locating figures from two media but within the same materially defined historical epoch, I avoid the pitfalls of the other five studies cited. I cannot make broad claims for the cultural based solely on literary expressions, nor can I, be-cause my historical frame is so insistent, reduce historical occurrence to an aestheticized procession of forms.

This first section anchors my study in concrete economic and social prac-tice. The succeeding sections, "The Natural" and "The Modern," detail the gradual cultural tendency to abstract matters of material life into increas-ingly mystifying ideological terms. In these sections, Raymond Williams's truism that "certain forms of social relationships are deeply embodied in certain forms of art" (148) fueled my investigation. I found that works of the imagination that claim "realism" assert a material and social world already made and that such texts, within a given historical situation, draw readers/viewers to them through their neatness of structure and their as-sertions of "the way things are." Thus, in part 2, the naturalist text—here Dreiser's *Sister Carrie* and Edwin Porter's *The Great Train Robbery* and *Life of an American Fireman*—can be seen as assuming the existence and persis-tence of the mass-produced commodity and therefore as concerned with the naming and marketing of that object. In part 3, "The Modern," we can see D. W. Griffith (in *The Birth of a Nation*) and Ernest Hemingway (in *In Our Time*) devising strategies of expression that attempt to remove the commodity from its economic basis altogether. They offer it as a reifica-tion, a pristine object in and of itself, acontextually aestheticized and highly intellectualized.

In each section, then, the materials I consider in relation to my chosen texts reveal this process of increasing mystification within the material context of successive capitalist formations. Part 1 draws on economic, tech-nological, and labor history; part 2 brings in historians of mass culture, including advertising; part 3 deals with the culture of professionalization, including that of modern psychology and historiography. In this list, I point out the changing elements of my discussion, as I move, as is appropri-ate, increasingly to superstructural matters. But in each case I reiterate the connection of these increasingly mystified and mystifying expressions to the "realist" cultural project I detailed in part I. Thus, Hemingway's *In Our Time* does not merely assert the terms of modern psychology, but also the specific strategies of scientific management. Similarly, Griffith's *The Birth of a Nation* does not simply recapitulate a form of historical investigation, but is also complicit in the specific contemporary social acts of segregation.

In ways my study draws on an earlier work, Jackson Lears's *No Place of Grace* (1982), a study that is culturally insightful and historically grounded. His meticulous tracing of the resistance to modernity that occurred among a body of upper-class Americans suggested to me that looking at key texts as the expressions of enthusiasm for modern life might be a mistake. Indeed, my conclusions largely complement Lears's in that I trace a range of cultural practices that belong more considerably to a nascent upper-middle class which, while not resisting change in a manner akin to that of older elites, attempts to find ways of restricting it in a specific manner, thus asserting the need to maintain crucial elements of an older social order.

In this study I emphasize the fallacy of considering realism in its various permutations as the textual culmination of the democratic impulse. My reason for doing this is not to create a response of despair or to assert inevitability. At the core of this study is a belief that out of critical consideration of the assumed natural structures of everyday existence can come possibilities that truly are democratic. In its usual application, the Gramscian idea of hegemony is used as a means of explaining how entrenched social and economic groups rule by coercion and not by violence. The process I consider conforms to this description in that the realist text, in my view, promotes ideological limitation and compliance. But by elaborating the terms of this coercion, I seek to bring about its dialectic alteration. In Gramsci's definition, hegemony also constitutes a practice that negates and alters this coercion. As Gramsci's interpreter Walter Adamson explains: "The hegemonic level represents the advance to a 'class consciousness,' where class is understood not only economically but also in terms of a common intellectual and moral awareness, a common culture. . . . What [Gramsci] did argue was that the attainment of an alternative hegemony was necessary before one could even hope for a 'complete' revolution" (171). This alternative hegemony is based on a level of critical awareness that cuts through previous forms of mystification. My intention is to elaborate these modes of cultural coercion in anticipation of their eventual status as archaeological curiosities.

PART ONE

The Real

TWO

William Dean Howells

and the Order of Progress

It is the intention of this chapter to reconsider the cultural event named *literary realism*. In the United States, the social conflicts of the last thirty years of the nineteenth century culminated in structures of social and economic organization that have promoted the hegemony of a capitalist class into our own time. I situate this literary mode in its historical context to reveal it as a part of that history, as an expressive device that seeks to promote the values of order and continuity. In this view, literary realism works *with* the other ideologically loaded tropes that promote the persistence and dominance of that class: positivism, elitism, aestheticism, sexism, racism. Thus, it produces and reproduces the political and cultural agenda of corporate liberalism.

Corporate liberalism is an ideology and a method of social and economic organization that employs the government as a means of promoting consensus and continuity by allowing it to provide the basis of the modern welfare state through what its proponents called "positive government." The rationale behind such a vision of government, as Martin Sklar explains, is to assure "the greatest possible preservation of private initiative and private property ownership, as against state direction and ownership." He goes on: "On this basis, upper- and middle-class leadership could preside over progressive reform as an alternative to reform or revolution from below. Party politics could be sustained as a mode of inter-class alignment and cooperation, rather than its being permitted to divide along class lines, with all the apocalyptic implications" (38–39). At the core of such a program is the concept of rational management. Progressivism couched its manipulations in the philosophy of positivism and the rhetoric of order. Progressives asserted the efficacy of their methods by coopting the term "efficiency" and defining its managerial strategies as "scientific." In this managerial model passions of the age could be tamed in the interest of a specific concept of order—but one which hid its ideology behind its ruse of objectivity.[1]

While it is true that American literary realism often does employ figures of other than an elite class as its object, this literary mode, I believe, is best understood as a device that works to accustom Americans of the Gilded Age, primarily those of the older elites and the emerging middle class, to the ideological verities of corporate liberalism. By reaching out to such an audience, realism speaks primarily to the converted and the easily converted, individuals whose interests are served by this particular social perspective. The realist text seeks compliance and represses dissonance. Its methods of asserting its relation to the real largely result from its use of a philosophy of composition that mimics and anticipates the precepts of the positive social sciences, and it thereby engages in a similar process of objectification and containment. Literary realism, then, as a cultural phenomenon produced and reproduced the assumptions of corporate liberalism: rationality, continuity, and the efficacy of a bureaucracy of technocrats.

My primary means of defining this method of writing is by focusing on the novelist and critic William Dean Howells, whose influence in the world of letters and beyond peaked in the last quarter of the nineteenth century. He had made the cause of realism his own by the mid-1880s with his "Reviews and Literary Notices" in the *Atlantic Monthly* from 1868 to 1881; but his most focused and sustained assertions of the realist method were pronounced in his "Editor's Study" columns in *Harper's New Monthly*, beginning in early 1886 and ending in March of 1892. In these columns Howells explicitly codifies the critical terms of this movement, and in his various novels of this period, he further considers his realist precepts.[2] In addition to examining Howells's critical writings, I will look closely at *The Rise of Silas Lapham* (1885) in order to explore the ideology of his method. This novel, as Donald Pease notes, was central in establishing Howells's reputation as a novelist and has been a key text for a variety of critical methods since it appeared. Though the novel does not exactly conform to the outlines defined in Howells's critical writings, it stands as his fullest fictional expression of the realist agenda.[3]

Connecting Howells with the realist movement in American letters is not a means of declaring him its inventor. Many of the characteristic features of this form appear as early as the 1850s and 1860s in works by Elizabeth Barstow Stoddard, Rebecca Harding Davis, and Frederick Douglass, for example. Writers such as Davis, Douglass, and Stoddard provide compelling visions of American social life by integrating objective description of extreme economic circumstances and subjective discussions of suffering.[4] Indeed, all these authors use the descriptive mode of composition to typify the oppressions of incipient industrialization, discrimination against women, and racism. Howells's cultural legacy was to preside over the homogenizing of this form into an increasingly distanced vision of American life, a vision that reified concrete reality by asserting a world already made. Howells's realism relates to this earlier version but shifts the emphasis of this project from contestation to confirmation. Howellsian realism shows the correctness of the textual devices that assert the objectivity of this form while providing a vision of a world that can be rationally managed by an enlightened class.

William Dean Howells's effective career as a novelist and critic fits perfectly into the era generally described as the Gilded Age, a term devised by his friends Samuel Clemens and Charles Dudley Warner to name the last thirty years of the nineteenth century. This central figure in that world of American letters achieved prominence through his ability to manage the politics of his profession and because his particular view of writing (he would call it literature) so well expressed the historical moment of the rising managerial class in America. Much as Progressive politicians averted the bald statement of their own class interests when they put forth their plans for restructuring American social life—they generally couched their rationales in terms of "common good" or "efficiency"—Howells, both as writer and as a critic, buried the historically specific cultural agenda of realism in the rhetoric of transcendence. His critical writings readily conflate the scientist's fact with the philosopher's truth as he makes his realism a method for revealing nature: including an essentialized concept of human nature. According to Howells, the realist "cannot look upon human life and declare this thing and that thing unworthy of notice, any more than the scientist can declare a fact of the material world beneath the dignity of his inquiry. He feels in every nerve the equality of things and the unity of men; his soul is exalted, not by vain shows and shadows and ideals, but by realities in which alone the truth lives" (*Criticism and Fiction* 15). In doing so the realist asserts, through the tropes of realism, not only that literature can and must reflect actuality, but also that the actuality of late nineteenth-century America was at its core beneficent and stable—if a keen observer could see through to its focal qualities.

The movements of Howells's life in many ways typify the broader social movements of Americans during the period after the Civil War. As America was in the process of becoming a primarily urban nation, so did Howells gradually move to larger and larger cities. The writer, born in Martinsville, Ohio, in 1837, after a peripatetic childhood in which he moved to various small towns and cities in Ohio, gravitated toward larger metropolises: first in Ohio—Columbus and Cincinnati—and then in the Northeast—to Boston and New York. Like most Americans involved in this process of moving to population centers, Howells was driven by economic motivations. He came to Columbus as a political reporter for the *Cincinnati Gazette* in 1856, moved to Cincinnati to become the city editor for that newspaper in 1857 and returned to Columbus in 1858 to write for the *Ohio State Journal*. In 1865, upon returning from a consular post in Venice, Howells settled in Boston to work at the *Atlantic*. As New York houses increasingly dominated the American publishing industry, Howells after 1888 began to spend substantial amounts of time there and made that city his primary residence from 1890 to his death in 1920.

While the general analogy applies between Howells and the mass of Americans in motion in the late nineteenth century, at a more refined point of comparison it begins to break down. Unlike most Americans, Howells exerted considerable influence on a cross section of American culture. For example, in 1861, when many Americans of modest means were being conscripted to serve in the Civil War, Howells was sailing off to Venice. By then he had already published a number of poems in the *Atlantic* and the *Saturday Press* and, perhaps more significantly, a campaign biography of Lincoln. Ohio governor Salmon Chase, among others, recommended Howells to Lincoln's secretaries John Nicolay and John Hay for a consular post. Howells himself wrote to the poet-politician John Hay in June of 1861 to promote his chances, knowing that Hay was familiar with his poetry and seeking to capitalize on his (limited) celebrity. This appointment served as the springboard for Howells's future success: it established him as a rising young figure in the world of American letters and introduced him to the avenues of power in America. It also signified Howells' political savvy and ambition. Throughout his life Howells traveled in circles of political power and achieved distinction within those circles. Hay himself, a man whose political fortunes ascended throughout the nineteenth century and into the first years of the twentieth, remained a friend of Howells after this initial encounter.

Rather than fitting the common romantic conception of the solitary artist, Howells was very much a man of the world. He sought to merge art, economics, and politics through his thoughts, words, and deeds. Realism expresses this synthesis in its conception, mode of dissemination, and desired effect. It was a method that reproduced the ideology of corporate management, a product for the booming magazine market and disseminated in that market, and a means of promoting the persistence of a political and economic elite. Critics who accept the Howellsian definition of the "common" do so at the risk of reproducing his mystifying attempt to make this explicitly worldly literature transcendent.

His political intentions and savvy mark his career. In his 1860 visit to Boston, for example, his first impulse was to contact the influential James Russell Lowell. Explains Kenneth Lynn, "He had decided that James Russell Lowell was the first writer he would try to see. The decision was not made on the ground of literary preference but because Lowell was the editor of the *Atlantic Monthly*, and, as such, was one of the prime authority figures in Boston culture" (*William Dean Howells* 92). The gesture of seeing Lowell typifies Howells's lifelong impulses. Howells was a figure who was powerful in the often intertwined worlds of American letters and American politics of the Gilded Age, attaining and maintaining relationships with Presidents Hayes (his wife's cousin) and James A. Garfield, while often intervening to assist in the political appointments of his fellow writers, such as Bret Harte. Howells was able to repay his friend John Hay by helping to patch up a political feud with Hayes, and thereby assisted in Hay's appointment as assistant secretary of state in 1879 (Monteiro and Murphy 38–39).

Howells's access to power and the way in which literary realism figures within the broader expanse of this era of American history in no way alter the fact that he became skeptical of the direction of American social life in the last years of the nineteenth century. Though we can plot the development of this skepticism from the event of the Haymarket riot in Chicago in 1886, this ebbing of faith became pronounced some time close to the turn of the century and focused on the occupation of the Philippines. Indeed, Howells's response to the Haymarket bombing also allows us to see his strategies for addressing the chaos caused by class struggle, strategies that also define corporate liberalism.

On May 4 a bomb exploded in the midst of a labor rally as the police attempted to disperse it: one policeman died and six were injured. The Chicago police immediately rounded up seven known German anarchists. Four were hanged in the autumn of 1887. In his writings and letters Howells took an ardent and unpopular stance for the commutation of the death penalties of the seven. While Howells certainly behaved admirably in this circumstance, he did not support the political goals of these anarchists:

rather, he felt that they had not received their fair due from the American judiciary system. In a letter to John Greenleaf Whittier on November 1, 1887, in which he tries to enlist the poet to his cause, Howells writes, "The fact is, these men were sentenced for murder when they ought to have been indicted for conspiracy" (*Letters* 3:198). This case defined for Howells the existence of class antagonisms in America and the need for disinterested mediation to redress such antipathies. If the judiciary system could not remain impartial, then some form of social corrective must arise. One may look at the rest of his political life, which included his literary pursuits, as the search for this corrective. Initially he felt that a renewed emphasis on the essential goodness of American life could restore unity. Later, he was not so sure.

As he ties the acceptance of the realistic method to a more stable society, one better able to co-opt radical alternatives under the idea of rationality, realism becomes for Howells a means of conserving his hierarchical vision of America. That is, rather than proposing a radical alternative to the inequities of capitalism, he seeks a way to enable Americans of all classes to adapt to a world where change will be minimized and therefore accepted by a "progressive" cultural elite. Indeed, elements of this elite define the terms of this progress. Thus, in Howells's top-down vision of social organization, the naturalization of the tenets of rationality as the common sense of the upper classes virtually assures their becoming a general cultural imperative. A powerful means of accommodation was the moral force of literature; he wanted to make "literature a very serious thing which can become morally indifferent only in an age of moral indifference" (*Editor's Study* 33). Howells himself equated realism with enlightened government and romanticism with the failure of the state. For example, he criticized the Illinois state's attorney in the Haymarket case, Julius Grinnell, as having "gifts of the imagination that would perhaps fit him better for the functions of a romantic novelist than for the duties of official advocate in a free commonwealth" (*Letters* 3:202).

Despite his doubts about the judiciary system's ability to conduct fair trials and his questioning of the producing, capitalist class's ability to avert warfare, he retained some belief in existing American institutions. Howells did, however, feel that American life had to be rationalized in order for its institutions to retain their centrality. For Howells, to correct the weaknesses of the system under the stresses of industrialization and economic consolidation meant the subjugation of class differences in the interest of working toward the common social good, i.e., the persistence of a top-down social and economic system but in a more humane form. In accommodating some notion of the welfare of the underclasses, Howells fit the terms of the liberalism of his day, but he was by no means a partisan of the laboring classes. For that matter, he also criticized the reactionary elite. In an 1884 letter to John Hay praising his reactionary novel, *The Breadwinners,* Howells wrote "that the workingmen as workingmen are no better or wiser than the rich as rich, and are quite likely to be as false and as foolish" (*Letters* 3:89). Howells, then, promoted what he felt were the ideologically neutral tenets of progress and continuity and had little sympathy for the irrational or, in his equation, the romantic.

Prior to this period, and most visibly in the 1870s, during his tenure as an editor at *Atlantic,* Howells generally aligned himself with the older, more entrenched voices of American culture, joining a number of Boston's most exclusive social clubs, writing a campaign biography for Rutherford Hayes, and presiding over a journal that, while willing to include western writers, generally maintained its New England emphasis. Kenneth Lynn also notes his expressions of nativism and his alarm at the perceived threat of the wandering unemployed, after the panic of 1873 (*William Dean Howells* 144, 225). Viewing this conservative tendency allows us to comprehend the form his political protest took later in the century and shades the ideology of his pronouncements on realism. That is, between the seventies and the mideighties, Howells began to see the disruptions occurring in American life as more entrenched and their cause as more fundamental. Once Howells perceived that the turbulence of social change was rooted in the economic disparities of the new American industrial order, and that they could neither be denied nor easily physically repressed, he devised a philosophy by which they could be managed.

This is not to say that his reform impulse does not exist before the mideighties: it leads back to his involvement in the liberal Republican Party in the seventies and defines Howells as a member of the movement that laid the groundwork for the Progressive era. In an 1872 editorial in the *Atlantic,* Howells asserts that the goal of this movement is "to evolve order out of chaos, government out of anarchy" (in Montgomery, *Beyond Equality* 379). Howells and others who inhabited this wing of the Republican party sought, among other things, civil service reform and a reduction in tariffs, reforms that were also part of the later Progressive agenda. This wing also asserted the philosophy of managed change found in the later movement. The liberal Republicans, explains David Montgomery, "sought to bring under the sway of science the management of the social order itself. . . .

When Liberals moved to the labor question, the science of progress and the science of human relations converged. Their road to social progress scrupulously avoided both legislative and trade-union coercion; it moved instead through cooperation and rising productivity" (*Beyond Equality* 382–83).[5] These philosophies and policies were at the center of the Progressive movement as it achieved power around the turn of the century, and Howells's affiliation with this earlier group helps us to see his ultimate political dispositions as a broader application of his earlier concept of reform. By locating Howells within the context of late nineteenth- and early twentieth-century reform movements, we can see that his vision of literary realism is only one part of a more encompassing worldview. In a general cultural context there also exists a relationship between literary realism and broader applications of positive management. Howells, like most reformers of his class, placed continuity and order at or near the center of his political intentions. Literary realism was but one part of a larger social strategy to replace disruption with rationally managed change.

In the years following the Civil War, American literary realism developed as a form appropriate to the material emphases of modern life and moved away from the otherworldliness of romanticism. Realism naturalizes the authority of a worldview derived from corporate liberalism by showing how this perspective is correct and able to find (but not create) the real. In employing selected elements to support ideologically weighted positions, these works are discourses like any other; however, their philosophy of composition and resulting narrative strategies potently plead for their cultural agenda. This occurs because these literary texts ceased to invest their power in the expression of allegorical abstractions, as authors made discernible efforts to limit the explicit presence of such abstractions in these works.

In this period, however, realism was but one mode of literary expression among a range of different types of texts. Howells wrote mostly for the genteel middle and upper classes, competing directly with the popular romances also read primarily by these groups. There also existed the dime novels, consumed—and in great quantities—by the working class. Howells's realism asserted the need for the capturing of the actual, which was moral. He devised a method of composition that could entice its targeted audience to read *with* the novels, as these texts apparently reproduced a world similar to the one in which its genteel readers lived, but somewhat less conflict-ridden. In *Mechanic Accents,* Michael Denning describes how the highly dramatic dime novels speak to different readers and situate them more complexly, on "a field of cultural conflict where signs with wide appeal and resonance take on contradictory disguises and are spoken in contrary accents" (3). This conflict arises from the way in which these works mediate between the classes who produce them and those who consume them, and it raises the question of the extent to which the working-class consumers of such a product could control and adapt its meanings.

Realism, however, invited no such dissonance, even as Howells's felt need to promote this literary mode and narrowly define it suggests his anxiety. Alan Trachtenberg has called these critical writings "a steady flow of reviews and screeds in defense of the real" (*Incorporation* 184), but they also characterize an offensive action as well, a cultural program to make a type of literature preeminent for a particular body of readers and thereby to assist in the ordering of America from the top down. Howells did not seek to win over the working classes, who voraciously read other types of literature: his writings sought to influence those readers of the rising managerial middle class and to ally this class with an older proprietary elite. Howells's vision of the realignment of readers perfectly mimics the strategies of Progressive politicians who sought to create a modern leadership class from the new managerial class and the enlightened heirs of older cultural elites.

In the late nineteenth century, with the increasing centralization of the American populace and the development of technologies that allowed for relatively inexpensive printing and binding, a boom in the production and consumption of books took place. Immediately before the Civil War and until the turn of the century, machines that folded, sewed, and printed books at previously unknown speeds became widely used. The output of titles by American publishers grew from 2,076 in 1880 to 6,356 in 1900. Works of fiction titles published rose during this period, from 292 in 1880 to 616 in 1900 (Tebell 675–92). With the increase of reading in the U.S. and the importance of fiction in the market, Howells promoted realism as a means of influencing a targeted—but vast—audience.

Indeed, since fiction could and did take a range of possible forms and possible audiences, Howells feared that imprudent readers would become imprudent leaders, led astray by the fabulations of romance. In the last decades of the century, bestsellers ranged from *Ben Hur* (1880) to *King Solomon's Mines* (1886) to Rudyard Kipling's *The Light That Failed* (1891) to *The Red Badge of Courage* (1895), suggesting that literary realism, at least by the mid-nineties, was a potentially popular form but that it was generally less popular than romantic adventures. Works such as *Ben Hur* and *King Solomon's Mines* were but two titles among a number of quasi-historical romances that attained a broad readership around the turn of the century; others included *The Prisoner of Zenda* (1894) and *Quo Vadis* (1896).[6] As a critic, Howells did his part to create the proper emphasis for his readers. Though he did not review Kipling's *The Light That Failed*, a general comment on his earlier achievements recognized that while "some qualities in Kipling's tales promise a future for him[,] there is little in the knowingness and swagger of his performance that is not to be deplored with many tears; it is really so far away from the thing it ought to be" (*Editor's Study* 278–79).

Works of literary realism did not sell in nearly the quantity of these works of adventure and romance, a fact that brought forth Howells's comment. In the *North American Review*, a somewhat less prestigious journal than *Harper's* or the *Atlantic*, he declared in 1900 that the popular historical romance "will in a measure and for a while debauch the minds and through the minds the morals of their readers. . . . That delicate something that we call tone, whether intellectual or ethical, must suffer from an orgy of the kind it would suffer from an excess in opium or absinthe" (*As Critic* 306). Howells's sense of calamity warns his broader middle class of readers in terms that suggest the ardor with which he viewed his cultural calling. He reaches out to the extent of his possible audience as though on a mission.

Yet, this gesture should not be interpreted as an appeal to a mass audience. Indeed, Howells does not elicit such a broad following. Howells neither addresses the mass of readers in his columns nor writes for them in his fictions. *Harper's New Monthly* (and the *Atlantic Monthly* for that matter) belonged to a group of older literary magazines that targeted readers who identified with or were actually part of an entrenched genteel tradition. The editorial decisions of such journals, in which Howells as an editor was instrumental, were often based on criteria other than broad commercial intentions. Christopher Wilson locates this type of magazine in the last quarter of the nineteenth century as the place where "traditionally fell the mantle of taste, and it was here, more often than in newspapers, where young authors looked for literary and philosophical trends of their times" (41). From the price and availability of the books they bought, Wilson characterizes these readers as "mostly Northeastern, mostly well to do" (43). Howells's critical gesture is to rescue the mores of the upper and middle classes from the low pursuit of the fantastic. By engaging the realist text, these readers could, in Howells's view, see the facts of American social life before them and use their reinforced sense of order to maintain their positive direction. In an impassioned 1887 essay Howells entreats, "The light of civilization has already broken upon the novel, and no conscientious man can now set about painting an image of life without perpetual question of the verity of his work, and without feeling bound to distinguish so clearly that no reader of his may be misled, between what is right and what is wrong, what is noble and what is base, what is health and what is perdition, in the actions and the characters he portrays" (*Editor's Study* 74). He thus asks readers to internalize his critical merging of morality and representation in deciding what to read and how they should read it.

Howells insists that realism is both a product of the world and a force in the world. In the former case, the materialist emphases of this aesthetic reveal themselves in the first "Editor's Study" column, in March 1886, when Howells declares that fiction should "regard our life without the literary glasses so long thought desirable, and . . . see character not as it is in other fiction, but as it abounds outside of all fiction. This disposition sometimes goes with poor enough performance, but in some of the books it goes with performance that is excellent; and at any rate it is more valuable than evenness of performance" (2). Howells defines the world itself as the proper object of the realist text. He asks that works break with prior conventions of literature and capture, through their use of visible aspects of the world, actuality itself in its natural form. Howells attempts to institutionalize through critical canon the realist (moral) author as a positivist scientist, one who through his wisdom and precision of vision accurately and objectively observes the world, records its facts, and draws out clearly their ramifications. Such a "science" of composition would simply capture the fact of the world and present it. As we shall see in the next section, this neutral apparatus does not exist either in human or technological form. Yet, to offer such a structure may create an illusion of formlessness. If a text reproduces a culturally based worldview while banning the source of that view from the work itself, the result, in both form and content, may seem like an immanent projection of the world itself. Howells seeks precisely this illusion, as he bans the author from the text, calling authors who "sympathize" with their characters "primitive" (28), and praising Henry James's "artistic impartiality" (*As Critic* 66).

He emphasises method above achievement and suggests that late nineteenth- and early twentieth-century cultural fascination with technical accomplishment, making the novel something like a complex machine that a mechanic may assemble. This departs significantly from the literary criticism of the most influential American critic of the antebellum period,

Edgar Allan Poe, whose focal criterion for literature was emotional effect. Howells termed the critical writings of Poe "well nigh worthless." He also felt of Poe's creative works that "if they were written today, most of them could not be taken seriously" (*Editor's Study* 97). In contrast to Howells's plea for rationality, Poe asserted the emotional depths to which good art could lead its readers. Howells's emphasis on technique seems to demystify the composing of literature by showing the apparently simple method by which it should be made.

But for all his apparently democratic rhetoric, Howells's aesthetic and social vision concerns itself with hierarchy and contains its own central mystifications. The most obvious distinctions are the qualitative textual differences between realism and romance. Howells makes these distinctions polar: he contrasts his realism's fidelity to the world with romance's distortion: his mode's truth and its opposite's falsehood; above all, the clash between these literary movements becomes that between morality and immorality. But there exists another, more subtle scale that Howells inscribes, a scale that defines the role of the modern critic as an arbiter of taste—and therefore morality. In his initial *Harper's* column in 1886, in his opening paragraphs, his first critical act is to describe, though with a somewhat humorous tone, the hierarchical relationship between the named "editor" of the "Editor's Study" and the reader.

> The editor of the Study proposes to sit at fine ease and talk over with the reader—who will always be welcome here—such matters of literary interest as may come up from time to time, whether suggested by the new books of the day or other accidents of literary life. The reader will, of course, not be allowed to interrupt the editor while he is talking; in return the editor will try to keep his temper and to be as inconclusive as possible. If the reader disagrees with him upon any point, he will be allowed to write to him for publication, when, if the editor cannot expose the reader's folly, he will be apt to suppress his letter. It is meant, in other terms, to make the study a sort of free parliament, but for the presiding officer only; or a symposium of one. (1)

This variation on the romantic convention of the "genteel reader" deformalizes the reader-writer compact in tone while it states the actual terms of public hierarchy in content. The editor chooses the objects and terms of discussion by the authority of his position and, though the humor of this paragraph exposes the disparity in power between the positions of writer and reader and seems to undercut it, subsequent writings reveal that Howells writes as an expert who respects this hierarchy. Indeed, many of Howells's edicts on the appropriate shape of fiction seem to address not readers of magazines but authors who have written or would write fiction.

For example, in his discussion of Armando Palacio Valdes, Howells, as is frequently the case, goes from the particular to the general. The resulting statements characterize the appropriate perspective of the novelist in terms of the text's point of origin, the philosophy of composition that generates it: "Let not the novelist, then, endeavor to add anything to reality, to turn it and twist it, to restrict it. Since nature has endowed them with this precious gift of discovering ideas in things, their work will be beautiful if they paint these as they appear. But if the reality does not impress them, in vain will they try to make their work impress others" (225). A reader would find little about the work itself in such a statement. Howells addresses himself to the composition at its germ. A reader, then, would very possibly find herself craning her neck from a curiously oblique angle to see how she fits into such a conversation. Howells's address becomes a portion of a dialogue between experts on which a reader may eavesdrop but in which she may not participate. Similarly, Howells also addresses other critics from time to time, distinguishing his own practice from "nearly all current criticism as practiced among the English and Americans [which] is bad, is falsely principled, and is conditioned in evil. . . . Being itself artificial it cannot conceive of the original except as abnormal" (268). In such assertions Howells, despite his self-deflating asides, claims his place among a class of experts, at its apex. The stance of the critic, then, places him at the top of a class that knows what is correct and is duty-bound to lead those who do not to the truth. Readers eavesdrop on conversations between experts; thus they learn "first-hand."

As an expert in the realm of fiction, Howells equates the normative real with the ordinary; but we may ask whose ordinary life fits his description. In posing such a question, we see the class biases of literary realism recur. For Howells, the norms of American life present themselves to any casual observer. He assumes that his own vision represents the realm of disinterest and that in order to achieve the realist effect a viewer must gaze as he does on the actualities he perceives. When he declares that "the true standard of the arts is in every man's power; and an easy observation of the most common, sometimes of the meanest things, in nature will give the truest lights" (*Criticism and Fiction* 11), he submits that all may see the world that he sees if they also adopt his class-based ideologies. That is, the source of the norm becomes the rationalist bourgeois male. Those who would not define the real in a comparable manner become extraordinary and romantic. For example, in his 1891 review of Mary E. Wilkins Freeman's *A New England Nun and Other Stories,* a volume that offers a distinctly female point of view, but also one that adheres to many of the methodological dictates of Howellsian realism, Howells expresses an almost predictable ambivalence. "There is apparently a conflict of purpose in her sketches which gives her art an undecided effect, as in certain of them where we make the acquaintance of her characters in their village of little houses, and lose it in the No Man's Land of exaggerated action and conventional emotion" (*Editor's Study* 321). Though Howells does not detail these exaggerations, I assume that he finds them in Freeman's portrayal of the potentially disruptive deeds and emotions of her women protagonists. Actions that question the right and correctness of rationalist males fall outside the Howellsian realist agenda.

This is not to say that Howells is perfectly consistent in his assertions and judgments of the real. Indeed, he is quite generous in attributing realist qualities to works that to my twentieth-century eyes seem to fall beyond his definition. Yet, on balance he promotes those who primarily conform to his dictates and diminishes those who do not.

Howells's committment to the agenda of the rising middle class is one of the elements that distinguishes his vision of realist literature from that of his French counterparts, particularly Balzac and Zola. While French realism was also tied historically to the rise of the bourgeoisie, it did not necessarily promote the interests of this class, and when it did so it found terms that were not as didactic as Howells's. Howells's act of definition is distinctly American in its repression of theory and its assumption of the desirability of an unproblematized concept of the norm. Indeed, the aesthetic credo of art for art's sake was fairly important to the French realists, as they generally preferred to adopt the stance of the distanced observer. Howells's ideas of morality and service break down this distance in one sense, as he insists on the social role of realism. His critical judgments reveal his estrangement, willed or inherent, from both Balzac and Zola. He calls Balzac's *The Duchesse de Langeais* "false to life, false to art" (21) while he makes similar comments about *Père Goriot* and *Cesar Birotteau.* In his discussion of Zola's *La Terre,* which he calls Zola's "latest and perhaps awfullest book," he declares that due to its sordidness "it cannot remain valuable as literature, but must have other interest as a scientific study of French life under the Second Empire" (126).

American literary realism serves as the aesthetic movement that, along with a variety of material practices, promotes the cultural agenda of corporate liberalism. It is important to recognize the ideological service done by Howells and his like in defining the dominant directions of twentieth-century American life. But it is also vital to see that the broad changes that occurred in American life around the turn of the century were accomplished not simply by hegemony but also through physical force. While literary realism promoted the correctness and rationality of a cultural strategy of containing chaos by couching a class agenda in the terms of objective good, it is crucial to keep in mind that this ideological practice worked in concert with specific concrete acts; physical coercion at times accompanied this ideological entreaty.

The exemplary hanging of the four Haymarket anarchists likely had a far more direct impact on political dissent than twenty "Editor's Study" columns. Then, too, the suppression of the Homestead Strike in 1892 and the Pullman Boycott in 1894 showed the disposition of industrialists to employ violence to achieve their ends and the willingness of the government to intervene on the side of capitalists. As Melvin Dubofsky notes, "By the end of 1892 the lessons drawn by workers were sufficiently clear. In most cases, by then, labor lacked the power to challenge concentrated capital. Where workers had the short-term ability to stalemate their employers, the state usually intervened and tipped the scales in favor of capital" (50). Although its cultural power should not be overstated, literary realism, then, is most revealing when looked at in relation to material history.

True to his nineteenth-century material context, Howells's realist project suggests the honing of words into a form appropriate for the marketplace. His vision of realist literature's particular shape, and his repeated assertion of it, evoke the process of standardization and differentiation necessary for the success of any new product. That is, he seeks a certain recurring aesthetic but values innovations that distinguish works from one another.[7] His place in this process emulates that of an industrial manager. He assesses the product and its effect on the market. Howells employs relatively mass-produced and mass-disseminated journals to advertise and market his conception of truth—which is designed to produce social good. We may find evidence of the realism promoted by Howells in a range of diverse authors of the late nineteenth century. Writers such as Sarah Orne Jewett, Stephen Crane, Hamlin Garland, and Frank Norris acknowledged his direct or indirect influence. Howells also served as a confidant to both Samuel Clemens and Henry James. He at times edited their work and spent considerable hours with them discussing the aesthetic goals of literature. Indeed, though both men finally leave Howells's somewhat narrow view of realism behind, in their earlier works a perception much like Howells's emerges.[8]

All of this suggests the power and influence of Howells and his ability to disseminate the dictates of realist fiction. While his role as a critic and editor was indeed important, it is his fictions that complement his other writings and provide his ideological dispositions with their most entrancing form. In his prominent work of literary realism, *The Rise of Silas Lapham*, form and content well express the political goals of this literary movement in a way that further illuminates his critical writings. This work actively effaces its authorial presence and confirms the solidity and power of the world's surfaces, while it thematically fosters orderly change.[9] *The Rise of Silas Lapham* instructs the reader in the rationality and desirability of the positive truths it apparently unearths.

The narrator maintains his relative distance from the narrative, matching appropriate symbols with appropriate characters. In this action, he does not show himself excessively but is able to rely on circumscribed cultural meanings of concrete objects to define the highly abstract idea of character. This is a book about relative stasis: characters function from reduced definitions of being and valuable objects are treated as though their material worth transcends time and circumstance.

The Rise of Silas Lapham is a meditation on the realistic credo. The novel shows various social and economic forces at work and traces its title character's move from rags to riches and back to relative rags. Lapham is first a producer, then a speculator, and at last a victim of his own speculation. This journey takes him from the country to the city and back to the country. Howells dramatizes the natural ascension of a tier of characters and a narrator who define modern America. He works to accustom its middle-class readers to a vision of social change from which they benefit, but to some degree these ideological assertions occur in terms that misstate historical conditions. Howells steers the novel between its various extremes; it is for a system of concrete value, but against inordinate paper gains. It is for prosperity, but against conspicuous consumption. It seeks a moral universe, but only in cases where morality truly reveals the logic of material life. Set amid change, the novel emphasizes continuity and helps to define a new morality, one in which concern for self takes precedence over concern for others. It thus elaborates the ethos of developed capitalism and the basis for consumer society, even as Howells attempts to constrain the actual emergence of such a fluid economic and social state. As Howells wrote this novel in 1884 and 1885, America's economy was in the midst of enormous structural alterations. Explains Alfred Chandler,

> In the quarter of a century following the completion of this Census [that of 1880], the family-owned factory was transformed in many industries into a vertically integrated, multifunctional enterprise. . . . In 1880 nearly all manufacturing firms only manufactured. . . . By the first years of the twentieth century, however, many American industries were dominated by enterprises that had created their own distributing organizations. . . . The large industrial firm thus became a primary agent for large-scale distribution as well as large-scale production and, indeed, became a critical link connecting the two. (*Changing Economic Order* 272)

Part of this process of consolidation and growth was the demise of family control of the day-to-day activities of these large enterprises, as professional managers now came to operate them. Primarily, however, this structural change did not result in wholesale upheaval of class positions. If you were born into the monied class, chances are you would stay there. As an economic novel, Howells's work expresses these large-scale shifts of the American economy in its broad plot outlines. We see the effects of unregulated railroad monopolies, the problems of undercapitalized, smaller manufacturing concerns in times of economic stress, and the demise of the family-run enterprise of Silas Lapham. Indeed, Silas's fortune vanishes due to his inability to steer his business in the direction Chandler characterizes, from family business to modern, vertically integrated corporation.

But as it succeeds in reflecting the broad movements of its age, the novel represents the economic fortunes of the older members of its central families atypically. *The Rise of Silas Lapham* traces the downward mobility of each older generation, as the Bromfield Coreys slide toward economic scarcity, while the Laphams plunge to it, but this social movement, according to demographic studies, occurred rarely among people of this class, at a rate of about 12 percent (Thernstrom 53). Howells's emphasis performs a distinct dramatic function, as it creates a kind of tension in the plot and allows for the depiction of contrasting situations, but in asserting the extraordinary as typical it fails Howells's own tests for realist fiction. Howells's distortion elucidates a part of the ideological project of the novel.

By emphasizing the passing of the older Coreys and Laphams from the center of modern economic life, Howells apparently confirms the mimetic function of his novel. As a work of and about the Gilded Age, *The Rise of Silas Lapham* chooses to reflect the period's turbulence by representing social movement through a specific taxonomy of change, in a way that misstates the incendiary class conflicts of the day. This historical conflict resulted from the economic chaos of industrial consolidation, but in Howells's novel disruption occurs as the continuity of blood is replaced by the relative discontinuity of merit. Howells reproduces the national fiction of equal opportunity by leaving this older generation with no wealth to bequeath.

Howells's Boston of this period was at a point of cultural change relatively typical of American cities, as the process of industrialization began to generate social disruption, the political hegemony of its traditional elites began to be contested by recent immigrants, particularly those of Irish origins, and the city's population became more fluid than it had been in the past, turning over by one-third in a given ten-year period.[10] Yet, for all the changes in the way Yankees from leading families made their money—now from railroads and complex interlocking enterprises formed into holding companies rather than from shipping and relatively simple finance—these same families still dominated virtually every phase of social and economic life. This predominance was relatively assured by their actions in the preceding three decades. "By mid-century, the Boston elite controlled commercial, financial, and manufacturing enterprises which held sway throughout New England, generated wealth at an unprecedented rate, and thus contributed to the establishment and maintenance of Brahmin prominence and identity in the decades to come" (Story 4–5).

In his meticulously documented *The Other Bostonians*, Stephen Thernstrom provides a vision of a city where mobility was possible but limited, a place that had been far more economically dynamic in relation to the national economy in the antebellum years, a city where the upper classes had not yet ceded any aspect of control to other emerging groups. "There were definite rigidities in the occupational structure, a series of barriers that impeded mobility and perpetuated inequality. The level at which a young man entered the labor market strongly influenced the course of his subsequent career. His point of entry into the occupational competition strongly influenced the course of his future career" (257).

Yet, though Howells's representation of this context overemphasizes its fluidity, the figure of Silas is relatively typical of a class of native-born Protestant migrants to urban life and conforms to the Howellsian notion of the real. Lapham begins his life in Boston well placed on the economic ladder and goes on to ride the industrial boom in the years immediately after the Civil War to a sizable fortune. His intended move to "the water side of Beacon Street" in Boston also typifies the movement of the upper-middle class in the seventies and eighties. The Back Bay of Boston was filled and developed between 1870 and 1900, providing housing for what Samuel Bass Warner terms "the rich and prosperous segment of the middle class" (17). However, these core material facts are devices to give the broader political vision of the book a similarly concrete status, a status that Howells enhances formally. His desire to mask his coercive intention and to assert the immanence of his text reveals itself in the work's first pages and inscribes his reflections and fabulations as indistinguishable.

Much like plays and films that seek to avoid the intrusive presence of a discursive narrator, but which for the sake of their narrative require more explication than is contained within the effective action of the presentation, *The Rise of Silas Lapham* begins with an interview of its protagonist. The journalist Bartley Hubbard questions Silas Lapham for a newspaper column. This device limits the extent of authorial intrusion in this opening chapter—which is not to say that the narrator becomes invisible; he remains available if we seek him out. However, he limits his explicit presence. Bartley Hubbard becomes a device for eliciting the true Lapham, but the work of the journalist fails to capture him. We see that Hubbard comes to his interview with distinct preconceptions and a flawed vision of how truth is ascertained. The interview's language is far from the rhetorical conventions of Lapham and inserts the pretensions of their author. The design of the article more or less sticks to facts but arranges them in a way that fails to "picture" Lapham.

We also know that Hubbard is a "potential reprobate" (*Rise* 8) and that Lapham's "burly simplicity had amused him" (21). Hubbard's appearance in this chapter is intended to elevate neither the emerging craft of journalism nor its practitioner. Bartley exists both to elicit the vital elements of Lapham's personal narrative and to contrast the journalist, obtrusive and immoral, with the knowing, and effaced, realistic narrator.[11]

With the narrator buried in the background of the text, the novel offers its vision of modern American life. This vision includes definitions of commerce, morality, and a managerial class that ably recognizes the positive truths of the world. The narrator belongs to this class and speaks for it with power. This novel shows how to derive actual and natural truths not simply by viewing with mechanical precision but by seeing things as they *really* are. The difference between these actions is that between process and result; one may look, but not see correctly. The narrator, then, is simply a guide to the natural truths of the world, which are available to the wise observer.

The realistic project as defined by Howells hides an historically specific and class-bound vision of truth behind the edifice of empirical fact, as it attempts to fuse morality and material reality. Writes Howells the critic, "[T]he works that represent and body forth human experience . . . can always afford a refined pleasure and can often . . . convey a refined truth" (*Editor's Study* 21). The narrator of *Silas Lapham* instructs the reader morally while paradoxically asserting the transcendent values of the material world. The illusory luster of surfaces fails to mislead him as he shows us how to find true value, which is the moral aspect of objects. This process of elaborating worth by reifying it places this undramatized, effaced figure in the novel's physical background but at its ideological center.

Having debunked Hubbard's journalism, Howells positions his realist narrator to define the facts of the novel's focal characters. Central to these definitions is the apparently automatic equation between aesthetics and class, with aesthetics cast as a timeless entity that individuals either innately know how to judge or will never comprehend. This is not to say that class is simply a matter of aesthetic acuity, for it also requires wealth; rather, such awareness underlies elite status. Thus, the older Laphams and Irene remain beyond social rescue. Their failed judgment is applied to furnishings, frescoes, books, architecture, and clothes. For Howells, such ignorance is absolute and significant of a necessarily lower social order. Indeed, this is one of the ways in which Howells makes vital distinctions between the old-money Coreys and this aspiring family. Shaming descriptions and judgments of ugly objects seem designed by their absolute certainty to secure a community of taste with middle-class readers who would not want to appreciate the aesthetically offensive.

James M. Cox notes, "Knowledge of literature is the chief possession that marks the distinction between the world of the Coreys and that of the Laphams" (122). While I find Cox's emphasis excessive, I do agree that the Harvard-educated Tom Corey, the son of the focal upper-class family of the novel and arguably the center of the book, is elevated by his ability to recognize worthy reading material. Early in the novel, when Tom visits the Laphams' summer house in Nantasket, he spies a copy of Eliot's *Middlemarch*, which prompts a brief discussion of literature. Corey is clearly a reader of novels and familiar with Eliot's works, as to a lesser extent is Penelope. Irene is barely curious, while Silas declares, "I can't get the time for books." Persis, a former Vermont schoolteacher, also expresses her skepticism of novels: "My mother called them lies. And I guess she wasn't so very far wrong about some of them" (88). Later, Tom provides a list of authors suitable for the library in the Laphams' new home to Irene, who cannot "see how anyone can keep the poets and historians and novelists separate in their minds" (114).

That Howells determines character by judging an individual's ability to read worthy novels suggests where his sympathies lie. Since the audience for a (worthy) novelist is not the Silas and Persis Laphams of the world—the nonreaders—but the Tom Coreys, we may see how this work speaks to a certain class by offering a narrator and a group of characters who confirm the truisms of that group's role in American social life. That is, he asserts that status flows logically from worth and that some people, whatever their material attributes, defy civilization. Further, Howells illustrates that the proprietorship of this rational class is a social good and the hope of the future. Since it is a sign of superiority to read worthy novels with intelligence, a point he makes repeatedly in his critical columns, it is no wonder that Tom gradually makes his way to the center of the novel.

The practice of defining class not by money but by an intangible such as aesthetic taste—this narration makes it a matter of recognizing aesthetic quality—is very much within the domain of late nineteenth-century social history. Appreciation for the arts became, in the estimation of those of the upper classes, a means of defining the civilized and a means of civilizing those who as yet had not fallen under the sway of high culture. As Laurence Levine argues in *Highbrow/Lowbrow,*

> To "hold the faith while social forms are bending" sums up succinctly what the champions of culture in the late nineteenth century felt their function was. It was not merely the audiences in the opera houses, theaters, symphonic halls, museums and parks they strove to transform; it was the entire society. They were convinced that maintaining and disseminating pure art, music, literature and drama would create a force for moral order and help to stop the chaos threatening to envelop the nation. (200)

Howells himself wrote in an 1878 *Atlantic* editorial that to avert "general mediocrity" those "who believe in culture, in property, and in order, that is in civilization, must establish the necessary agencies for the diffusion of a new culture . . . a better culture . . . a culture of a higher order" ("Certain Dangerous Tendencies" 385–402). In *The Rise of Silas Lapham*, Tom Corey serves as something of a missionary to the lower class, though we find that certain elements of that class are more fit for instruction than others.

At the moment when the novel reveals the distinction between the Laphams and their class and the Coreys and theirs in its most precise way— when the Laphams attend a dinner party at the Coreys' home—discussion of fiction again serves as the means by which Silas is shown to be inferior. Novels are discussed by guests who have attained the class to which Silas may only aspire. Indeed, as they discuss literature they move beyond the commonplaces exchanged between Tom and Irene, and even of those bantered between Tom and Penelope. The elite characters of this set-piece echo almost word for word Howells's own critical writings.

The ethics of the novel, and correspondingly of life, are first declared by Reverend Sewell:

> The novelists might be the greatest possible help to us if they painted life as it is, and human feelings in true proportion and relation, but for the most part they have been and are altogether noxious. . . .
>
> And the self-sacrifice painted in most novels . . . is nothing but psychical suicide, and is as wholly immoral as a man jumping on a sword. (197–98)

This statement foreshadows the angst that will come when it is revealed that the somewhat clever Penelope, and not the beautiful Irene, is Tom's choice for a wife. Howells employs a romantic situation that includes many of the elements of sentimental fiction—mistaken identity, unrequited love, the clash between sisters over a suitor—in order to show the efficacy of the realist dictates of management. Indeed, the choices detailed in this phase of the novel are between the "self-sacrifice" Sewell disdains or a more rational approach. The former is the romantic, "literary" response, while the latter is the pragmatic, the "real."

Sewell's statement closely associates the minister with the author, restating Howells's critical term that "the tests of literature should not only be more practical, but more ethical" (*Editor's Study* 92).[12] Later in the scene at the Coreys, when the men have retired to the parlor to smoke cigars and drink brandy, the Coreys' cousin, Charles Bellingham, about whom we know nothing but his high breeding, reiterates: "The commonplace is just that light, impalpable, aerial essence which they've never got into their confounded books yet. The novelist who could interpret the common feelings of commonplace people would have the answer to 'the riddle of the painful earth on his tongue'" (202). In contrast, we find of Lapham that "there was a great deal of the talk he could not follow" (201).

The elder Corey, Bromfield, also participates in the various discussions of the novel and reveals himself a thoughtful and knowledgeable appreciator of the arts. This is somewhat problematic in that Corey, while certainly possessing all the correct affiliations of his class, is in the process of watching his fortune shrink, and his family must either find new money or persist as symbols of a family and an age passed by. Corey himself evokes a lost age. His family has made their money in the shipping and textile businesses— endeavors that were basic to Boston commerce in the century prior to the Civil War—but Bromfield lives on the capital that he has inherited. This fortune is shrinking because of the accelerated cost of living, caused by the dynamic, if erratic, economic growth of postbellum America. While Lapham has money but no taste, Corey has taste but a shrinking fortune. His son will have both, as Tom adapts to the conditions of modern economic life and perpetuates the family line through his ability to involve himself in its materialism. We find that though taste is indeed vital to status, it cannot absolutely supersede money. In the world of the novel, downward mobility is far more easily attained than upward, as one may lose money but it is very difficult to acquire taste. Explains Corey, an authority on such matters: "It is very odd that some values have this peculiarity of shrinking. You never hear of values in a picture shrinking; but rents, stocks, real estate—all those values shrink abominably" (95–96). In this platonic twist of logic, aesthetics are forever while monetary wealth can ebb. Howells emphasizes through Corey what otherwise might be lost in the machinations of plot: the value of money may not be absolute, but on the other hand, if you can have it without selling your soul, it is rather desirable.

Curiously, individuals of Corey's class and background overwhelmingly tended to retain their financial preeminence in Gilded Age Boston, shifting their capital to areas of appropriate growth. As noted earlier, downward mobility of such figures was extremely rare. Corey's descent, then, becomes an emphasis by which Howells foists a perception of an age on his readers. Through the waning of Corey's fortunes, Howells makes the distinction between the old monied classes who fail to modernize their orientation and those who do. This emphasizes that modern life is a meritocracy in a way that contrasts with demographic data: in the novel those who retain status do so deservingly. Corey is also used to assert the closing of the distinction between a professional upper middle class and an older aristocracy.

Tom Corey, Charles Bellingham, the architect Seymour, and the Reverend Sewell—the last two achieve status through their occupations and their wisdom—sit at the same table comfortably. This vision of a meritocracy well conforms to the broader ideological outlines of corporate liberalism: the rhetoric of this movement justifies its domination of American life by emphasizing its ideology over its genealogy. This older elite and a newer managerial class dominate, in the world of this novel, primarily through the fitness of their ideas, ideas that any right-thinking American should have.

The Laphams' plot to move from the realm of the merely wealthy to that of the transcendent upper class takes the shape of building a house in a part of Boston that is more prestigious than their current neighborhood. Says Persis, "There's got to be something more than money, I guess" (30). That something is characterized by their house, but its precise nature escapes her. Since in this realistic work recognizing true value is the basis for wisdom, Persis's ignorance dooms her: the Laphams will never ascend.

"There ain't a sightlier place for a house," says Silas in reference to the water side of Beacon street (32), thus showing his instinctive comprehension of the means by which status is achieved in late nineteenth-century urban America. In order to move into desirable social circles, Lapham must concoct some display of his wealth. Lapham declares of his earlier life, "I didn't know what the Back Bay was then" (11), but now he knows its public meaning and asserts this in his newspaper interview with Bartley—a gesture toward self-advertising that announces the need for his shift in residence. This era marks the beginning of the modern economic age, an age where public expressions of being take precedence over less ostentatious matters of private definition.[13] Yet, by using the house as a means for the marketing of reputation, Howells employs a substantial and fairly stable symbol, very different from McTeague's gilded tooth or Carrie Meeber's clothes.

Since the house is concocted to display wealth, its design must create the right impression.[14] Fittingly, Lapham decides to replace the master builder, whom he initially instructs to reproduce the style he had often viewed in his "inspection of many new buildings," with an architect. Lapham shifts his alliance from the skilled craftsman of the past to the specialized professional of the future by employing a man who designs houses but does not build them.

The narrator characterizes this decision with the same condescending tone toward the Laphams that has marked the novel from the beginning. The architect is thus aligned with the narrator, Tom Corey, and Reverend

Sewell, because he "was able to conceal the shudder which [the Laphams] must have sent through him" (40) when they announced their conception of their house. The narrator constantly distances himself from the Laphams through these judgments of their indecorous behavior and treats the architect, Mr. Seymour, with reverence. He includes him in the pivotal social event of the novel, the Coreys' dinner for the Laphams, and values him as an artist even when it seems possible that he may be ridiculed as a leech bleeding his client. Indeed, Seymour is employed as a figure to assure readers of this class's ethos of careful and steady progress, telling the assembled guests that he thinks not only that Lapham's house is "prettier than the Coreys'," but also that, as a matter of fact, "it's better built" (192).

Howells's use of the figure of Seymour is exemplary. The architect joins the aesthetic and the material in a way that he as a novelist would like to. This reverence for the architect developed as a cultural event in the last three decades of the nineteenth century, making individual architects into celebrities. "For the first time a handful of architects even became generally known to the American public and were considered important cultural figures" (Handlin 101). This is the age of the celebration of Stanford White, Henry Hobson Richardson, and Richard Morris Hunt. Howells himself was well acquainted with such figures, as his brother-in-law William Rutherford Mead was a renowned architect in his own right and a partner of White's. As realism is the literary method that asserts cultural continuity by offering the iconography of the real—that is, the materially available and "objectively" valuable—architecture emerges as the ultimate plastic art, aestheticizing the idea of the urban landscape, the scene of America's future, while it works in the most solid of materials: mortar, brick, and wood. Seymour's house provides a material equivalent of Howells's ideal realist text: it is light, natural, and possessed of large windows with exemplary views. Seymour himself describes the triumph of modern architecture in a way that echoes Howells's literary criticism: "What we've done is largely to go back of the hideous style that raged after they forgot to make this sort of house. But I think we can claim a better feeling for structure. We use better material, and more wisely; and by and by we shall work out something more characteristic and original" (192). The expression of "hideous style" could easily be applied to Howells's bête noire, romanticism, as the technical notion of structure and the modulated idea of "characteristic" suggest the realism advocated in his critical writings.

We see the house performing its function almost immediately, as it is encountered by Tom Corey, the love interest of the two Lapham daughters and the type of social prize that status will bring. This accidental meeting attests to the power of place in establishing the social contacts aspired to for the girls. That the house is unfinished makes it an ambiguous symbol, but it exudes promise as a plot device. Tom, with his greater powers of observation and subtler sense of value, does not display himself or look out on the street side of the structure. He gazes at the less peopled and more "natural" view of the Charles River. In doing so he gazes in the manner that Howells himself describes in an 1884 letter praising the setting sun's "glory over the Back Bay" (*Letters* 3:108). Once again we see Howells's act of identifying with a class of characters who reproduce his own social position. These hard class distinctions are further asserted by Lapham's discussion of value and aesthetics. He explains, "You can't have a nice house for nothing. It's just like ordering a picture from a painter. You pay him enough, and he can afford to paint you a first class picture; and if you don't, he can't" (55). The fact that Lapham believes that true quality can be bought is the telling statement of his ultimate inability to recognize it when he sees it. Indeed, he never comes to realize the true worth of his house, as the narrator tells us much later that though he has been somewhat educated in aesthetic value by the architect, he remains ignorant: "it appealed to him as an exquisite bit of harmony appeals to the unlearned ear" (310).

Realism, then, presents a world of objectified meanings, but one where value is relatively fixed.[15] It asserts the value of owning but not necessarily of consuming. We may see such an emphasis as typical of the strategy to minimize dislocation in a time of economic and social disruption. Indeed, such a gesture of moderation seems moot from the perspective of the present, where owning and consuming have become virtually synonymous. Howells's attempt to hold a line of moderation suggests that he also was aware of how easily the elevation of objects and ownership becomes the act of discarding and consuming. The naturalist writers will elevate the act of consumption, but here there is a greater emphasis on stability.

Howells's novel defines a moment and projects the future: therefore the question of who will marry whom and produce the next generation is pressing. In this romantic portion of the novel, recognizing the distinction between true beauty (Penelope) and its simple physical expression (Irene) becomes a device for eliciting realism's necessary containment of desire in the service of social order. The question posed by the novel is whether its characters (or its readers) possess the ability to contain such desires. We see these actual strategies in the narrator's prose, as he names Irene's physical allure, then immediately disclaims her overall worth. For example, he tells us that "she dressed well, perhaps too well"; and "she began for the first time to form ideas which she had not derived from her family, and they were none the less her own because they were often mistaken" (27). Within the project of realism, Irene must be devalued because, if her ability to incite remains intact, the very social chaos that realism seeks to contain will go unfettered. As Leo Bersani explains, "Desire is a threat to the form of realistic fiction; it can also disrupt novelistic order. The nineteenth-century novel is haunted by the possibility of these subversive moments and it represses them with a brutality both shocking and eminently logical" (66). Howells uses the romance between the Lapham daughters and Corey, and its romantic conventions, to show explicitly that the requirements of order dictate that passions be tamed.

Tom recognizes Penelope's quality from the first, not isolating her physicality because he is unable to isolate her presentation from her essence. Things that are good look good, and those who have the ability to recognize this are the nobility of the new America. Fittingly, Silas and Persis remain oblivious to the true object of Corey's intentions, as do his own parents. Penelope attracts Tom with, among other features, her ironic manner, which repeatedly deflates pretensions, including Mrs. Corey's (164–68) and her father's. Her speech strategically reduces those who fail to embody the spirit of realism, and as Tom is a force of affirmation, she is initially a necessary force of negation. She does not serve as an index of unfettered desire. Rather, she appeals more to the intellect and to reason. To choose her over her sister implies a rational process and not simple vision and instinctual response. That the reader can *understand* this choice makes him or her an accomplice in it.

The morality of Tom and Penelope continuing their romance becomes one of the focal points of the novel's last 150 pages. This section contains the work's most conclusive statements of right and morality. None of the Coreys or Laphams are able to resolve this problem of the heart, though Penelope almost does when she asserts, "Well, I *have* a right to him, and he has a right to me. If he's never done anything to make her think he cared for her—and I know he hasn't; it's all been our doing,—then he's free and I'm free" (229). Penelope's resolution is blurted out in a passion, and she is unable to act on it. Yet, her insight seems to elevate her above the others and suggests her place on the fringes of the class of Tom and his peers.

Just as the Laphams consulted an architect when they needed a house, they consult a clergyman, Reverend Sewell, when there is a question of ethics. Of course, the enlisting of the clergy for nontheological matters is a distinctly modern gesture. The clergyman has ceased to be strictly a religious figure; with the decline of religion as an organizing system of beliefs in American life, he has moved into a civic role. Reverend Sewell has previously enlarged upon the social responsibility of the novel in general and now steers this one toward a fitting conclusion. The Laphams have no knowledge of his doctrinal beliefs, and yet Silas "likes the looks" of Sewell (238).

Sewell details a strategy for resolving this problem:

> One suffers instead of three, if none is to blame. . . . That's sense, and that's justice. It's the economy of pain which naturally suggests itself and which would insist upon itself, if we were not all perverted by traditions of the shallowest sentimentality. . . . [W]e somehow think it must be wrong to use our common sense. I don't know where this false idea comes from, unless it comes from the novels that befool and debauch almost every intelligence in some degree. It certainly doesn't come from Christianity, which instantly repudiates it when confronted with it. (241–42)

Sewell's theory of the economy of pain resolves a question of ethics with simple mathematics. As Wai-Chee Dimock explains, this formulation is "a model whose claim rests on its ability to conjoin the moral and the economic" (67). Sewell's sense of ethics provides the most articulate expression of realism's philosophical perspective, a vision that becomes exemplary in its recapitulation of the agenda of the modern technocrat and its potential to resolve the book's various dilemmas. As desire is fettered by rationality in the choice of Penelope, all forms of disruption may be so calmed.

Reason effectively resolves the love triangle of Irene, Tom, and Penelope. The latter two marry and Irene remains with her parents. Unfortunately for Irene's marriage prospects, her parents now reside in Lapham, Vermont. Rather than a moral triumph, this step backward symbolizes the Laphams' lack of fitness for modern life and their inability to figure the economy of pain. Silas is the victim of several circumstances beyond his control—economic contraction, the emergence of a competitor in the paint market, the accidental burning of his house on Beacon Street—but he also suffers significantly from his inability to reconcile pragmatism and ethics. Indeed, in opposition to Sewell's simple formula, Lapham struggles interminably with the morality of certain business actions.

Lapham's long-standing moral dilemma begins with his relationship to his former business partner, Milton Rogers. The undercapitalized Lapham had taken Rogers on in his paint business in the days after the Civil War. Rogers supplied that capital, but failed to approach the paint business itself with the ardor of Lapham. Explains Silas: "I was loaded with a partner that didn't know anything and couldn't do anything, and I unloaded; that's all" (47). At the end of their business association, Lapham left Rogers with a modest profit, but nothing like the profit he would have realized if he had maintained the partnership over the coming years.

If one accepts the premises of capitalism, there is nothing wrong with Lapham's actions. He enlisted an investor with no particular expertise in an enterprise that ultimately ended in profit. However, under the suasions of Persis, when Rogers comes to borrow on the basis of collateral stocks, Lapham agrees to the loan. As he does this Lapham says, "I don't *think* I ever did Rogers any wrong, and I never did think so; but if I *did* do it— *if* I did—I'm willing to call it square, if I never see a cent of my money again" (132). In holding Silas to this high ethical standard, Persis attempts to maintain the business practices of an earlier stage of capitalism. She sees the relationship between Lapham and his partner as personal and not strictly financial. Thus, her sense of responsibility to Rogers extends beyond the mathematical considerations of profit and loss. Lapham, a man of more worldly experience, senses that Persis is wrong but, as he has no countervailing ethos, allows himself to be worn down by her sentiments.

His transactions with Rogers would be of no particular import were it not for the contraction of the American economy in the late 1870s. As Lapham sees his fortune shrinking, he finds he needs to realize some return on his loan. Since the collateral Rogers placed in Lapham's hands was initially merely ceremonial, the fact that he seeks to use it to stave off bankruptcy changes the nature of the transaction, which is transformed from a debt of conscience to a business practice of questionable wisdom. Even Persis sees the transaction in a new light in this time of need, admitting, "I'm to blame for that . . . I forced you to do it" (276). The desire for return reframes the question of right and wrong in Lapham's dealings with Rogers when they were partners. Either morality is strictly situational— one may do the right thing so long as it doesn't impinge on business success—or there was no wrong. Under duress even Persis admits this. The Laphams seem pretty well divided as to which condition applies. Since they cannot decide, they are unable either to write off the cash and the moral debt or to attempt to salvage some financial return in any way possible.

This indecision prevails when Lapham attempts to sell a milling property he has accepted from Rogers. Once again the novel introduces a distinctly early nineteenth-century view of business ethics in its treatment of the transaction between Lapham and Rogers. The properties have been accepted by Lapham, both because he senses he has some moral debt to Rogers and because he might realize a profit on them. However, since the most valuable of these properties, the mill, stands by the tracks of a major railroad, its value is fixed by what the railroad chooses to pay for it. If the mill's owner were to refuse to sell at the price offered by the railroad, the railroad would likely raise freight rates to a crushing level. Thus, the property turns out to be worth somewhat less than Lapham had anticipated. The problem with the railroad is treated as a bit of skullduggery on the part of Rogers by Lapham and his wife, as they believe that the ethics of the situation provide that Rogers should have fully informed them of this nuance to the transaction. However, since no offer has been made by the railroad, this injury remains theoretical for a time, even as Silas and Persis treat it as something more.

Interestingly, the more pressing question of ethics is a much broader one: that of the railroad's unfettered power to squeeze smaller businesses. Howells leaves this matter unexamined, as he once again reveals realism's disposition to naturalize what *is*. The railroad is treated as a fact of the landscape, as Rogers and Lapham go on to split ethical hairs.

To further cloud the moral basis of Rogers's and Lapham's actions, the former finds a party of Englishmen, acting as agents for a utopian community, willing to buy the mill for a price that reflects Lapham's original conception of the proerty's value. Lapham, feeling that he has been wronged (which suggests that he no longer believes that Rogers needed to be paid back and that no injury had been committed), discloses fully the problem of the railroad's interest in the property in order to be clean where he feels Rogers is sullied. The interested parties do not care, explaining: "[T]he loss, if there is to be any, will fall upon people who are able to bear it— upon an association of rich and charitable people. But we're quite satisfied there will be no loss" (325). Lapham asks for more time to debate the moral subtleties of his position.

As he debates the fine points, Rogers himself asks to buy the property— which he will then sell to the Englishmen. This gesture further clouds the morality of Lapham's position, as his responsibility for the properties after he sells them is questionable. Lapham does not answer this offer, but debates the ethics of it all night, reaching no resolution by morning. When he reaches his office that morning, however, the letter with a concrete offer from the railroad has arrived. This offer leaves his debate moot: now he must either be a party to cheating the clients of the Englishmen, or take the loss. Since the ethics of this position are clear, he does the latter.

Lapham has yet another chance to rescue his paint company when he finds an investor who is unaware of the emergence of a competitor with a better product that costs less to produce. Lapham tells him of the existence of this competitor and assures his own ruin. He feels bound by the ethics of disclosure, extrapolating from his own transaction with Rogers.

All of this agonized debate over the morality of business provides an antithesis to Sewell's neat and pragmatic economy of pain. Lapham is unable to figure out what is right in the first case because he has no theory to guide him. If he had applied the economy of pain, he would not have entered into any further transactions with Rogers, as he would have seen clearly that he owed him nothing, having lived up to the letter of their business relationship. In the transaction concerning the mill, if he had applied the economy of pain he would have sold the property, since he has been informed that none will suffer if he does. Further, even his transaction with the investor would have been saved by a narrow application of the economy of pain. One would have suffered while many would prosper. In addition, there seems no fixed law requiring either the repressing of information or the revealing of it.

His inability to apply the mathematics of suffering to business leaves Lapham a victim of his own premodern ideology. To see this novel as the triumph of morality requires a most peculiar vision of triumph. Lapham is ruined financially and not particularly ennobled. The novel marks his retreat from Boston. "For his nerves there was no mechanical sense of coming back: this was as much the end of his proud, prosperous life as death itself could have been. He was returning to begin life anew, but he knew, as well as he knew that he should not find his vanished youth in his native hills, that it could never again be the triumph that it had been. That was impossible, not only in his stiffened and weakened forces but in the very nature of things" (353). His return to Vermont is a failure, his failure to apply the economy of pain. In Penelope's application of this doctrine is her salvation, and the only resolution the novel offers. She and her similarly modern husband, Tom Corey, will go on to define the future.

As the concept of the economy of pain is one that might have salvaged Lapham's fortune and defined him as a modern entrepreneur, Sewell comes to provide the doctrinal center for the novel. He represents the strain of liberal Protestantism in the Gilded Age that makes the management of irrational impulses its primary concern. Donald Meyer calls the defining doctrine of this movement "individualistic piety," a term denoting the responsibility of all classes to effect a world where class conflict will be replaced by cooperation—in sum, an ethos of order. Explains Meyer:

Early social-gospel leaders were uneasy about disorder from below and about the limits of evangelism upon the new industrial classes. They were uneasy in other ways too, which divided them more decisively from liberal apologists for the new order. From the standpoint of the past, anarchy in the late nineteenth century was advancing as much from above as from below. By no means adequately justified within the old moral logic, men of immense new power and organizations of unprecedented scale and influence had appeared within the community. The context for the Protestantism of individual piety—whatever its theology—was not only a social economy in which each generation could expect to rise, but also a social economy in which the classes that had risen could expect to hold their positions. (30)

Thus, a doctrine of personal responsibility governed by an overriding recognition of the need for order underlie the gestures of containment emphasized by Sewell and Howells. The very act of intellectualizing spirituality builds upon the transcendental movement of the 1830s and 1840s, but replaces the mysticism of that movement with a means-end pragmatism. Indeed, Sewell's equation recalls the Christian social visions of such Gilded Age thinkers as Richard Ely and Laurence Grondlund and the socioreligious visions of Walter Rauschenbusch and Washington Gladden (Howells's neighbor). Conflating Christianity and sociology was very much a Gilded Age strategy for addressing the disruptions of the time. In this union we see the social terms of Howells's aesthetic vision, a perspective that also joins the terms morality and fact. In these related worldviews, morality becomes that which preserves a narrow material order. Realism—social, political, and literary—becomes a strategy of managed change that preserves as much of the existing social order as possible. Which is not to say that realism is a philosophy of reaction: it promotes adaptation to perceived inevitabilities in order to maintain the hierarchies of an orderly world. In effect, it eliminates from consideration desires that cannot find a socially appropriate expression, and unrealized desires are vanquished in the interest of order. Says Sewell, "We can trace the operation of evil in the physical world . . . but I'm more puzzled about it in the moral world" (364). Sewell resolves this mystery by introducing a morality of physical result, subordinating internal factors to visible ones.

Silas does not fall for lack of trying. Only as he teeters on the verge of ruin does he replace his moral advisor, Persis, with a more suitable financial counsel, James Bellingham. Bellingham, the heir to an entrenched Boston family and the uncle of Tom Corey, gives Lapham the bad news in a direct and concrete manner. Indeed, while Lapham knows about paint, Bellingham, a far more modern figure, comprehends markets. Fittingly, this financial manager provides the economic application of the economy of pain, as he summarizes Lapham's position in a conversation with Tom Corey: "Whether [Lapham] can be tided over his difficulties remains to be seen. I'm afraid it will take a good deal of money to do it—a great deal more than he thinks at least. He believes comparatively little would do it. I think differently. I think that anything less than a great deal would be thrown away on him" (301). Bellingham's judgment proves true within the novel, but it is an insight that Lapham resists to the end.

By soliciting Bellingham's advice, Lapham moves toward bringing his enterprise into the modern industrial age, an age of consolidation, mass production, and mass distribution. Indeed, his business is ultimately bought out by a West Virginia concern that has New York capital behind it and is able to produce a better product more cheaply. Lapham's Boston years emerge as an anomaly, a period where the decentralized production of goods by small, family-owned concerns momentarily had access to major urban markets. However, this moment soon passed, as American industry entered an age of mass production and distribution. The concerns that defined this age did so through the rationalization of this vertically integrated process. Lapham lacks both the capital to amass such a concern and the organizational skill to oversee such an enterprise; therefore, he retires to the sidelines. This conclusion provides the change and continuity of Howells's social vision and an appropriate resolution for a realist novel. The Laphams are no longer focal in the new economic order but are represented by Penelope, who has adapted the shrewdness of her rural antecedents to the modern age. Similarly, Tom possesses both the lineage of the Coreys and a vision of modern life that allows him not simply to rest on his inheritance, as his father has, but to assert positively his nobility in a productive way, by entering a business endeavor. The union of Penelope and Tom symbolizes a synthesis of various positive strains of the past joined to produce the shape of the future.

In *The Rise of Silas Lapham,* Howells reveals the politics of his favorite literary form. He critiques a passing industrial class and an older elite, as he affirms and empowers a new class. This emerging elite is related to these older upper classes, but has adapted to the demands of modern life. Explains Martin Sklar of the turbulent last decades of the nineteenth century: "Out of the crisis there crystallized an emergent class leadership reconstituting itself on the basis of large corporate wealth, organization and power, and attaching to itself leaders and service savants from other social sectors—smaller business, politics, the law, the academy, the press, science and engineering, the churches" (32). Literary realism anticipates and assists in the ascension of this class by reaching out to its middle-class readers in expressions that produce and reproduce the positivist, top-down equation for enabling social order. This equation allies the Tom Coreys and James Bellinghams with the Seymours and Sewells to assure a well-ordered America where taste, morality, and managerial acumen combine to minimize the social role of the less skilled. This is not to say that such a strategy eliminates the producing classes from the social picture, only that these classes need to efface themselves in this particular model of order. Howells neither reaches out to these working classes nor represents them in a significant way. Realism is a philosophy of continuity and an ideological construct that declares the necessity of a society managed rationally and efficiently, terms that this novel and Howells's critical assertions associate with a modern definition of morality. Thus, realism asserts the ethics of its ideology.

THREE

Thomas Edison

and the Machine That Sees

In mid-June of 1891, as Howells reached the last year of his tenure at
Harper's Monthly, an article by George Parsons Lathrop (Nathaniel Haw-
thorne's son-in-law) heralded the newest invention from the laboratory
of Thomas Edison. Lathrop's description, which appeared in yet another
of the Harper brothers' publications, told of a device that "in one total
effect . . . reproduces with absolute fidelity and naturalness the movement
as well as the form of the original object" (9). For those of us who look
upon the flickering images of early cinema and are struck by their technical
imprecision, Lathrop reminds us of the way in which they were viewed in
the late nineteenth century. He goes on to evoke this marvel with language
that recalls Howells's aesthetic goals for realistic literature: "Edison's machine . . . reproduces the movement and appearance of life with such truth
of action that if colors could only be given at the same time, the illusion
that one was looking at something really alive would be absolute" (10). This
article was perhaps the first published description of cinema and reveals the
nature of its allure. In late nineteenth-century America, written narratives
that asserted their power to capture reality and to represent it compellingly
appealed to a particular body of writers, publishers, and readers for their
apparent ability to inscribe as fact the transient material realities of the day.
This idea of fixing fact contained at least an implicit effort to restore order
to a culture in the midst of visible social disruption. This hope of order was
particularly compelling for the guardians of middle-class culture and for a
number of its participants. Moving pictures promised a higher realism, as
they offered the immediacy of the iconic image. Indeed, as practitioners of
positivist methods in the social sciences proclaimed their ability to capture
reality itself, the invention of a machine that seemed to observe the world
in a perfectly neutral manner seemed further to support their intellectual
and ideological goals.

The presentation of fact was an immediate imperative of this new medium. Initially, cinema was conceived not simply as a means of entertainment but more prominently as a device for dispensing information of various types. The "documentary" film, defined as a presentation that primarily seeks to reveal some material aspect of the external world, was a popular practice of early cinema. Indeed, as the eminent film historian of this period, Charles Musser, has pointed out, film in its early form "was used primarily as a visual newspaper" (*Guide* 11). Later, the newsreel remained a staple of theaters in the era before television. The strategies by which early cinema asserted the factuality of its image, both textually and extratextually, define part of the legacy to subsequent American narrative film and its ability to inscribe its viewers in a particular ideological system. When subsequent "fictional" film is considered in light of its historical antecedents, its power as a means of dispensing "information"—that is, ideologically neutral fact—emerges.

If realistic literature restricted the form of its texts by pronouncement and cultural coercion, cinema did so by technological practice—a material expression of such coercion. The impetus to develop a mechanical system for taking continuous pictures and reproducing them on a large screen seems very much a late nineteenth-century desire in its complementary elevation of the visual and the technical. As the materialist impulse of the Gilded Age resulted in a broad emphasis on productive power over all other human characteristics, so did cinema provide a window through which to watch distilled action. Reese Jenkins, a noted historian of technology, explains: "In Edison's time most people regarded photography as 'objective,' recording the visual facts to be retrieved later at will" (159). He goes on to find that this desire to store reified moments was central to Edison's quest for machines that possessed "mechanical memory," including the phonograph and the motion picture apparatus.

> The systems of sound and motion recording fit with the philosophical tenor of the age. An antimetaphysical, positivistic view, which placed exclusive focus upon objective data, permeated the culture and fostered the enthusiastic and rapid development of such "nonsubjective" recording systems. These marvels of technology and science not only provided absolutely new experiences to masses of people, but they also possessed a presumed integrity congruent with the philosophical goals and values of the era. ("Elements of Style" 159)

Thus, these machines expressed the American cult of technology, while they also produced and reproduced the ideologically mystifying notion of objectivity. From a more critical perspective, the concept of data that informs this Edisonian project becomes reifying and a means of removing such facts from the influence of individuals. This estrangement is complemented in early film practice by the distanced perspective of the camera, which allows viewers who are so inclined to assume the culturally superior place of the distanced scientific observer, even as the screen image may provide a complementary voyeuristic titillation.

The material fact of cinema's form may make its content seem even more natural and inevitable than that of the literary text. Its technological basis appropriately expresses the power of the machine, as its solidity apparently elevates it above human error and displays the means-ends rationality of what Jürgen Habermas terms "technocratic consciousness".[1] However, such an uncritical view merely restates the common modern assumptions that equate technology with progress. In this narrow view, the history of such machines is limited to the statements that specifically explain the mechanical development of the techne. Machines do have a history, and technology is very much a product of culture. Cinema embeds its history in its apparatus, and it is in examining the specific form and history of that machinery that its meaning may emerge.

The first successful large-screen projection of a film in America occurred in the fall of 1896. This culminated a flurry of activity that had begun in 1877 when the still-photographer Eadward Muybridge took successive plates of a trotting horse in the interest of reproducing that motion in pictures. In 1879 he did so with the zoopraxiscope, which projected the revolving plates. In 1882, in France, Etienne Jules Marey introduced a chronophotographic gun with which he attempted to capture the movement of birds in flight. In 1887, Hannibal Goodwin used celluloid film for the first time. In 1891, W. K. L. Dickson, working at the Edison laboratories in West Orange, New Jersey, produced the kinetograph (the subject of Lathrop's article), a machine much like the moving-picture camera as it exists today. In the winter of 1895–96, two projecting machines appeared, one produced by the Lumière brothers in France, the other by Thomas Armat and C. Francis Jenkins in America. In January of 1896, the Edison Company entered into an agreement with Frank Gammon and Norman Raff, film entrepreneurs in their own right who had bought the rights to Armat and Jenkins's machine, to manufacture the projectors and supply films for it.[2]

This spate of activity, directed toward making a machine that seemed to capture movement and one that could project that vision, coincided almost precisely with the attempt in American letters to produce a science of composition based on positivist definitions of reality. If we look at the center of the realistic project in literature as having occurred in Howells's "Editor's Study" columns at Harper's from 1886 to 1892, we find that it falls neatly between the efforts of Muybridge and those of Armat and Jenkins. Film, like its literary cousin, derives its essential precepts of what is valuable and "real" by the same reduction that marks the philosophical basis of Progressivism. That is, in its material emphasis it reproduces the objectivist perspective found in such historically germane concepts as "efficiency" and "positive government." This form presents and re-presents the assumption that a human may be fully comprehended by observing his or her actions scientifically, that is, objectively. Because of its lack of an explicitly reflexive dimension and its representation of an increasingly common worldview, film also displays the results of those actions as immanent facts resistant to fundamental alteration.

Like realistic literature, cinema was the product of a class comprising, or allied with, the Progressive experts who sought to structure American society with their top-down notion of order. That is, the development of cinema and its ultimate commercial prominence resulted from those who believed in the efficacy of its technological reduction—including the capitalists who funded the cultural dispersal of films. As cinema went to the large-screen format and a model of economic dissemination that required mass production of films, in 1896 and 1897, film stock became virtually a monopoly of the Eastman Company, and it remains so today (Musser, *Emergence* 130). Indeed, in American cinema the figure of Thomas Edison as a corporate sponsor stands at the center of the enterprise. He operated the laboratory in which much basic research occurred, acted as an organizer of the varying avenues of technological development, and influenced cinema practice at several key moments in the early history of the medium. When Raff and Gammon began to market Armat and Jenkins's projecting device in early 1896, they judged that their best commercial strategy would be to enlist the cooperation of Edison. They justified their decision to Armat: "No matter how good a machine should be invented by another, and no matter how satisfactory or superior the results of such a machine invented by another might be, yet, we find that the great majority of the parties who are interested, and who desire to invest in such a machine, have been waiting for the Edison machine, but would hold off until they found what Edison could accomplish" (quoted in Musser, *Nicklelodeon* 59).

Edison's efforts to control the new medium found expression in his persistent legal harassment of his competitors. This was a common corporate strategy of the Edison Company, as the litigation department of the corporation became, in the years after the turn of the century, one of its most active components. Its centrality suggests the emphasis of the company. While Edison enjoyed the public prestige of an "inventor," his primary corporate intention in this era was to file federal patents in the broadest language possible and then to defend them aggressively. Rather than fostering invention as a broad imperative, Edison actually worked to thwart it legally. His intention was to use the legal codes governing intellectual property to maintain his economic preeminence in emerging fields of technical innovation. The legal department also "provided useful information for the laboratory by reviewing all relevant patents in the field and monitoring the technical advances of the competition" (Millard 178), suggesting the ways in which the vision of progress that functioned in the Edison laboratory was largely an economic one and primarily served the needs of the parent corporation. As André Millard writes of this period and of the Edison Company in particular,

If pure science is defined as basic research to discover new knowledge without the motivation of future profit, there was little science in industrial research. . . . In corporate laboratories intellectual freedom was often reined in by budgetary requirements and scientific freedom undermined by the need to keep the advantage gained by research. The work of the staff was primarily dictated by corporate strategies and not by scientific considerations. Research meant working towards specific technological goals. (158–59)

In the area of motion pictures, Edison's ongoing battery of lawsuits, begun in 1897, culminated in the formation of the Motion Picture Patents Company in 1909, in which the Edison and Biograph Companies pooled their patents and required all film producers in America to operate under their license. The legal power of this holding company was enhanced by Eastman Kodak's refusal to sell film stock to unlicensed concerns. The Patents Company maintained its domination until 1913. By 1918, the Edison Company had sold its motion picture business, its power eclipsed by those with more "nerve and capital" (Millard 293). Considering the terms of corporate prominence in American cinema around the turn of the century, and particularly the centrality of the Edison Company, one can see that the companies involved generally employed the strategies of other manufacturing concerns of the period. Large producers in the cinema industry attempted to restrict access to the marketplace and rationalize their own process of production and distribution. Indeed, we may look at early cinema practice as primarily a series of strategems organized around market imperatives that merged economic and editorial goals. Whether in the lab or behind the camera, the technicians and entrepreneurs of the early cinema, like Howells's realist narrator, effectively asserted the boundaries of cultural discourse by either normalizing or marginalizing the objects they represented.

The development of American film form was an event of broad cultural import and not simply a matter of technological history. The coincidence of the emergence of the cinematic apparatus and that of literary realism provides evidence of an elite class, to which Howells and Edison belonged, attempting to assert a specific form of continuity within a culture in the midst of disruption. While the Howellsian model enlisted the mediation of responsible civic leaders to bring about its moderating social ends, the methods of Edison were somewhat more direct. Cinema, in the predominant model employed by Edison, offered a broad appeal to various classes by basing its terms in a technological concept of "progress" that seemed to transcend ideology. As a pioneering device in the creation of a truly mass culture, cinema provided the guardians of culture with a device that could offer didactic principles implicitly. Indeed, since its inception the cinema has been the site on which those with competing visions of American life have fought ongoing battles. That the products of the film industry provoke such controversy reaffirms the medium's power to instruct; that the industry's primary impulse to promote continuity is not sufficiently conservative for some Americans comments directly on the effective range of American ideological debate.

As highly visible and widely acclaimed technological products had the potential ideological effect of producing and reproducing their own form of causality—reducing reflection and emotion to the simple mechanical model of actions producing more actions and reactions—it seems fitting that there would emerge an apparatus which would reproduce that reduction. The cinema was such a machine. It idealized the objective observer as it projected seemingly inevitable chains of action and reaction made into "science." It did all of this by employing the technology of the age: it used synthetic material for film stock and motor-driven cog/sprocket technology for its camera and projector, making it a machine that possessed both metaphoric and actual powers. It seemed to reproduce the world in fact as it provided vital testimony to the power of technology.

Initially it was the form of the apparatus that attracted experimenters and viewers. It is not merely a reading of the cinematic device which allows one to find its scientific basis, but also a consideration of its birth. Two central figures of the late nineteenth-century development of cinema were both, to some degree, men of science. Etienne Jules Marey was a professor of natural science at the Collège de France, and Eadward Muybridge was a professional photographer who ultimately produced motion studies for the College of Physiology at the University of Pennsylvania. Each developed their early form of camera as a means of capturing animals in motion, in order to reproduce that movement and analyze it carefully. They believed that such studies would reveal the essence of their object, as they equated kinetic movement with being. This equation may be appropriate as it applies to animals; however, implicit in these studies is the basis for the reduction of humans by the same method.[3]

Both Muybridge and Marey believed in the precepts of the modern scientific method. They looked upon facts as existing independently of human perception and sought a neutral device to capture this data in its natural form. They intended to create a machine that effected an inhuman—that is, technological—perspective and sought thereby to remove the problem of subjective vision from objective science.

This ideal, however, is ultimately unattainable. No matter how one attempts to efface the human basis of perspective, it still exists. Just as we can find the realist author hiding behind the illusory immanence of his or her literary text, so we can find not only the person pointing the camera but the men creating cinema. As a product of a specific cultural tradition, the cinematic apparatus did not reproduce the disembodied abstraction of sight. It merely re-formed a culturally based manner of organizing space and masked it by removing any explicit human presence.

These codes of perspective found normatively in cinema employ the formal characteristics of renaissance painting, a tradition with its own cultural history. Explains Jean-Louis Baudry: "Contrary to Chinese and Japanese painting, western easel painting, presenting as it does a motionless and continuous whole, elaborates a total vision which corresponds to the fullness and homogeneity of 'being,' and is so to speak representative of this conception" (42). Cinema normatively centers its image and places its viewer at eye level, hence creating the centrality of the observer, as he or she becomes the physical and metaphysical center of its engulfing image. This formal inscription of the viewer creates the intense illusion of subjectivity, as one seems to create the text immediately, from the atmosphere itself, and watches in subjective isolation. The image is clearly outside of the viewer and inscribes itself as a priori fact, as it simultaneously proclaims its objective quality. The viewer's complementary experience of subjective isolation and an objective image is the ideological basis of realist thought.

This condition of alienation from others within a universe of objective elements—that is, a world of facts that stand outside of human affect—*is* the condition of modern urban/industrial life as it is historically defined within the context of American capitalism. However, that it has taken the form it has may be traced to the specific devices of the rising technocratic elite—and cinema is one such device. The particular methods of industrial practice, both economic and technological, that occurred in the late part of the nineteenth century and came to define modernity in America were devised as a means of concentrating political power, not of democratizing it. Thus, mechanization as it occurred in large industries, such as the electrical and textile, became (if it was not initially) a means of mystifying the process of production and placing control over the shop floor in the hands of largely absent white-collar managers. This is not to say that this process of wresting control from workers simply stemmed from the form of new technologies. Rather, it resulted from a combination of the particular modes of technology employed and the specific ways in which they were imposed. David Montgomery finds this process of centralizing authority in managerial hands "a conscious endeavor to uproot those work practices which had been the taproot of whatever strength organized labor enjoyed in the late nineteenth century" (*Workers' Control* 27).

If we consider that cinema might have been a medium that was far more broadly participatory at its point of production and reception, then the specific conventions of presentation and reception traced in this chapter might not have developed along the lines noted. Indeed, cameras and film stock might have been widely available and halls of presentation bustling places where a range of films made by a range of filmmakers could be shown in a variety of ways. But since it was and is inscribed within a specific culture dominated by particular material and ideological practices, this medium's reproduction of that culture's system of exchange assumed the contours of the natural. Cinema at the point of its technical formation was conceived as means of making money for its owners, and its subsequent forms of practice have been developed to further that end. The act of buying a ticket and entering the hall where the image is projected becomes an act of consumption that occurs unquestioningly; and yet, by looking at the various codes that govern this notion of mass culture and mass consumption, we may see their outlines and pose questions that erode their illusory immanence:

What if there were no motivation for profit? What if the goal of entrancing an audience were not central to the enterprise? What if our modern notion of entertainment were more active? In looking at cinema at the turn of the century, it is also hard to ignore the fact that, from its inception, cinema's usual (commercial) form has largely mimicked what was then an emerging industrial practice: viewers sit still and in the dark observing a world already made, much as industrial workers sit inert and isolated at their machines. Cinema, in its dominant commercial expression, was and is a powerful ideological medium that both reflects and creates the human situation of modern American industrial life.[4]

As we look at the late nineteenth century, we find Americans in positions of influence lamenting a culture that has lost many of its ideological points of reference and seeking an appropriate worldview to reduce modern life to a series of commonsensical truisms, truths that may act hegemonically and substitute for critical thinking. The center of this view was a culturally inscribed definition of the term "rationality" that in effect meant the maintenance of older social hierarchies with the assistance of a new technocratic class for the end of order—but which was mystified by the interjection of a notion of a common good. This term rang with the ideological "neutrality" of science, yet could be bent appropriately and displayed widely by those with access to modern mass communication systems. Jackson Lears, in his study of the period around the turn of the century, has found that this concept was particularly malleable. For example, it served the apparently antimodern Arts and Crafts movement, which consisted of "business and professional people . . . from the aloof patrician Charles Eliot Norton [a longtime friend of William Dean Howells] to the flamboyant former soap salesman Elbert Hubbard" (61). These elite figures could employ the idea of rationality, with equal facility, to explain the need for their movement and to advocate centralized corporations:

> The final irony was that, despite the craft movement's origins in antimodern discontent, most of its leaders worshipped at the shrine of economic growth. And most fell victim to the evasions and self-deceptions of the dominant culture. In the name of individualism many hailed the vision of a future society modeled on the giant corporation. They shared that enthusiasm with the corporate liberal ideologues who had formed the National Civic Federation in 1900 and had begun to coalesce around Theodore Roosevelt. Roosevelt's ad-

vocacy of the strenuous life jelled with the Arts and Crafts program for individual regeneration. Both urged the cultivation of supposedly primitive traits as a path to greater efficiency in modern life. (96)

Cinema assisted in asserting the class interests of an entrenched group as objective truths. As we watch the various shifts in the medium's dominant practices, we may see the assimilation of these truths.

Had cinema been the device Muybridge and Marey sought, it would not have attained the ideological power it did. Rather, it would have been localized in creating "truths" at the cultural margin of science. But the primary use of the apparatus as a tool of scientific inquiry had all but ceased by the turn of the century. As early as 1895, Marey had conceded that "the image appeals more to the imagination than the sense" (6). In 1901 he noted, "Animated projections, interesting as they are, are of little advantage to science, for they only show what we see better with our own eyes" (quoted in Robert Sklar 9). Marey intended, as a man of science, to create a superior eye without a human attached. His scientific failure was his political achievement, as he produced merely a machine that saw as an acculturated human. This device is the essence of a propaganda machine, performing precisely the function of naturalizing and then reproducing ideology. Bill Nichols explains: "Ideology appears to reproduce not itself, but the world. It proposes obviousness, a sense of 'the way things are,' within which our sense of place and self emerges as a self-evident proposition" (2).

Muybridge agreed with his French counterpart and as early as 1888 discussed with Thomas Edison the possibility of linking sound and cinema to recreate performances by Edwin Booth and Lillian Russell. This conversation stimulated Edison's interest in cinema and marked the moment when he began to devote a portion of his industrial resources toward its development. It also seems to have oriented his notion of film practice. This conversation suggests that Muybridge too had altered his thinking regarding his machine, seeing it as a mode of entertainment with great commercial possibilities. Indeed, even as Muybridge worked for the University of Pennsylvania from 1884 to 1887, his photographs of humans and animals in motion suggest that he was already having doubts about the "science" produced by his machine. These shots include a collection of nudes in various athletic actions, such as running, playing cricket, and riding horses. Though the scientific community of the era seems to have taken Muybridge's work quite seriously, when viewed today these frames seem whimsical and evoke an artist's play, not a scientist's study.[5]

Yet, if the cinema did not produce an image that was of use to scientists, whose careful scrutiny found flaws in it, such imperfections were not immediately apparent to the less careful vision of a mass audience. By the last decade of the nineteenth century, the impulse to perfect the machine was not driven by scientific curiosity, but rather by the spirit of commerce. The Edison Company sought to display the kinetoscope at the Columbia Exposition of 1893 not as a curiosity of science but as a wonder with commercial potential. Indeed, the final form of the machine was determined by a vision of the marketplace. Initially Edison felt that large-screen projections were an economically limited mode of presentation, theorizing that such a mass audience would reduce the demand for the machine itself: If hundreds of people could view one image at the same time, then the market for the machine would be limited. He therefore emphasized the kinetoscope, which entertained but one customer per coin. At first, Edison's strategy seemed apt. Gordon Hendricks records that through the fall of 1894 "the profits of the Kinetoscope Company appear to have been solid" (20).

This marketing strategy ultimately failed, which suggests that Edison did not at first fully realize the appeal of his machine. Cinema could not produce these miniatures and have the ideological impact it did. By 1896, Edison concluded that the large screen was the future of the medium and bought Thomas Armat's device for starting and stopping the film on a projector. Large screen presentation offered a more compelling image than that available through the kinetoscope. It enveloped the viewer, as it recreated a worldview that many could watch simultaneously and mutually verify. One of the first large-screen projections of the film image, at Koster and Bial's New York theater, caused a contemporary journalist to remark that it "amazed the spectators . . . [with its] wonderfully real and singularly exhilarating . . . moving lifelike figures."[6]

With the emergence of large-screen projection came a range of types of presentations. These included vignettes of staged action (usually self-contained) and excerpted elements of plays or other familiar narratives. Most commercially prominent among presentations in the first years of large-screen American cinema were two apparently opposed types of film content: one presented visual illusions while the other apparently revealed actualities. Both initially relied on the wonder of the machine itself for their attraction, which allows some insight into the manner in which audiences approached this new form of entertainment.

In ways, of course, all cinema was magic. It miraculously presented visions from another time and place as if they were occurring before the viewer's eyes. Such mastery of the seeming absolutes of nature was indeed miraculous and transformed even prosaic actualities. As Tom Gunning points out, "Clearly, the fascination and even the realism of early films related more strongly to the traditions of magic theater (with its presentation of popular science as spectacle) than to later conceptions of documentary realism" ("'Primitive Cinema'" 4). The late nineteenth-century spectacle of the cinema machine at work endowed even the most ordinary street scenes with an element of wonder. Still, the "trick" film as it developed over the next decade or so asked for a somewhat different audience response than that elicited by more concrete presentations.

Erik Barnouw notes, "In the year 1896, magicians on every continent suddenly added a new and astounding attraction—the miracle of the century, the wonder of the world—'living pictures.' Within months it dominated all other wonders" (3). If the machine was extraordinary, the initial method of practice by these magicians was remarkable only in that it was so prosaic. The apparatus was apparently employed as a simple recording device. That is, much as Muybridge and Marey had used an earlier version of the machine to record the fact of animals and humans in motion, so did magicians use it to present the fact of their illusions. These tricks were strictly visual and effaced the prestidigitators' more complex actions, in a way similar to the manner in which realist literature showed the characters' actions but effaced their and the author's rationale. Magicians performed their acts before the camera, which was set stably in front of them at an ideal distance and fixed to center the performer. This form of presentation was relatively short-lived and gave way to a method of practice that either enhanced old tricks or created new ones. This method also had a short life. By 1904 the Biograph Company's promotional bulletin for the film *Bewitched Traveler* reassured exhibitors by declaring that it contained no magicians. Eileen Bowser documents the decline of American trick films after the turn of the century and their eventual demise:

About 26% of the 1900 productions were trick films; about 20% of the 1901 films; about 21% of the 1902 films (but here the number of Biograph films copyrighted in 1902 for which we don't yet have production dates may have slightly increased this percentage incorrectly); and about 10% of 1903 films. After 1903, there were only four or five trick films a year, at least among American films. Camera tricks continued to be used, not as the raison d'etre of the film, but as one of the tools of the medium. (6–7)

From the perspective of the performer, one can see the gradual development of insights and conclusions that parallel those of Marey and Muybridge. At first, magicians treated the cinema as a reliable recording device. That is, they trusted its ability to record and present the actuality of the world. They let the camera run continuously and record their tricks, in essence functioning as the ideal viewer who merely observes but never probes. It was next employed to posit the factuality of events that were not taking place. "Magicians" understood that it was possible to create tricks solely on the screen. That is, disappearance was so easily managed by employing the cinema as an aid that it became a convention of the trick film.[7] For example, in a film like *The Strange Adventures of a New York Drummer* (1899), a conventionally dressed man is shown to his room by another man wearing what appears to be the garb of an innkeeper. The innkeeper then disappears and reappears, as does the furniture in the room, and finally the drummer himself is stuffed into a trunk. The innkeeper reveals the trunk as empty, before the drummer reappears. Similarly, a film like *Uncle Josh's Nightmare* (1900) uses many of the same tricks of disappearance: a figure dressed as the devil vanishes and returns, as does the room furniture. Another common trick film featured decapitation. In *Mary Queen of Scots* (1895), for example, a performer in appropriate dress submits to apparent beheading. Such illusions required little of the skill of a live show and made such magic easily performed. Finally, the use of cinema expressly as a tool of magic ceased to intrigue practitioners of illusion. If one devotes his or her life to producing visual illusions through elaborate methods, then a machine like the camera has limited appeal once it is deemed unreliable. Magicians learned that the image was not of the world, but a formalized projection of its surfaces. Such an approximation was finally not good enough, and the image was discarded. In this, the dominant film presentation was moving from spectacle to narrative.[8]

Audiences, however, approached the magic of cinema from a different perspective. The audience of early cinema did not see the camera on a tripod stopping and starting or the frame being cut and spliced. It could not spy the performer's head being submerged or the furniture being removed when the camera ceased operating. What they saw were seemingly plausible presentations of decapitations and disappearances. But how could this be? Certainly this new form of entertainment was not bringing about the wholesale mutilation and disappearance of its performers. When in the first phase of filmed magic magicians offered only their stage acts, the seeing-is-believing axiom on which the cinema relies was not severely tested. How ever, with a glut of more extreme presentations, audiences were confronted with two possibilities: either the image of the projector was illusory, or people were vanishing and being killed. The logical conclusion, the former, was also somewhat unsettling. If we look at the realist aesthetic as flourishing in response to a culture's desire for a fixed reality, the act of calling into question one of the major expressions of that reality was disturbing. Further, as a metaphoric expression of the power of science, technology, and rationality, the screen image stood for more than itself. Audiences responded to this rupture of form and content by largely avoiding films that expressed it.

In a parallel practice, another school of early filmmakers employed their machine as a device to capture the fact of the world (as opposed to the fact of illusion). They did this by filming events that appeared continuous and often led to some plausible conclusion; hence, they posited that what was on the screen was the entire fact of an event. These scenes were shot from a fixed perspective, with the subject or subjects usually placed at the center of the frame and including his or her entire body. The image, then, seemed to assert the fact of a singular view and a correspondingly definite reality. This method may be seen as a necessary phase of the medium in asserting its vision. This mode of presentation entices not through curiosity, but through certainty. Hence, the more absolute and closed its perspective, the more desirable. Early cinema often offered nonnarrative slices of life, frequently of urban streets and recreations. A typical pre–twentieth-century slice-of-life presentation is the Edison Company's *New York Street Scenes, 1896–1898*. Crowds mill about and an occasional elevated train appears, but no singular attraction jumps out to command a viewer's focus.

This persistent focus on city life in cinema and realist literature suggests that the dominance of the positivist worldview is tied to the social phenomenon of urbanization. The broad dissemination of any ideology is much more efficiently accomplished if its subjects are densely massed. As the nation entered the twentieth century, its population was for the first time proportionately more urban than rural, as people moved from farms and from abroad to American cities. Realist literature and early cinema overwhelmingly focus on urban locales: they define this increasingly common experience as a norm and make it seem, if not familiar, then inevitable. These forms operate as a method of indoctrination, but likely one whose objects—of all classes, to a degree—willingly participate.

While those involved in the financing of realist literature and cinema of this period had an agenda based in the naturalization of their class-based perspective as "reality," and those who read realist novels generally came from the same class as those who produced them, the audience of cinema was somewhat different. As several recent studies of the reception of late nineteenth- and early twentieth-century American cinema have noted, the development of the cinema as mass-market entertainment depended on its ability to transcend class distinctions at the point of reception.[9] Unlike the novels Howells praised, early films sought to appeal to all elements of both the middle class and the working class. The urban actuality spoke to a common, though not universal, desire among Americans to align themselves with the values of a dominant culture. As Elizabeth Ewen writes in her discussion of the role of early cinema in the lives of immigrant women, "Film as a component of mass culture became a mediation between an historic uprooting and an unknown and threatening urban society" (S65). In this mediating role, cinema assisted Americans of all classes in assimilating a particular vision of modernity. Cinema helped its patrons find a place in the present by encouraging them to use the screen as a device for "finding themselves." "Local views," offering moving pictures of sights in the immediate locale of the place of presentation, were a particular attraction of this era of cinema practice. Audience response was enthusiastic, and to take commercial advantage of their popularity, exhibitors often added them to their programs of actualities of marvels (Musser, *Nickelodeon* 65–66; *High-Class* 109–11). Those who consumed these texts, which have little narrative appeal, sought to confirm their world by matching it with that documented by the normative eye of the camera, and they took pleasure in their ability to do so. Whether this disposition was a matter of confirming the hegemony of one's own class or, from the perspective of one beset by this hegemony, of identifying as concrete the social relations of the period, viewers actively looked to the screen to see themselves and the objects they knew existed outside the film image. This broad-based desire for validation of visual experience makes the late-century, middle- and upper-class–based notion of a fixed and limited empirical reality an entrancing interclass ameliorative to the rigors of urban/industrial life. Indeed, the cinema has the potential to define as natural and inevitable the social disruptions that feel so alien.

The role of cinema in acculturating Americans to this new world was no accident. Thomas Edison had a distinct vision of America, and since the Edison Company played an essential role in the definition of early American cinema's form and content, Edison himself looms large in its history. Though, as various film historians have noted, Edison did not really invent any aspect of the apparatus. Indeed, some historians have credited its invention to W. K. L. Dickson, a technician at Edison's laboratory. Edison did, however, organize the development of technology both inside and outside his lab.[10] To argue that Edison's limited technical involvement makes him irrelevant to any discussion of cinema's technology denies the nature of modern invention. As David F. Noble notes,

> After achieving considerable financial success in the invention of stock tickers for Western Union, Edison had set himself up in Menlo Park, New Jersey, with a well-equipped laboratory [the cinema was developed at a better equipped lab in West Orange] and a permanent staff 'to spend full-time in making new inventions.' . . . Edison's investigations were inextricably informed by economic considerations; as in all engineering work, the profit motive did not lie behind the inventive activity, but was bound up in it. (8)[11]

To deny Edison's role is to accept the mythology of the inventor as a solitary tinkerer laboring to build a better mousetrap, a mythology that surrounded Edison himself. Certainly, by 1888 Edison had become far more an industrialist than a tinkerer. As technicians such as Dickson worked for him at his West Orange laboratory, explains Thomas Hughes, he was increasingly "concerned about mass production, labor saving, and unit costs. The principles he was applying were those of the production engineer and capitalist, not the master inventor and applier of electrical science" (92). In his specific work on the cinema, he proceeded much like any modern corporate head devoted to the research and development of new products: he bought patents that contributed to the development of large-screen cinema and sponsored research by his employees, including Dickson, to that end. With the emergence of the apparatus in 1896, he also provided films for this new entertainment. Edison's control over form and relative importance in the presentation of content makes him a central presence in any consideration of early cinema. Though in 1897 the Lumière brothers of France enjoyed a dominant share of the American exhibition market, they withdrew their products at the end of that year when Edison threatened a lawsuit.

In 1896, Edison's empire of invention was showing signs of weakness. His magnetic method of milling iron ore had proven commercially unsuccessful and resulted in monetary losses. Further, the controversy over the method of producing electricity—by direct or alternating current—had been virtually settled, with Edison's direct method losing out. In 1889 he had lost a large portion of control over the power industry with the formation of Edison General Electric. In 1892 this company was merged into a trust by J. P. Morgan, thereby cutting the man widely known as the inventor of the electric light out of the industry's ongoing wealth. With the money he received from his stock he sought to perfect his forays into entertainment: the phonograph and the cinema.

Edison's loss of control over the method by which electricity would be supplied to the masses was largely the result of his methodological limitations. Edison was a man who eschewed theory for practice: he believed in the empirical method. The abstract nature of disseminating electrical current on a large scale was beyond the limits of his imagination. This limitation was quite apparent to those with more evolved scientific training, such as Charles Steinmetz and Nicholas Tesla, who had worked for Edison but resigned over disagreements regarding money and method. Cinema, then, became proportionately more attractive to Edison.

Edison's metaphoric importance in modern American cultural history has been well chronicled by Wyn Wachhorst. Wachhorst notes that 1889 was the "pinnacle of Edison's life and career" (90); subsequently, the inventor fought a rearguard action to protect his wealth, reputation, and cultural image. It is no wonder that the movies attracted him so, providing a means of shoring up all three. The medium became an area of interest, not as pure science, but as the embodiment of the meaning of Thomas Edison, which included, according to Wachhorst, "the gospel of technological progress, the rural Protestant virtues (hard work, initiative, perseverance, prudence, honesty, frugality, etc.), the success mythology of the self-made man, individualism, practicality, anti-intellectualism" (3).

It is instructive to consider precisely Edison's central role in shaping cinema and the results of his direct influence. Edison's ideal was to link image and sound for the purpose of engaging mass audiences, either as individuals or as aggregates. As early as 1888 he sought to link sound to image, but scrapped the project because he was unable "to make a phonographic recorder which would be sensitive to sound at a considerable distance away, and which would not show within the range of the lens" (Clark 178). When faced with this technical problem, he had to decide on one form or the other for mass entertainment: either a device that offered only sound, or the silent film. He decided on the latter, reasoning that the eye, the empiricist's primary means of knowing the world and the essential vehicle of the positivist reduction, was the preeminent sense. He declared, "Light travels quicker than sound, and the eye absorbs ideas instantly" (quoted in Clark 178).

As with Howells's realism, the values of positivism define the formal properties of the medium. We find the eye as the center of meaning, not through an unreasoned act of emphasis but distinctly chosen in preference to a machine which appealed to another sense. In his explanation, Edison reduces the entire process of acquiring knowledge to the passive idea of absorption through a single organ. Further, in keeping with the illusion of the authorless text, the film image must also appear as if it has sprung from the world itself. A microphone may not appear in the frame, as it would intrude on the vital illusion of immanence, an illusion that would make the medium seem, as in Howells's words, "let appear, not made appear." In perceiving the demand for realism as well as the need to posit it through seemingly factual and immediate presentations, the Edison Company consciously sought to limit the possibilities of productions that would neutralize the appeal of its new medium.[12]

If we see Edison as a central figure in the early days of the industry, then the content of films produced by and distributed through the Edison Company is instructive. These films overwhelmingly presented images that would not call into question the factual vision of the machine. These short productions centered an immobile camera on a subject who performed an activity with a logical continuity to the point of completion. Initially, these images were of rather ordinary scenarios, which diminished their emphasis on film content as they asserted their form. They could entice a crowd only for a limited period of time, as their form is indeed the assumed inevitable form of everyday vision. The question became, then, how to create extraordinary visions which would not undermine the machine's illusion of fact.

One answer was the first phase of film magic. Interestingly, a famous film by the Edison licensee Vitagraph, *The Vanishing Lady*, illustrates the conservatism of the parent company. The film was produced by Vitagraph, and copyrighted by the Edison Company in December of 1898. It shows its audience a magician (his identity is expressed by his dress and demeanor) approaching a woman, who is positioned slightly deeper in the frame. He then produces a curtain, which he places before her and which hides her from the audience's view. When it is removed, the woman has vanished. Due to the imposition of this covering, we do not see the device of the trick, or even see the act of disappearing. Rather, we simply view a trick which is defined as such by pro-filmic codes. That is, if the male in the shot were not a magician, we might not know how to apprehend the trick correctly. Since the actual vanishing is unseen by the viewer, the seeing-is-believing axiom is unchallenged, as this manner of illusion places no undue attention on the means of presentation.

This particular film was very similar to one George Méliès produced in France in 1896. Explains Lucy Fischer: "The 'plot' of the film is simple: a lady in full Victorian garb is seated in a chair, against the background of an ornate, elaborately molded wall. A magician (played by Méliès) drapes her body with a fabric cover. When the cloth is removed, the lady has disappeared, and much to our horror, in her place is a skeleton" ("The Lady Vanishes" 339). The difference between the two films is that Méliès substitutes a skeleton for the lady, making it a trick not of disappearance but of transformation. Disappearance asks only a suspension of disbelief regarding place and time. It does not ask an audience to consider the prospect of a fundamental alteration of substance. Further, a disappearance may be explained away by a number of rational considerations: maybe she escaped through a trapdoor in the stage; maybe she ran away as the audience's vision was masked by the curtain. The imposition of the skeleton, however, sets up the same situation created by magicians who, in a later stage of American production, asked audiences either to believe the unbelievable or question the device which presents it. To suppress that type of query, Edison and others offered a less fantastic image.

Such presentations show the limitations of content in early American cinema. Further, by emphasizing the medium's power to capture the world, they assured that the market would demand such images. As the device itself lost its intrinsic ability to enchant, matters of content became more important. That is, actualities of everyday life ceased to provide the entertainment they did initially. Producers looked for factual presentations that would not question the machine's vision. These newer films offered the realism of the extraordinary, as they focused on ethnic curiosities. For example, films such as *Buck Dance* (1898) and *Watermelon Contest* (1899) offered black performers behaving according to broad racial stereotypes, dancing in the former and eating watermelon and spitting out the seeds in the latter. In the 1896 *Morning Bath,* the behavior of the black performers is less stereotypical but also subject to racist interpretation: the black woman centered in the frame bathes an infant in a washtub and then rather roughly takes the child out. She smiles as the infant cries. Indians also appeared in early films which similarly inscribed them according to the broad contours of cultural stereotype. In the *Sioux Ghost Dance* (1894) and the *Eagle Dances-Pueblo Indians* (1898), performers who appear to be Indians dance ritualistically before the stationary camera. In the 1898 *Parade of Buffalo Bill's Wild West Show,* the spectacle of Indians in native costume is once again employed as a curiosity.

In this vein, one of the other likely subjects of early cinema was human sexuality. Titillating images offered all of the visceral excitement of magic without disrupting the veracity of the medium. One of the first major events of large-screen film was the presentation of the May Irwin and John Rice *Kiss* in 1896. This short tableau consists of a relatively close (for late nineteenth-century cinema) shot of a man and a woman lubriciously kissing. Drawn from a Broadway play and employing stage actors, it provides an image both common and extraordinary. In the manner of this era, it effectively blurs the boundaries between private and public life—in the same way as the realistic novel. The kiss ceases to be an expression of intimacy between two people and instead becomes a performance for mass consumption. Other popular pre–twentieth-century films in this vein included scenes of scandalously dressed (by contemporary standards) women dancing, beach scenes featuring "scanty" bathing costumes, and variations on the theme of the male intruder and the woman preparing for bed, such as in *The Old Maid and the Burglar* (1899).[13]

Cinema had the power to create the currency of cultural exchange in this increasingly distended social milieu of American life. It could endow things, as Howells does Silas Lapham's house, with objectified values that transcend their private meanings. A woman's body ceased to be her particular physicality but is inscribed as her totality, the purpose of which was to excite the generalized male viewer.

In ways, these types of film refer back to the hopes of Marey and Muybridge. These "curiosities" primarily occur after the apparatus's initial stage of naturalization, but at a point where its vision and the assertion of its ability to fix the actual were still somewhat tenuous. The camera and, by virtue of its representation of the camera's view, the projector serve as eyes that have the ability to view the extraordinary, but these scenes, while uncommon, are nonetheless certifiably real. The cinema functions in a manner consonant with the aims of science; it reveals the fact of aspects of life unavailable to the ordinary eye. The distinction between the early practice of Marey and Muybridge—both initially focused on animals—and these later uses of the apparatus is that here it is trained on humans, but humans of a particular type. In its emphasis on people it suggests the social sciences. As we have seen that the form of the image objectifies in a manner appropriate to the conditions of modern American life, so it follows that significant among the objects it creates would be those whom contemporary racist ideologies would term human, but of a particular order. If animals, lacking an inner life, are a relatively appropriate subject for the camera to reduce to mere behavior, so it follows that actions of a particular stereotypical nature

by human "curiosities" would ease audiences into this manner of objectifying themselves and others. That is, these ethnic performers come to
the screen pre-objectified by racism, and therefore they create no rupture
between form and content. Similarly, one of the features of the tableaux
concerned with sex was the objectification of women's bodies. The realistic
medium of the cinema normalizes the spectator as the dominant gender
and thus inscribes the body of a woman as an object of the male gaze's curiosity.[14] They thereby provide a bridge to the positivist manner of beholding
the world.

Also among these early films with more affective content were restagings
of various prize fights, performed in Edison's Black Maria studio in West
Orange, New Jersey. Such restagings, according to Raymond Fielding, included Michael Leonard and Jack Cushing (1894) and James Corbett and
Peter Courtney (1894).[15] These bouts provided a view of life similar to
those noted above, as they introduced people on the margin of American
society performing in a stereotypical way. That is, they show recent immigrants to America engaged in elemental acts of violence. These films have
much of the same exotic allure as an Indian ghost dance but perhaps more
visceral appeal.

Also quite important in early American cinema were "documentaries" of
war scenes. After the sinking of the *Maine* in February of 1898, films that
purported to be of that ship appeared. Films of war-related titles produced
by the Biograph Company, Edison's major rival, proved so successful that
the Edison Company sent a cameraman on William Randolph Hearst's
yachts to gather comparable footage. After war was declared in late April,
films of troops, though not in combat, proliferated. These films benefited both the war effort, in their ability to galvanize public support, and
the film business, as new theaters included film programs and audiences
grew. Arguably, film was also instrumental in the elevation of Theodore
Roosevelt to national hero and president, as films of him were a popular
aspect of programs. As the war in Cuba was soon over, films of it gave
way to those concerned with the Philippine "insurrection" of 1899–1901,
which maintained patriotic fervor and provided further subject matter.
In the same years the Anglo-Boer war also titillated American audiences,
who supported the British cause with a fervor that matched their cheering
for the United States. The use of films to rally popular support for what
seem in hindsight dubious imperialist adventures highlights the distinctions between cinema and realist literature of this period. While Howells
and Clemens lamented the myopia that allowed such militarism and the

jingoism that accompanied it, producers of films saw profits, and audiences experienced uncritical nationalism. Indeed, David Axeen finds the ideological resonance of these adventures in the Pacific and the Caribbean lodged in the terms of their particular rhetoric of "civilization," a rhetoric that speaks to a core of inscribed cultural belief. "Military and police actions from 1898 to 1902 gave the modernizing elite dramatic support for conclusions that it now urged on the public: . . . that war and empire would force new men and more progressive ideas on national attention; and that improvements in the United States military establishment had obvious applications to the 'progress of civilization' in general" (485). In its early years, film was a spectacle of the powers of technology to assert the concrete actualities of American life. One element of such an assertion was an embedded statement that celebrated the machine itself and that equated technology with progress. The cinema thus became the machine that celebrated the machine of civilization—in this case expressed by the atavism of war.

These films instruct us in distinct ways. Some of these productions were actually composed of footage taken on location; however, many were simulations, often shot in the hills of New Jersey by Edison. Sometimes these simulations appeared quite authentic, sometimes not, but this seemed to matter little to audiences, who accepted these films whatever their relationship to actual events as if they were fact—if their content were politically correct. Contemporary accounts note that such scenes "awakened enthusiasm" and were "warmly received."[16] The medium, rather than merely reflecting fact, now consciously created it, though the distinction seems to have been lost. What appears to be true is that the terms of that which was asserted as fact were bound by audiences' expectations. In the films of these American colonial adventures, it was necessary to cast the role of good and evil appropriately. The Spaniards or Filipinos needed to appear villainous, the Americans justified. Films showed the execution of these villains, victorious flag raisings, and Dewey's naval victory in Manila Bay, among other stirring scenes. In portraying the Boer War the same extremes held true. Films generally showed the noble English vanquishing the barbaric Boers.[17]

In his discussion of early film exhibition in Rochester, New York, George Pratt provides a description of audience response culled from newspaper reports:

> Audiences left no doubt as to their opinions and preferences. They expressed an approval by hearty clapping, endorsing Queen Victoria during the Boer War, although they might have disagreed with British

policy in South Africa. A Biograph film of Victoria's visit to Ireland in 1900 "was tremendously applauded. . . . It is evident that Queen Victoria's popularity has not been seriously affected by recent events." At other times rage lashed out, as it had once in the case of a Lumière view of the Spanish infantry, shown late in 1896 and "greeted with a storm of hisses, aptly illustrating the condition of the American mind on the Cuban question." Feelings boiled into greater aggravation more than a year later during a Biograph showing in 1898, and a Spanish warship view had to be eliminated from their program. "At first the audience hissed and with every performance there were indications of an approaching storm. Finally the gallery gods showed their disapproval with potatoes and other garden truck, and as the management did not care to start a grocery, the obnoxious picture has been permanently removed." (53–54)

In this manner, we see the historically specific politics of realism—which are distinctly aligned with Progressive notions of continuity and class hierarchy. The cinema effectively provided a cultural bridge into urban/industrial life and did so through the power of its images to appeal to the mass of disrupted Americans. Indeed, the figure of Edison at the center of the development of film form and content provides a mythic presence resounding with conservative intention. Though Edison himself eschewed American politics, he did so from the position of technocratic superiority, a stance that recapitulates that of the Progressive expert. He professed an uncritical patriotism and opposed the initiatives of organized labor, feeling that workers were overpaid and undermotivated (Millard 292). In the period from 1909 to 1914, as his control over American cinema crested and waned, Edison wrote of his ongoing faith in technology and the tenets of efficiency, including his idea to place music on a "scientific basis." He also made various statements expressing his admiration for the German methods of industrial production, never questioning its increasingly militaristic application.

Edison symbolized material progress, the embodiment not simply of technology but also of the technological reduction of thought. As such, his own words further refine that worldview. In a 1922 lecture he articulates his vision of modern education in a manner that distills his thought and speaks to his specific cultural impact:

I believe that the motion picture is destined to revolutionize our educational system, and that in a few years it will supplant largely, if not entirely, the use of text-books in our schools. Books are clumsy methods of instruction at best, and often even the words of explanation in them have to be explained.

I should say that on the average we get only about two per cent efficiency out of school books as they are written today. The education of the future as I see it will be conducted through the medium of the motion picture, a visualized education, where it should be possible to obtain one-hundred per cent efficiency. (*Diary* 78–79)

Edison assumes the unquestioned value of hard facts as he inscribes the inert, unquestioning student into his system. By linking his vision of the motion picture to his perception of education, he sheds light on the ideological underpinnings of film. To Edison, cinema is a means of indoctrination, which he equates with education. Indeed, one of the stated intentions of the Patents Corporation was to produce films that would be of service to American society, including educational films (Millard 223). His ideal was to minimize or eliminate abstract matter, including the word, from American life. This emphasis on the concrete and on training over education echoes the general terms of educational reform in this era. Indeed, Edison's vision recalls the importance of business leaders in devising the terms of school reform around the turn of the century and their relative success in making the urban school a place for the training of industrial workers. Like Edison, business leaders employed the terms of efficiency and productivity as a means of asserting the efficacy of their program (Oakes 30–32).

Edison's notion of education fleshes out the implications of the realist mode. Howells never articulated such a reduction, but the basis for it is embedded in his notion of literary realism. That is, as he proposes the world be reduced to its surfaces, he reduces knowledge to that which can be attained and confirmed by the visual sense. He thus reduces analytical thought in the positivist way. As literary naturalism and modernism further Howells's doctrines, their vision of man echoes that of Edison.

The roots of cinema show us its basis as a machine designed to view animals. In Edison's perspective, its ultimate application evokes visions of rats in a maze—except the rats stand on two legs and speak. Edison, as a one-man embodiment of the ideology of modern American life, promotes a vision that is distinctly anti-intellectual and views humans as nonreflective, machinelike entities who may be "trained" efficiently by reducing them to and by the visual sense. Like the realist narrator, the cinematic apparatus defines which surfaces are important and treats its rationale as self-evident.

In some ways Edison's ideology was prescient, in some ways typical. His legend defined the early twentieth century, even when his strictly empirical method had displayed its limits in his own research. Yet the suppression of theory and the substitution of doing for thinking as a value marked the emergence of modern American life. We may see this early stage of realism as a means of defining the reduction of people to objects and the world to that which is visually apparent, and as a purveyor of a worldview that began to smooth over ruptures in American social life.

PART TWO

The Natural

FOUR

Sister Carrie

and the Natural Power of Things

When Doubleday and Page published *Sister Carrie* in the fall of 1900, literary realism was far from moribund. The general principles of composition defined by Howells could be found in any one of a number of works, including the nonfiction of muckrakers Jacob Riis and Lincoln Steffens, the poetry of Edwin Arlington Robinson, and the fiction of Kate Chopin, Stephen Crane, and Frank Norris, among others. These precepts also found their expression in the still-simple narratives of the burgeoning American cinema. To assert that Howells had lost the war for the hearts and minds of Americans is a very narrow literary-historical judgment. Indeed, Howells's compositional method, with its emphasis on visually available materials and its efforts to join a notion of morality with the modern dictates of expedience, defines an epistemology that is common to twentieth-century American life. Critics who cite this failure base their conclusions on the fact that the sale of popular romances dwarfed those of realist novels. However, when literary realism is considered as an expression that produces and reproduces the normative voice and method of the technocratic reformer, its cultural centrality emerges. Among middle-class reformers the tenets implicit in Howells's vision became even more focal to the reorganization of American life in the years immediately following the turn of the century, as the Progressive political movement that had burgeoned on the local and state level in the nineties now found its national expression through the voice of Theodore Roosevelt.

If the Gilded Age revealed a culture in flux, the first years of the twentieth century suggest a move toward stability under the apparently rational guidance of Progressive management: "The Progressive ethos—rooted in evangelical protestantism, now turning to the task of delivering the cities from sin; committed to social science methods because they could eradicate social conflict; opposed to the evils of big business but accepting of capitalism itself; devoted to collectivist, interventionist solutions, confident they would not destroy individualism—was distinctively native, urban, and middle class" (McCormick, "Public Life" 107). To some degree, this marked the fruition of Howells's social ideal—though by the time it came to fruition Howells no longer believed faithfully in its efficacy, having become disillusioned with the cant of capitalism and the imperialism that accompanied it.

Literary naturalism is an expression that represents the historical and cultural shift away from the concept of morality embedded in realism. This is not to say that this morality vanishes, only that its centrality is in the process of being displaced by more mechanistic notions of causality and a diminishing of human agency. In the years around the turn of the century, social policy was increasingly justified by its efficiency rather than its beneficence, with these terms assuming a kind of equivalence.[1] In literary terms, the distinction between Howells's realism and the naturalism typified by writers as diverse as Edith Wharton, Henry Adams, and Jack London, to note just a few, is a matter of degree, not of kind. A concept of orderly progress lies at the center of realism, and realists explicitly declare that their philosophy is one of nature and not of the text. But by dwelling excessively on the distinctions between these two literary methods, critics may largely ignore their broad philosophical similarities.[2] Where realism presented the power of things as a proposition to fix value according to the rational tenets of a newly forming social order, naturalism vociferously, almost stridently, declares the fact of the material basis of American social life and derives a system of value from that fact. Central to this system is a belief in the inevitable power of the world's surfaces to typify being; indeed, this idea so pervades the naturalist text that individuals may lose their integrity, as human characters tend to be reduced by a system of value based on appearance and acquisition.

In his critical writings, Howells insisted that an affirmative expression of Christian morality inform contemporary fiction. Yet, as a novelist recognizing the forces of modernity, he employs a compositional method that so emphasizes the world's surfaces that it diminishes the power of abstract ideals to alter material life. In *The Rise of Silas Lapham,* Howells heralds the rise of a new morality of expedience. In the dictates of naturalism we may once again see the grafting of ideas of order onto the dictates of materialism. Naturalism furthers the assertions of Howells's novel and declares the power of such logic to define a social life that has already been determined—but somehow by nature and not by humans. Though naturalist authors may lament the new order of social relations, the protests in their narratives are ultimately ineffectual, and their vision of the world largely asserts not the coming of a new social order but the intransigence of the existing material order. The reformist impulse of naturalism is textually subordinate to the strident announcement of the necessity of pragmatic behavior, suggesting the gradual, if uncomfortable, act of assimilating the increasingly behaviorist ideology of twentieth-century industrial life.

While Howells argued long and hard for his program of literature, believing in the desirability of its ultimate social effects, there is no such polemicist for the social good of the naturalists. The most that Theodore Dreiser, a focal naturalist author, is willing to claim is that he provides "a picture of conditions done as simply and effectively as the English language will permit" (*Uncollected Prose* 164). Dreiser emphasizes the positivist methodology that is central to Progressivism's ideology, but he lacks the movement's optimism regarding the ability of reformers to reorder the world rationally. Like the social science model of analysis that informed late nineteenth- and early twentieth-century programs of social amelioration, naturalists objectify the world in order to derive its facts of human behavior: unlike the activist social science model, no plan is devised by which such behavior can be adjusted. In naturalism, the reified descriptions of social life defy alteration. Thus, in Edith Wharton's *The House of Mirth,* Lily Bart can neither fit the social world as it exists nor produce an insight that would allow her to reconceive herself and her social context—and therefore must die. This is also true of Frank Norris's McTeague, Jack London's Martin Eden, Kate Chopin's Edna Pontillier, and countless others who occupy the center of naturalist texts. In contrast, realism reveals a vision of social life that, while reified, has not yet assumed its hardened and pervasive character: Silas Lapham is allowed his refuge in Vermont, and Huckleberry Finn may move to the western territories.

In social terms, the era when Howells codified his realist text, the last quarter of the nineteenth century, was defined by galvanizing acts of public violence and an apparent, if not actual, disorder. In contrast, the first years of the twentieth, when naturalism became ensconced, were marked by relative stability. Where the Gilded Age had offered the railroad strikes of 1877, the Haymarket Riot, the Pullman Strike and Boycott in 1894, and the populist revolt, the twentieth century, prior to the first World War, had no such dramatic events. Labor battles such as the Anthracite Coal Strike of 1902 could be arbitrated with the assistance of the federal government, in marked contrast to the previous disposition of government to send troops to suppress labor physically. Indeed, Progressivism largely succeeded in institutionalizing a class of experts who would bypass the democratic process and dictate policies that they scientifically had found suited the common good. Samuel Hays notes of this adjustment, "A vigorous and purposeful government became the vehicle by which ideals derived from an individualistic society became adjusted to a new collective age" (*Conservation* 271). Thus, the Progressive impulse was to mediate strikes when they disrupted public good, to break up or manage trusts that operated inefficiently, and to legislate industrial and social policy that minimized class upheaval, by accommodating the rural and industrial underclasses with concessions that would co-opt their anger and not substantially disrupt hierarchies of power. As Arthur Link and Richard McCormick have noted of Theodore Roosevelt, "He reserved his most caustic criticism, not for radicals, but for blind business magnates who defended the status quo against all reform whatever. Such men, Roosevelt believed, were fools who risked a revolution without knowing it" (36).

Beyond the accommodations of Progressivism, however, we may also consider that by the turn of the century Americans were beginning to accept the terms of modern life, even if they found these conditions onerous. The ideology of Progressivism derives from a worldview that places power in the hands of a class of experts who can comprehend the facts of the world and make appropriate, rational adjustments in its condition. The larger system of the world, however, remains as a hard fact that defies alteration. But what about the mass of Americans who felt they had no access to such information and no formula for comprehending it? There are a number of explanations for the relative quiet that occurred after the turn of the century. Prosperity in the first decade of the twentieth century had replaced the erratic economic cycles of the Gilded Age. Systems of managing workers and of their actual coercion had been devised specifically to thwart the efforts of radical elements within organized labor to alter relations of production. With the defeat of the Populists in 1896, there existed no organized political entity to confront the hegemony of the two major parties.[3] But as a complement to these we may also offer the mass-disseminated expression of the efficacy of science and the wisdom of its neutral interpreters, devices the burgeoning managerial class employed to diminish the laboring class's idea of its own power. The extent to which these devices worked is subject to debate, but they were a regular feature of journalism and advertising around the end of the century.[4]

Dreiser expresses a worldview related to that generally construed as the dominant perspective of Progressivism, but he does not belong to the reform movement in the manner that Howells did until around 1890. Unlike Howells, Dreiser produced no body of materials that reveals his affiliation with the rising managerial class. He knew no presidents and controlled no patronage. Dreiser was the son of an itinerant religious family that never quite found what Howells referred to as "the smiling aspects of American life." They drifted in relative poverty, encountering various calamities along their way. Indeed, his sister Emma's ill-fated relationship with the much older L. A. Hopkins provided the model for Carrie and Hurstwood. Theodore also had his ups and downs. Unlike Howells's well-mapped ascent through the American class system to fame and wealth, Dreiser's career traces no such arc. Like Howells, Dreiser had some success as an editor of magazines and as a writer of articles, but it was generally a success of the second order and often followed by periods of failure. He wrote for newspapers and up-and-coming journals of a more distinctly middlebrow variety, such as *Ainslee's* or *Success*. In his work for the former he met Howells and then renewed that acquaintance for an interview in the latter. He also wrote a piece on Thomas Edison, a figure who captured his fancy, for *Success*. Dreiser's career as a journalist, though, had its problems, less because of his lack of ability than because of his lifelong difficulty in maintaining amicable relationships. His editorship of the journal *Ev'ry Month* came to an abrupt end in September of 1897, leaving him unemployed. He edited the somewhat lurid *Broadway Magazine* from spring 1906 to June 1907, when he was fired by a publisher who wanted more control. But perhaps his most widely known career setback was as a novelist, when *Sister Carrie* flopped in 1900. This resulted in three years of despondence and sporadic employment, a portion of which is recounted in the recently published memoir, *An Amateur Laborer*.

Dreiser's journalism of the nineties reveals a line of intellectual questioning that expresses many of the philosophical stances typified in *Sister Carrie*. As a journalist who later wrote novels, Shelley Fisher Fishkin tells us, Dreiser benefited from "two developments": "(1) the popularity of color or feature stories and (2) the new emphasis on 'facts'" (95). While a newspaperman he often "reported" in a style employing the newly wrought conventions of objective description; as a feature writer he often wrote of biological processes and new forms of technological wizardry.[5]

For all its recurring emphases, Dreiser's intellectual life defies the imposition of a simple pattern. In 1894, while working as a journalist in Pittsburgh, Dreiser discovered the writings of the social theorist Herbert Spencer, particularly Spencer's *First Principles,* which he later claimed "quite blew me, intellectually, to bits." Yet Dreiser's biographer Richard Lingeman notes that his copy of the book "contains marginalia—'not true,' 'nonsense,' 'yeah!'—that suggest that Dreiser did not swallow it whole" (144). The Spencerian doctrine proclaims that all matter progresses toward an increasingly complex state of perfection, propelled by an unknowable force. Given this logic of the universe, those humans possessing inherent characteristics of fitness prosper and reproduce while those of lesser qualities vanish from the species. For Spencer, the intrusion of human agency into the determined order of social existence was both false and dangerous, since progress and personal success had been foreordained. At best such intrusions wasted effort; at worst they disrupted universal logic. In the Spencerian view, social life, whatever its inequities, was always justified simply by the fact of its existence. Indeed, the harsher it was for some, the more apparent the truth of this misapplication of Darwinian theory was to its proponents.[6]

Though Dreiser was struck by his introduction to Spencer, to emphasize the Spencerian element of his thought as a key to his worldview misstates the case. Says Ellen Moers in her treatment of Dreiser's thought:

> Spencer's assertion of the uncertainty of all knowledge proved a spur rather than a barrier to the acquisition of scientific information. Because of its ultimate mysteriousness, such knowledge seemed no more accessible to the expert than to the unspecialized inquiring mind (of which Spencer himself provided the ideal, because largely self-taught, example). . . . To Spencer's influence in America can be directly traced the flowering of popular scientific education outside the academy at the end of the century. One product of it was the publication by Appleton of their distinguished International Scientific Series, of which Dreiser himself was a beneficiary. (139–40)

Thus, rather than being a doctrinal follower of Spencer, Dreiser employed a Spencerian stimulus to develop a vision of the science of social life.[7] At the time he wrote *Sister Carrie,* in the fall, winter, and spring of 1899–1900, the major doctrines intriguing Dreiser were a modified Spencerian system and a degree of Christian moralism. As other critics and scholars have noted, the narration of *Sister Carrie* problematically blends apparently distinct voices, which gives the novel, in the view of some readers, a certain lack of coherence. This narration has been typified as the clash of the new realism with the older convention of sentimentality (Petrey). It has also been explained as the sign of Dreiser's presence, his means of representing the "inaudible realities of the new America" (Trachtenberg, "Who Narrates?" 115). Both these analyses strike me as accurate, though the latter speaks more focally to the novel as a historical production. I would, however, take this second assertion one step further and find that this double narrative voice expresses the two strands of Progressive thought. Dreiser's mix of scientific method and Christian doctrine was precisely the philosophical mix that defined the ideology of this by now highly influential political movement. Thus, when looked at within an historical context in which the currents of an age are driven by a closely aligned ideological formation, Dreiser's narration becomes typical rather than extraordinary, and the relative incoherence of his novel a reminder that this set of beliefs did not always join seamlessly (McCormick, *Party Period* 269–72).

Sister Carrie dramatizes the inability of the moralizing dimension of its narrator's voice to steer events to a satisfying conclusion. Carrie's economic success illustrates the rewards available to one who assimilates effectively the vulgar values of American life. In the novel's final scene, as Carrie rocks in her chair, the narrator addresses her psychic disquiet: Carrie, "shall you dream such happiness as you may never feel" (369). He laments her inability to comprehend the truths of the social world—as the narrator does—and act in a way that is not simply acquisitive but socially responsible. Yet Carrie's material elevation reveals the limits of the narrator's social ideal. Clearly, Carrie is better off than when she began life, and she has done far better than Hurstwood. The narrator's telling of her relative discontent does not minimize the shown social effects of Carrie's instinctual system of values—a vital emphasis in a work that relies on its visualization of the world and denies the agency, but not the perspicacity, of abstract moralizing. Dreiser has the intermittent voice of a reformer, but not the heart of one.

In *Sister Carrie,* Theodore Dreiser explores the implications of Howells's and Edison's notion of realism and extends it polemically. Where both early cinema and the realist novel employed their media to confirm the power of surfaces and the inevitability of positivist truths, they did so by asserting these truths implicitly. That is, they effaced the human presence behind the text in order to assert the immanence of its presentations. *Sister Carrie,* as an expression of literary naturalism, assumes that its readers have already accepted the essential tenets of literary realism. Dreiser asserts (as did Howells and Edison) that reality is empirical and seeks out the nuances of the material world to show its meanings. He does not disrupt Howells's vision of the realist author but extends it by assuming the power of objects to define the virtual sum of a human being. Indeed, this further reliance on visually available symbols expresses an aesthetic logic much like that of early cinema. Its practice of freezing character into objective moments of definition lends itself to cinematic terminology: Carrie is found in "scenes" that Dreiser's cameralike eye constructs out of the found matter of the world.

In order to effect these emphases, Dreiser risks breaking the text's illusion of immanence by instituting a narrator's voice showing the reader the generic facts that emanate from the scenes. This voice seems to transcend human dimension and offers the tones of scientific and moral omnipotence. It confirms the facts of social life, describes them as inevitable and natural, but seeks to adjust them to assure the persistence of a correct order. Dreiser's assumptions of the world and the text mirror Howells's emphasis on material life; however, his forceful presentation suggests that he began with the notion that the formal properties of realism had been naturalized and that he could now argue volubly for their implications. This method and philosophy of composition places his novel within the formal context of literary naturalism and evokes writers such as Hamlin Garland, Upton Sinclair, and Edith Wharton. All these writers attempt to document apparent social truths with a wealth of objective detail, employing a method analogous to that of contemporary social scientists. In doing so, they create a sense of social structure that inscribes it as fact and places its power beyond the hands of the humans represented in the novel. Indeed, though *Sister Carrie* may be *the* naturalist novel, these authors also often employ a form that features this narrative voice confirming the inevitabilities of social life.

The personal relationship between Dreiser and William Dean Howells has been well documented. Dreiser interviewed Howells twice, once for *Success* magazine in 1898 and once for *Ainslee's* in 1900. Amy Kaplan describes the differing tones of these encounters:

Dreiser's [first] interview with Howells reconstructs an idealized world no longer available to Howells's generation—nor indeed to Howells—a world in which literature is integrated into other ways of life, whether the rhythm of the country newspaper or an ambassadorship in Venice, and in which writing is a pleasurable form of artisanal work, whose value lies in community service. . . .

His second interview, "The Real Howells," consigns Howells as a "personage" to an outdated world. . . . Many critics have read this interview as a tribute to the man who should have been his most appreciative reader, or as a request for patronage, but Dreiser's most recent biographer, Richard Lingeman, more accurately characterizes it: "as if he were prematurely writing Howells's obituary." (108)

This movement of Dreiser toward and away from Howells well describes their personal and textual relationship. Lingeman notes that as Dreiser left Howells after the second interview, "Theodore must have fancied that the warm benevolence of Howells's patronage was enveloping him" (236). Yet, the biographer recounts, "Not long after *Sister Carrie* came out, Dreiser ran into Howells at the Harper offices. 'You know,' the Dean said, 'I didn't like *Sister Carrie*,' and hurried off" (300). *Sister Carrie* abandons the genteel guises of *The Rise of Silas Lapham* in its dramatized narrative and explores the "facts" of Howells's materialism. These novels are nevertheless similar at moments, as the moralizing aspect of Dreiser's narration recalls the earlier work's emphasis. This occurs when Dreiser adopts a perspective from which he condescends to his less articulate characters and comments on their failures of taste and behavior. Though Dreiser dramatizes a world where material values have achieved dominance, like Howells he asserts the need for a corrective that would place the ideology of Progressive reform at the center of his ideal social system. Howells could not see this similarity: he saw only immorality and an unacceptable expression of the realist project: he did not wish to stop and chat.

Recent discussions of the naturalist novel, and of Dreiser in particular, have focused on its expression of the changing economic circumstances of the late nineteenth and early twentieth centuries, and the means by which this novel supports and/or critiques them. Walter Benn Michaels says, "The power of *Sister Carrie*, then, arguably the greatest realist novel, derives not from its scathing 'picture' of 'capitalist' conditions but from its unabashed and liberal acceptance of the economy that produced those conditions" (*The Gold Standard* 35). In contrast, Rachel Bowlby argues, "Behind the attractive images of consumption, [Dreiser's novel] clearly shows up some of the peculiar disparities created by that institution [capitalism] in the form it took in the 1890s" (61). My analysis defines a middle ground between these interpretations. Dreiser portrays the underclass, but in his manner of doing so he makes his novel a cautionary tale about the economic fate of those who lose their enabling desires.[8] While Dreiser's novel assimilates the truisms of living and prospering in industrial capitalism in recognizing the power of desire, it dictates, however ineffectually, the preferability of a more intellectual cast of materialism. Carrie knows the social value of things but not their true value, a limitation that makes her, in the narrator's estimation, extraordinarily common. She has qualities that leave her materially successful but not intellectually fulfilled. Thus, rather than fully embodying the ethos Carrie represents, the novel mediates between it and a moderating concept, also found in Howellsian realism, of fixed value.

Dreiser's argument, however, is not narrowly economic; though his broader polemic encompasses economic considerations, he posits a world that redefines the very nature of being. As Philip Fisher notes,

> The world of Dreiser's *Sister Carrie* is composed of images of motion of which the most are not the horizontal motions of train rides, carriage excursions, trips to Europe and walks on either Broadway or the Bowery, but instead the tragic and vertical motions of rising and falling. . . . Of all of these motions . . . none so dominates Dreiser's novel as that of Carrie again and again rocking in her chair by the window. . . . A window theatricalizes experience both for the one rocking on the inside as well as for the passerby who glances up and sees the "pretty scene" of a young lady wistfully rocking at her window in the evening light. (*Hard Facts* 156–57)

While the novel expresses the validity of performance, it is not so fatalistic as to suggest the inevitability of cycles of motion, and therefore of good fortune and misfortune. Indeed, this may be the overriding political effect of the work: Carrie's "instinctual" sense of the value of the world's surfaces makes her something of a genius, however unintellectual she may be. We as readers, then, are inscribed in the same process of recognition, and we must see the worth of appropriate commodities as expressions of being or we may succumb to the power of a social system which casts us out as it does Hurstwood. Within the novel this system may be morally incorrect, but that it does define the work's representation of the terms of modern life is inarguable. Thus, *Sister Carrie* becomes a novel of accommodation, even if that act is not the ideal condition defined by its narrator.

The tenets of materialism and accommodation also lie at the center of the historical currents of the turn of the century. By the turn of the century the cultural emphasis of America had fully turned the concept of progress into a primarily material one. This equation was to some degree intentional, a matter of capitalist enterprise employing the newly expanding modes of mass communication to create a world in which it could prosper.

Mass-market magazines of all types included articles announcing that the seemingly alienating changes of life that defined modernity were really part of an ineffable process that could be identified by the apparently neutral term "progress." As Richard Ohmann explains, "Magazines helped readers understand how things work. . . . *Cosmopolitan* ran a "Progress of Society" section, and explained in detail how men had harnessed Niagara to produce electricity. Magazines helped middle-class people feel competent and at home in the world through a mediated comprehension of human action upon nature, and of nature itself as represented through science" (149). In addition, the advertisements that in some journals dwarfed copy told of a revolution in matter that had produced consumer goods of necessity and scientific distinction, ranging from soap to hair dye to tooth powder. As the century turned, capitalist production had co-opted the term progress and its range of applications and reduced its meanings to the world of goods and the triumph of its own vision of the relations of production. Progressivism is a means of reforming the visible abuses of such a system in order to preserve it. Dreiser's novel looks out upon a world where such a co-optation has already occurred, as it baldly states the "facts" of life.[9]

But even as *Sister Carrie* reproduces central cultural truisms, its production and reception were problematic. The production history of the novel, in brief, begins with Doubleday and Page accepting the manuscript in the spring of 1900. In the summer of that year, Walter Hines Page sent a letter to Dreiser attempting to renege on the contract. Apparently, Dreiser's treatment of Carrie's sexuality made him apprehensive, as the fictional character lives "in sin" throughout a good deal of the narrative. In addition, the author vexed Page by using actual names and places in his fiction. Both of these objections are comprehensible: the former due to fear of public censure, the latter out of deference to those who would have preferred that their names and establishments not appear in such a scandalous work. Dreiser persisted in having the publisher honor its acceptance and left many of the real names and places in the book. It was published in 1900, sold half of its run of one thousand copies, and went out of print. In 1907 B. W. Dodge and Co. reissued it and sold a respectable 8,500 copies. It also received enthusiastic reviews, which established Dreiser's reputation. As Lingeman notes, "The times were changing" (418). It has remained in print ever since.[10]

Sister Carrie dramatizes the rise of consumer culture even as it grieves over that culture's new centrality. The novel's impact relies on the reader's comprehension of the world of commodities, as it assumes not only that the objects of the world are meaningful, but also that the specific importance of these things is fairly obvious. In addition, the novel requires that the reader associate these objects, in all their resonance, with the book's human characters. If the reader fails to perform these operations, the book deteriorates into a morass of description of various mass-produced objects of the world. If the novel is read "correctly" it engages and affects. Thus, the novel not only comments upon a burgeoning system of mass production and consumption, but it also asks that its readers participate in such a system as the act of consuming the novel itself.

When the novel introduces Carrie, we can see from the sequence of relationships between the narrator and his object the manner in which he studies her. The work's initial paragraph establishes its terms and focus immediately: "When Carrie Meeber boarded the afternoon train for Chicago, her total outfit consisted of a small trunk, a cheap imitation alligator-skin satchel, a small lunch in a paper box, and a yellow leather snap purse containing her ticket and four dollars in money. It was August 1889" (1).

Carrie herself is first seen as an actor in this tableau, as the narrator notes her boarding the train, but she seems to freeze in the midst of this activity. The reader is aware of no further movement, as she passes no landmarks nor looks for a seat. She fails to effect any sequence of movements. Instead, the focus shifts to the objects which surround her, and from these her character begins to take on definition. We know that she is of modest means and background, due to the nature of her belongings and the contents of her bag. Her trunk and the description "total outfit" indicate that she is leaving her home permanently. Her ersatz alligator satchel suggests to us that she aspires to better things.

The objects described in the paragraph are assumed to be universally meaningful. If the reader has no knowledge of these objects, then they have no resonance and effectiveness in defining Carrie. Rather, their appearance at the beginning of a long novel as a means of describing its central character may puzzle someone opening the book. Dreiser assumes that readers are able to relate their own understanding of these objects to the descriptions found in the novel. This method supposes not only an understanding of the utility of these objects, but also a comprehension of them as means of self-definition. We know Carrie because we know what this imitation alligator-skin satchel means.

The relationship between Carrie and these objects is not clearly that of owner to commodity. While Carrie appears in the first sentence, which asserts her centrality in the paragraph, no description of her occurs. Neither is the fact that she owns these things stated. They are simply her "total outfit," a description that alludes to the objective status of these things as implements in the generic sense. They are things to use, and within the worldview of this novel, and indeed of the realist canon, behavior determines character. As such, it logically follows that the things used by a character take on a significance almost equal to that of the individual who uses them. Carrie's outfit has the objective status of found elements from the world, commodities with remarkable powers to define the self, but ultimately of only transient value, as the self is subject to change and takes on new commodities to define that change. While Carrie is clearly central, she is symbiotically linked to the commodity world. As such, she is an object among other objects, as her humanity itself becomes commodified and transitive.

In the next two paragraphs, the terms of this objectification come further into view, as the novel's form becomes clear. Paragraph two begins, "To be sure there was always the next station, where one might descend and return" (1). Paragraph three reads, "When a girl leaves home at eighteen, she does one of two things" (1). We know from the generic "a girl" and "one" that Carrie's experience is in no way unique to her. Rather, the novel commodifies this particular experience through using common objects to define character, as well as by employing broad statements to discuss the universal importance of Carrie's plight. In the ensuing paragraphs Carrie's centrality gradually diminishes. In paragraph two she is one among many who have taken this particular train ride from Columbia City to Chicago, and indeed, in this paragraph's second sentence Carrie is recalled with the pronoun "she." In the third paragraph, however, she becomes merely one girl among countless girls, and no word invokes her particular experience. The sequence of these paragraphs progressively objectifies both Carrie's being and her experience. She is initially defined by commodities; then she gradually becomes a commodity. The focus of this sequence gradually moves away from Carrie, the person with an individual perception and a unique experience of the world. Instead, as our point of view is manipulated, we move back from this character, and by our doing so her importance in the scene diminishes.

We notice this change in perspective because the core of the novel is so markedly visual. *The Rise of Silas Lapham* has some tendency to rely on the surfaces of the world to create its meanings, but it also employs dialogue more strategically than *Sister Carrie*. Dreiser's focal characters are far less articulate than those of Howells, and therefore the novel must show them acting and in frozen moments surrounded by their "things" in order to provide them with any illusion of fullness. Indeed, this mobile eye is necessary to seek out the material nuances that are so vital in defining these objectified humans. Further, this searching lens suggests the direction of narrative film form, as the strictly visual terms of that medium result in a similar reduction, and therefore the camera must become increasingly mobile to add objective nuance to the flat humans on the screen.

The process of objectifying the character named Carrie reproduces a vision of humans and goods that marks the rise of consumer culture in the early portion of the twentieth century. Because the boom and bust cycles of the late nineteenth century had produced chaos (between 1873 and 1897, there were fourteen years of recession or depression) a means of attempting to regulate production and consumption was being theorized to hedge against such disruptive cycles.

Rationalizing production was relatively simple compared to the mysterious process of creating demand for a specific product. In the former case, industries employed technological change and rational management to attempt to regulate the amount of goods produced. In the latter, less satisfactorily, the national advertising market was largely defined in the eighties and nineties. The creation of this market not only resulted in a boom in the amount of advertising, but it also changed the type of advertising, which often differed from the older, local type in its saturation techniques and in its psychology. Though many national advertisers considered it their duty only to inform their readers of the availability of their product, a distinct minority of American advertisers between 1890 and 1910 considered it their job to create demand by sensationalizing the advertised goods. Thus, "Wooltex Styles," in a 1905 ad in the mass circulation *Ladies Home Journal,* proclaimed in large type that they were "for the well dressed woman." Or a later Cutex ad could proclaim, "Every Day People Judge You By Your Nails." These two ads are typical of advertising strategies in appealing to women and the lower classes, groups that were generally considered less rational than the normative middle-class male. In these ads, rather than getting quickly to the point and emphasizing price, copy and pictures made the product the answer to an emotional need.[11] As one contemporary explanation went, "For a man an advertisement must be short and to the point. . . . For the women, on the contrary you can put in as much detail as you please; once a woman is attracted to an ad she will read it all through, no matter how long it is or how fine the type is" (in Curti 344).

The figure of Carrie Meeber reproduces the assumptions and methods of modern advertising. She is made by the mass-produced things that adorn her and becomes an embodiment of the course of a life of desires, a perfectly integrated mechanism for internalizing the ethos of consumption and externalizing its notions of fashion and desirability. While objectifying Carrie, the perspective of these opening paragraphs makes an explicit case for its worldview as the most expedient approach to this environment. The order of information related to the reader is generally objective. The gradual distancing of the point of view in these three paragraphs makes the case that the novel is not simply about the truth of this character's experience, but about the experience of this *type* of person, a group that in the circumstances of the novel's view (where self is an objectified commodity) may well run into the thousands. While Howells tentatively suggested the means by which his novels should be apprehended, Dreiser insistently tells us, by placing the narrator between the reader and the novel's plot. This interposed narrator asserts the fact of this text and functions in this phase of the novel as the voice of scientific certainty, not of authorial intrusion. Such a voice can appear because the realist form, through the cultural impact of Howells and his colleagues as well as that of the cinema, is in the process of becoming naturalized.

Yet as we read with the certainty of such judgments echoing throughout, an attempt to characterize the narrator's relationship to the action finds him not simply superior but actively condescending. His is the voice that tells how people as common as Carrie, Drouet, and later Hurstwood are drawn in by the self-defining forces of the world; yet from almost the beginning of the novel, he intercedes to tell of the need for "a counsellor at hand to whisper cautious interpretations" (2). This counsellor, then, possesses the intellect and distance to comment on their vulgarity from without. He says of Carrie in a way that echoes Howells's discussions of the Laphams' aesthetic sense, "Books were beyond her interest—knowledge a sealed book" (2). Whereas in *The Rise of Silas Lapham* Howells commented on his characters' lack of fitness for modern life by asserting their vulgarity, Dreiser declares his characters' typicality by asserting their ignorance. Yet, this moralizing narrator's distance from the narrative is so great that this voice seems unable to effect change. Indeed, it is difficult to see his comments as affirmative in any way; they come through as criticisms without resolutions.

Dreiser's method results in a novel about objectification and anomie. In this world, objects take on human functions, emotions are reified, and humans act like machines. A city may possess "cunning wiles" (1), "things breathe into the unguarded ear" (2), and clothing represents intellect. The novel confirms the existence of this world of commodities and acts out its drama within that world.

Carrie's relationships with Drouet and Hurstwood characterize the state of human interaction within this world. In both cases the novel focuses on the functional aspects of the relationship. Drouet buys Carrie clothes; Hurstwood provides social and geographic mobility; Carrie adorns their respective apartments and adds to their public appearance by being seen with them. The method of organizing the industrial workplace according to the top-down dictates of rationality and industrial efficiency becomes a working metaphor for all human relationships; a man or woman is a machine who can be fully apprehended by his or her behavior and whose essential value is productive. As David Noble notes in his study of the ideology of the systems of engineering that developed after the turn of the century: "Human engineering was the movement to control the human element of production at the individual and group level through the study and manipulation of human behavior" (264).

The specific nature of the relationship between Carrie and Drouet illustrates the functional interaction between them. From the beginning Drouet attracts her because he presents the possibility of producing gifts to consume. She knows this through her reading of the objective meaning of his wardrobe. As they travel to Chicago on the train he offers to show her the sights of the city. Her response indicates both the desirability of consuming these experiences and his attractiveness as a producer of these delights: "There was a little ache in her fancy of all he described. Her insignificance in the presence of so much magnificence faintly affected her. She realised that hers was not to be a round of pleasure, and yet there was something promising in all the material prospect he set forth. There was something satisfactory in the attention of this individual with his good clothes" (5). Indeed, the sum of Carrie and Drouet's interaction is true to these initial insights. He does produce the material prospects he promises and by doing so gains her attention. However, this does not guarantee her eternal fidelity; her interest will last only as long as his productive capabilities entrance her.

Perhaps the most telling scene of their relationship takes place when they meet by chance in downtown Chicago. He takes her to lunch at "the old Windsor dining room, a large comfortable place. . . . Drouet selected a table close by the window, where the busy rout of the street could be seen.

He loved the busy panorama of the street—to see and be seen" (44). As a novel that implicates its readers in a kind of urban voyeurism, the emphasis of the text is in "being seen." The passive form here expresses only the fact that a person sitting at this table would have the physical ability to peruse the street. In fact, though the next sentence indicates that Drouet loved to see as well as to be seen, the ensuing paragraphs never locate him in the act of looking at this busy panorama.

In his first meeting with Carrie, Drouet recognizes the quality of her physical attractiveness. The narrator notes this: "Carrie was really very pretty. Even in her commonplace garb, her figure was evidently not bad, and her eyes were large and gentle" (46). In addition to this description, the narrator has already noted that Carrie is "in possession of a mind rudimentary in its powers of analysis and observation" (2). Hence, Carrie does not *act* as an adornment, nor is she *interpreted* as an adornment by Drouet; the voice of the narrator tells the reader that she *is* an adornment. Drouet merely responds to the reality of that condition and uses her as she is best suited, displaying her before the window.

Drouet, by contrast, has the power to produce material goods. Again his inner life is logically ignored, as the text notes that he was of a type who had "a mind free from any consideration of the problems or forces of the world" (3). Defining him by his function seems a legitimate response to the reality of his character. The narrator locates him sitting at the table in the Windsor room and notes not his depth of conversation but that he "chattered on at a great rate, asking questions, explaining things about himself, telling her what a good restaurant it was." As if to equate his bodily noises with his speech, we find that "as he cut the meat his rings almost spoke. His new suit creaked as he stretched to reach the plates, break the bread, pour the coffee" (45). The depth of his humanity is further questioned by minimizing the acts essential to it. The form of the meal's presentation takes precedence over the content of the actual nutrition he derives from eating. Once again we see a world where even the simplest acts are commodified. Dining is a means of fulfilling a social role, not of performing a vital function. Speaking is a means of making appropriate noises, not of communicating. The final sentence of the paragraph notes that "he was a splendid fellow in the true popular understanding of the term," further defining him as a mass-produced being. This bit of commodified language seems accurately to describe a person whose individuality is so suspect that a term describing many describes him.[12]

Subsequently, as they leave the restaurant, the narrator records Drouet producing the economic reward Carrie has hoped for: he gives her "soft and noiseless greenbacks," as the narrator notes that "in his crude way he had struck the key-note. Her lips trembled a little" (47). The correctness of the novel's conception of human-as-machine is affirmed in this scene. Drouet proves his value by churning out the product he has been created to produce. Furthermore, the object that he produces takes on a sensuality that he himself does not possess. While Drouet is described in term of function, the money he gives Carrie has a sensuality, "a softness," that brings about an appropriately sensual response, as Carrie's lips tremble. In the world of this novel, where the difference between humans and inhuman things becomes indistinct, money possesses a quality like human skin (softness) and seems capable of making sounds, as if it were alive. Paper money, an object with no real value but only the symbol of value, takes on a meaning far greater than that of the character who possesses it.

Yet for all the dramatization of the power of money, this moment becomes an occasion for the moralizing voice of the narrator to intercede. He tells us that, though Carrie and Drouet are worshipful of currency, "the true meaning of money yet remains to be popularly explained and comprehended" (47). In this aside the narrator defines it as a "moral due—that it should be paid out as honestly stored energy, and not as a usurped privilege" (48). This notion of moral due seeks to replace Carrie's ethos of simple desire and consumption with a fixed system that defines worth as a concrete entity, a matter of performing actions with a distinct value. One might assume that this statement of "moral due" elevates the power of productive, physical labor and is therefore an attack on developed capitalism, where paper transactions allow capital to increase exponentially. But a closer analysis that considers the reformist expressions related to this phase of narration more easily aligns this assertion with the classist imperatives of the rising technocracy. Indeed, it is a statement that belongs in the mouth of Sewell the minister or Seymour the architect in *The Rise of Silas Lapham,* as both these figures speak to the necessity of differentiating the essentially valuable from the momentarily desirable. It reveals the wisdom of its moralizing social scientist and the necessity of incorporating the lower classes into its rational social vision, one that would displace excess energy—the fuel of social chaos—with knowledge of the facts of the value of the world's goods.

As in advertising, Dreiser's moralizing narration finds a woman as its prime object of instruction. Though this scene suggests that both Carrie and Drouet misapprehend the value of money, it is only Carrie whose ignorance merits comment. Similarly, though both Drouet and Hurstwood apparently share Carrie's passion for consumables, it is only she who is dramatized shopping and refining her ability to make astute judgments regarding the value of objects. In typifying Carrie in this manner (and I would include her Chicago friend Mrs. Hale and her New York friend Mrs. Vance in this category) Dreiser reproduces truisms regarding women in the turn of the century marketplace, as he also not only dramatizes the terms of advertising in his novel but recapitulates its critique by late nineteenth-century reformers, who questioned the social impact of unleashing the irrational impulses of women. As William Leach notes of the dramatic increase in mass consumption after the Civil War, "An index of the control many middle-class women had over the family budget, shopping gave them a measure of economic power they lacked by not working. By the 1880s the New York *Times* could report 'the awful prevalence of the vice of shopping among women,' an addiction, it warned, 'every bit as bad as male drinking and smoking'" (333).

As women increasingly did most of the consumer purchasing in America (80–85 percent by 1915), anxieties increased over their abilities to function responsibly, with public attention fixed on instances of overbuying on credit or shoplifting. Indeed, the publicizing of such acts served as a reminder that women's impulses required moderation through the imposition of male restraints. Thus, by the second decade of the twentieth century the male-dominated advertising industry was gearing its advertisements not simply to desires but to rational purchases—but in a way that would not influence the actual amount of money spent. "Economy rather than thrift became a virtue, and the upper- and middle-class American housewife practiced thrift by purchasing new products that were 'economical.' Indeed, appeals to economy seemed to grow almost in proportion to the apparent affluence depicted in the advertisements. Economy, however, as defined by American businesses in their advertisements did not mean saving; rather it meant getting your money's worth on your purchases" (Norris 86). Even the rhetoric of advertising had taken on a voice that dared not fly in the face of moderation. This notion of economy in consumption well recapitulates Dreiser's notion that money should mean value. Dreiser neither critiques capitalism nor embodies it wholly. He typifies, in his assumption of the moralizing impulses of Protestant reformers, a strain of its elite class of men who seek to regulate its progression and fix its social hierarchies. But he also represents the power of goods to define social life without human encumbrance.

As we conceive of Carrie as a consumer and a symbol of the transition to a social life based on the ethos of consumption, it is fitting that her barter transaction with Drouet reveal the astuteness of her initial judgment. He does produce relative material luxury and remains the commodity he began as; he never takes on an emotional or intellectual dimension. Carrie, however, does change. Her presentation becomes more luminous, as the quality of its trappings improve. She becomes more astute as a shopper even as she does not question the terms of transaction: money for sex. She is shown to differ from her suitors in that while she satisfies their narcissism through her physical beauty, this provides nothing in the world of transactable goods. Her beauty has less power to define the social life of men than their goods have to define Carrie's social ascent, suggesting Dreiser's reading of the turn-of-the-century hierarchy of cultural value. This, of course, is a selective reading on Dreiser's part. In another scenario her youth and beauty could be viewed as commodities consumed by men who seek to employ her looks to elevate their social appearance. Yet in Dreiser's world, Carrie is distinct from Drouet and Hurstwood in that they merely use her but she consumes them. This suggests the greater social utility of her womanly desires, as Dreiser represents the desire of things as more enabling than the encumbering lust for another person.[13]

As was the case with Drouet, the first thing Carrie notices about Hurstwood is his garments. The success of her relationship with Drouet has confirmed the correctness of this perception, seeming to prove the adage that clothes make the man. Her powers of astute observation allow her to notice that Hurstwood dresses better than Drouet, and in Carrie's world the possibility that he merely has better taste does not exist. If he has more fashionable garments it only follows that he is a better man—with *better* referring to his relative power to produce goods. Character is as character appears, and in *Sister Carrie* there is little distinction between clothes and flesh. Indeed, whereas Howells promoted the normative vision of the rising managerial class as the proper device for ascertaining objective value and meaning, the functional truths of Dreiser's world—those that are dramatized—while similarly objective, are mass-produced and mass-consumed. The realist novel explores the true value of objects as their moral value, even as this equation between realism and morality falters under the weight of its contradictions. The naturalist novel reveals that the value of objects must be known for the sake of correctly comprehending the facts of the world. Thus, Dreiser throws off Howells's illusions.

The narrator focuses on Hurstwood's objective qualities as he first meets Carrie and effectively discerns their component parts.

He was in his best form for entertaining this evening. His clothes were particularly new and fine in appearance. The coat lapels stood out with that medium stiffness which excellent cloth possesses. The vest was of a rich scotch plaid, set with a double row of round mother-of-pearl buttons. His cravat was a shiny combination of silken threads, not loud, not inconspicuous. What he wore did not strike the eye as forcibly as that which Drouet had on, but Carrie could see the elegance of the material. Hurstwood's shoes were soft, black calf, polished only to a dull shine. Drouet wore patent leather, but Carrie could not help feeling that there was a distinction in favor of the soft leather, where all else was so rich. She noticed these things almost unconsciously. They were things which would naturally flow from the situation. She was used to Drouet's appearance. (73)

The narrator in this scene dissects Hurstwood's clothing with a precision and attention to detail that indicate the correctness of approaching the world in this manner, as well as Carrie's increasing acuteness in deriving the meaning of a person's wardrobe.

Again, the text states the reality of approaching these symbols as the fact of a character's being. Carrie notices these things "unconsciously," as their meanings "would naturally flow from the situation," asserting the inherent importance of these adornments. Her astuteness allows her to translate these perceptions into objective meaning without consciously considering them. She does not see just shoes, but elegance and distinction. The presence of these qualities attracts Carrie. With her refined ability to associate the recognition of goods with the unquestioned desirability of economic mobility, Carrie anticipates what the pioneer of industrial psychology, Walter Dill Scott, termed the process by which "goods offered as means of gaining social prestige make their appeals to one of the most profound of the human instincts." Stewart Ewen comments on this remark, "The use value of 'prestige,' of 'beauty,' of 'acquisition,' of 'self-adornment,' of 'play' were all placed in the service of advertising's basic purpose—to provide effective basic mass distribution of products" (35). Though Dreiser's moralizing narrator critiques Carrie as a consumer, he fails to demystify the process of consumption. We are never allowed into the privileged space where modern advertising devises the terms of the system of value that spurs capitalist consumer culture. In effect, in contrast to that other novel of 1900, Frank Baum's *The Wizard of Oz,* we never get to go behind the curtain to see the wizard manipulating the levers.

On the day when Hurstwood finally comes to see Carrie in her rooms, she has previously been out touring the lavish neighborhoods of the city. This touring whets her appetite for more luxury than Drouet can provide and makes her susceptible to Hurstwood's greater possibility. That Hurstwood has no individuality, or that the nature of his presence is not what it seems to be, has no impact on Carrie. She possesses neither the tools to deal fully with the situation nor the inclination to look beyond the surface of their interaction. In fact, if she did approach the scene critically, she might find that Hurstwood is a married man who seeks to displace Drouet as her lover. She might also recognize his mediocrity and banality. Yet, the narrative goes on to state that Carrie has made no error of interpretation. The narrator declares the correctness of her response by asserting that although Hurstwood says nothing of importance, "People in general attach too much importance to words. They are under the impression that talking effects great results. As a matter of fact words are, as a rule, the shallowest part of the argument" (88).

Carrie's method of reading Hurstwood is initially correct as far as it goes. He is more prosperous than Drouet and can introduce her to a more refined market of goods. But she does not read that he is married, nor can she predict that he will decline. Within the logic of the book, however, these things are only of fleeting importance. His marriage seems primarily a residue from an older system of morality, primarily significant as an obstacle to his marrying Carrie. The emotional value of the institution of marriage is minimized by the fact that his existing marriage has not substantially encumbered him in his desire for and pursuit of Carrie. And if marriage is simply contractual, then why introduce a mechanism for binding Hurstwood and Carrie's relationship, one that is otherwise a matter of function? Similarly, even though Carrie does not anticipate the shrinking of Hurstwood's capital—both monetary and human—such a consideration based on the idea of the permanence of their relationship also lies outside this system of exchange: once shrinkage occurs, the terms of the relationship no longer exist, and it terminates—which is precisely what occurs. Carrie has consumed him and changed the nature of their transaction. She will not become a device for his support or anyone else's, as she is used but never consumed.

The logical figure to replace Hurstwood is Mrs. Vance's cousin, Bob

Ames. Ames stands out in the novel. He is provided with an intellectual dimension that no other character possesses. He is an engineer and inventor who at first appearance works for the electrical company and in his second and last has a laboratory on Wooster Street. Ames's appearance in this work, as distinctive and fleeting as it is, presents a number of textual problems. As he occurs for the first time in the midst of Hurstwood's decline (the chapter preceding his appearance dwells on Carrie's unhappiness with Hurstwood and the things he cannot provide) Ames seems like the next level of suitor and yet another symbol of Carrie's development. This relationship never transpires, however.

Like the narrator, Ames also contributes a critique of consumer culture to this work. As Carrie and Ames, along with the Vances, sit amid the splendor of the newly opened dining room at the Plaza Hotel, he remarks, "Do you know I sometimes think that it is a shame for people to spend so much money this way. . . . They pay so much more than these things are worth. They put on such a show" (235–36). A questioning of the value of the "show" of objects in a novel such as this could be a fundamental critique of its represented system of value. Indeed, the unconventionality of Ames's comments spark Carrie's interest in much the same way as Hurstwood's shoes did. "She felt as if she would like to be agreeable to the young man" (236). He goes on to introduce to Carrie the until-now foreign assertion that a man need not consume conspicuously "to be happy." Carrie's response is doubt, but "coming from him it had weight with her" (237).

In addition to his inquiry into the actual good of the display of modern American material consumerism, he also devises a hierarchy of theatrical performance. As with social display, there is "good" stage acting and that which is relatively worthless. In his second appearance a great deal of time is devoted to defining what this means. In Ames's estimation, genius is defined as the ability to voice the desires of those who cannot articulate their own. Carrie's destiny should be, according to Ames, to use the natural expressions of her face to represent "all desire." He tells her, "Now that you have it you must do something with it." He also informs her that this quality is perishable, saying, "If you turn away from it and live to satisfy yourself alone, it will go fast enough" (356).

Ames's statements regarding the concept and importance of value echo the narrator's earlier comments regarding the passing of bills from Drouet to Carrie. Ames also reiterates the narrator's disapproval of the conspicuous display of food, clothing, jewelry, and service going on in the restaurant, which occurs on the page preceding Ames's appearance. Beyond these two instances, the figure of Ames represents the dramatization of the element of the novel that until now has been located only in the narrator's voice. This convergence gives this character an impact disproportionate to his extremely truncated appearance and might suggest that the novel now functions primarily as a radical critique of the system it has so voluminously represented. Indeed, critics of the novel who ascribe to literary naturalism the agenda of leftist cultural critique often employ Ames as the central figure of their analysis.[14]

I would question this reading of the figure of Ames. Ames does not effectually develop a radical critique, and while he does articulate a vision of reform, Ames is neutralized, much like the narrator, by the natural power of a system already made. Indeed, readings that find the social power of this novel in the figure of Ames do so primarily as an expression of their own belief in the Progressive concept of reform and their acceptance of the term progress in its narrow turn-of-the-century liberal definition.

Ames's critique reflects the reformer's criticism of degree, not the radical's questioning of system. As his voice merges in ideology with the narrator's, we see Ames as the embodiment of the Progressive technician. For Ames the world has no mystery; his universe is defined by a notion of embedded laws of action and reaction that he must bring to light in order to avert the potentially dangerous condition of excess. He restates the narrator's concept of the morality of fair exchange, but more along the lines of a balancing of the economy of desire and not as a means of altering the relations of production that form such a system. Says Ames, "The world is full of desirable situations, but, unfortunately, we can occupy but one at a time. It doesn't do us any good to wring our hands over the far-off things" (355). As an engineer, Ames works in a world of discernible cause and effect. The economy of speculation conflicts with his materialist analysis. Indeed, in the popular economy of desire he perceives, the production of desire far exceeds an individual's ability to sate it. Such an irrational system of exchange, in Ames's view, results in unusable surpluses, of goods, of desire, and of unhappiness. Thus, like the managers and technicians who sought to balance production and consumption in order to ensure stability, so Ames looks for a similarly rational economy of exchange. But in no way does this entail any radical reorientation of market relations.

Revealingly, Richard Lingeman finds that Dreiser based the character of Ames on the figure of Thomas Edison, whom he had interviewed for *Success* magazine. According to Lingeman, Dreiser admired the inventor because "Edison was more interested in contributing useful innovations than in making money" (267). Edison was quite interested in making money, and presciently saw that, in producing new concepts of use, innovations could make lots of it. Dreiser has fallen for the ideological canard, one promoted by Edison's manipulation of his own image, of the neutral technician interested in pure science. Such a mystification reasserts the reigning vision of technology that denies its ideological origins. As David Noble asserts, "The development of technology, and thus the social development it implies, is as much determined by the breadth of vision that informs it, and the particular vision of social order to which it is bound, as by the mechanical relations between things and the physical laws of nature" (xxii). Dreiser's conception of Edison does not simply misconstrue the social production of technology but, as the preceding chapter asserts, it almost willfully misreads the man himself; this misreading, however, illuminates Dreiser's social vision. By romanticizing the figure of Edison, Dreiser shows the extent to which he participates in the rationalism of the day. Indeed, the association of Ames and Edison suggests the antidemocratic "resolution" that might be imposed upon this novel. Ames's triumph would be that of the expert, the seer into the objective laws of science. Indeed, his vision of Carrie as a serious performer suggests that this "natural genius" must sacrifice herself for the good of others. But this notion of good defines it only as the displacement of an excess of feeling in the interest of order.

As a reformer, Ames is every bit as ineffectual as the narrator. Dreiser keeps him from the center of the novel and further minimizes his role by limiting his appearance. Ames's effect on Carrie is also limited. He piques her interest, but he does not alter the mechanism of her desire. Indeed, the terms by which she expresses her desire for Ames are about the same as the terms by which she has sought Drouet and Hurstwood. Now the thing that attracts her is intellect and not shoes, but it remains a thing to use up, an object that "set Carrie's heart pounding" (238). There is little doubt that she would consume his intellect by making it into a thing, and that if he entered into a relationship with her she would alter his system of exchange and not the reverse. But Ames remains outside the popular economy of this novel and avoids any sustained involvement. Indeed, that he does not respond to her passion makes him personally significant but limits his social impact. Ames makes Carrie aware that there might be an existence that is not fueled by perpetual longing, but at the end of each appearance of Ames, the narrator informs us that Carrie did "nothing" (239, 357). In a novel that is so committed to the power of things, change cannot be theoretical, it must be actual. It is hardly redemptive for the narrator to address her with the lament "shall you dream such happiness as you may never feel" (369).

In a novel about the power of social life (which is equated with "nature") to form fully its own system, the agency of an individual is minimized. Indeed, Dreiser himself believes this in his determinist vision of social life. He writes in 1915, "All nature is supremely intelligent. It expresses itself amazingly without the aid of man" (*American Diaries* 129). *Sister Carrie,* then, reveals its Dreiserian notion of the immutability of nature. As a document of American modernity, it reproduces common assumptions regarding the significance of exchange and the power of goods; while it mounts its critique, it finally laments its own limited power in the face of the mass of documented natural facts. The novel solidifies social conditions as scientific truths. Dreiser furthers the assumptions of Edison and Howells and develops a vision of economic life that rigidifies its implicit system of value and shows how one may internalize the tenets of this system and succeed.

Perhaps the novel's initial commercial failure was due to Doubleday and Page's lack of marketing initiative, or perhaps it was due to the fact that American readers were not yet used to making the intellectual leaps the book required of them, that is, knowing the meanings of various common objects and being able to apply those meanings immediately to objectified humans. It is clear that the book has long captured an audience, despite the interventions of prestigious critics, such as Van Wyck Brooks, Stuart Sherman, and Lionel Trilling, among others, who sought to consign it to the ash heap of literary history just as it was receiving some attention from highbrow cultural figures such as H. L. Mencken and F. O. Matthiessen. It has been in print in a range of editions for almost eight decades. All these critics have attacked the novel on the basis of its vulgarity. This is by no means an incorrect perception. If vulgarity is defined as calling on the common knowledge of things, and as the reduction of humanity, then the work certainly conforms to that judgment, as it invokes American culture's fetish for objects. Yet, *Sister Carrie* is an engaging and affecting work that has been read and reread. Its power and influence illuminate the context in which it has succeeded.

FIVE

Edwin S. Porter

and the Facts of Intelligible Narrative

As American cinema grew as a mass medium in the first years of the twentieth century, it rapidly adopted the institutional structure of corporate
capitalism, while the films themselves, or at least those that enjoyed mass
production, distribution, and consumption, became increasingly expressive of the very model of bourgeois hegemony found in literary realism
and naturalism. Unlike those literary modes, however, the cinema in the
early century directs itself to a range of classes. As Miriam Hansen notes,

> If the suppression of class and ethnic diversity was in keeping with
> the cinema's pretension to a bourgeois public sphere, the effort to
> co-opt such diversity was more in touch with large-scale transforma-
> tions in capitalist economy. The film industry's aim was not to exclude
> the working class but to integrate them, allegedly into the democratic
> melting pot, yet more effectively into a consumer society of which
> mass culture was to become both agent and object. ("Early Silent
> Cinema" 154)

As literary realism and naturalism spoke most prominently to the members
of and the purveyors to a modern elite, they had the effect of reaffirming
that group's classist perspective. These affirmations included the wisdom
and normative power of the expert, the power of neutral science to ascertain facts, and the desirability of a moral sphere that promoted social
continuity. As film assumes its affective form, that of entrancing narratives,
it makes a range of similar assertions, but not quite so heavy-handedly. Distinct from its literary analogues is the early cinema's ability to merge with
the cult of technology that marks the historical moment. That is, it not
only reproduces the popular ideals of applied science, its technical basis is
of that very process. Thus, it offers the apparent immediacy of its primary

cultural assertion and, on a variety of levels, demonstrates the power of showing over telling.

American cinema in the first years of the twentieth century continued to develop narrative conventions similar to those employed in certain forms of American literature. Once again, I do not mean to suggest that those involved in the young film industry were directly influenced by the novel. Rather, the homologies we encounter may be traced back to the relationship of each medium to its particular cultural context, defined both narrowly and broadly. The line of historical sequence projects teleologically to the prominence of Progressive thought and the enthroning of the expert in the late twentieth century. It follows, then, that an examination of the cultural history of this line will reveal the use of related texts that valorize these developing and then focal cultural tropes. Early cinema defines the method of composing narratives that culminates in modern film form in America, and it is analogous to both literary realism and naturalism in many of its key features. As with Howellsian realism, its mimetic status relies on a relatively effaced organizing presence. Thus, it primarily represses reflexive references to its process of production. Like naturalism, its resonance relies on capturing of reified objects and freezing these images into apparently timeless units of meaning. As cinema moves toward the narrative structure modern viewers recognize as "natural," it, like naturalist literature, both preserves and alters the precepts of realism. As did Dreiser's novel, the form of early narrative cinema asked audiences to comprehend an increasingly flat definition of being. It also assumed the complementary primacy of objects as definitions of self. Indeed, in early cinema there is virtually no notion of human autonomy. As the single-shot tableaux of early film ceased to entrance audiences who had assimilated this early manner of presentation, the emerging narrative structure of cinema increasingly argued for and helped to naturalize the objectification and fragmentation of modern life.

Edwin S. Porter has been inscribed in film history as the creator of the process of "editing." Revealingly, the process that is described by this name is that which occurs at the point of production, as sequences of shots are assembled in an editing room under the guidance of their producers. This practice assures a relative uniformity of presentation. In many histories, this process of composing narratives out of sequences of related shots is seen as a natural outgrowth of the cinematic form itself.[1] Historians complement this notion of film's natural language with praise for Porter's particular genius. For example, Gerald Mast praises his "cinematic imagination," as he discusses the structure of *The Great Train Robbery* (43). Both visions, that of genius and that of inevitable form, deny the cultural component of reception. Porter and his method succeeded because his formal strategy was appropriate for his audience. In the nature of the cinematic appara- tus itself, there seems to be no element that suggests the inevitability of composing narratives by imposing a discontinuous form. Rather, since the moving-picture machine's original novelty was its ability to simulate natu- ral motion, it is noteworthy that in the brief period between its commercial introduction in 1896–97 and 1904–5, the fragmenting of its sequence of images would become a dominant form of presentation. During the period from August 1904 to February 1905, acted and staged films, which gener- ally were compositionally complex, accounted for 84 percent of all Edison Company footage (Musser, *Before the Nickelodeon* 282).

Looking at cinema within the context of the larger process by which American industry defined its modern practices of production and distri- bution, we may see the period in which Porter becomes significant, from 1902 to 1905, as one in which larger filmmaking concerns adopted methods of centralizing control similar to those of the largest American industries. In the period prior to the turn of the century, the rudiments of the Ameri- can film industry were largely disorganized. Equipment and films were as yet not standardized, distribution and production were erratic. Perhaps as a result of these problems of supply and the difficulties of the industry in turning out persistently enticing products, the business of film in the first years of the twentieth century was in severe commercial crisis. In response to this unstable financial situation, the industry rationalized its technical apparatus, with the widespread acceptance of the 35-millimeter format in film stock and projection occurring by 1903. In addition, in this period the three-tiered structure of production, distribution, and exhibition was devised. In the earliest days of the motion picture, exhibitors generally bought films from their producers, formed a program from a variety of one-shot presentations, and projected them on unreliable and often dan- gerous machinery. For example, a program possessing a rough unity might employ the recurring motif of the police chasing a criminal or a sequence of comic sketches (Musser, *Emergence* 179–89). By 1903, the rental of films had become commonplace, with distributors providing a bridge between the production company and the exhibitors. Further, projection machinery had become significantly easier to operate and was often run by a rela- tively low-paid technician. Perhaps most significant, however, was the way in which the nature of programming was altered. Porter may be seen as a figure from the phase of cinema when the production company standard-ized its product by assuming the editorial control over content that had previously resided in the exhibitor. Thus, while the one-shot films of the earliest cinema had often been collected, with varying degrees of audience approval, into impromptu narratives at the point of presentation, now edi-torial control was increasingly centralized in the production company. This took the form of films that were longer and consisted of a series of distinct shots joined together. By diminishing the editorial role of exhibitors, the young film industry moved toward the centralizing of the producer's au-thority over the presentation of his product in the marketplace. In doing so, cinema emulated the broader processes at work in large American in-dustry.[2]

In its early stage, film was considered a fairly low-cost product that re-quired its own drummers to disperse it over a far-flung and decentralized network of theaters small and large. Like hardware or dry goods, film was a product for which its producers were not yet sure of the existing de-mand. By the twenties, such a decentralized system of distribution and exhibition was no longer desirable. Like the steel and railroad industries, the American film industry had become something of a national necessity.[3] Indeed, by adopting the dominant model of vertical integration, the film industry joined the ranks of the modern large industrial corporation, what Alfred Chandler calls "the most powerful institution in America" (286). When viewed within the domain of the economic history of the Ameri-can film industry, the producer's assumption of editorial control becomes an aspect of an ongoing process of centralization. With the burgeoning of the American film industry (by 1919 the industry claimed it was the fifth largest in America, though this accounting was widely disputed, with one analyst situating it only in the top ten) came efforts to emulate other cen-tralized industrial enterprises. Indeed, in this transition we may see the manner in which those who controlled the industry had reconceived their enterprise. The film industry, still in its youth at the turn of the century, lagged behind other industries in its organization but gradually adopted the dominant model. This disposition to employ existing models of pro-duction also resulted in the next major organizational shift in the industry: by the mid-twenties, after a period in which various smaller companies were combined, the vertically integrated film company was increasingly the industry-wide goal. This meant that a single large corporation controlled production, distribution, and presentation of its films. The three-tiered organizational structure of American cinema was analogous to that operated in other industries of mass production and consumption; however, in industries such as dry goods and hardware it had occurred two or three decades earlier.

That the consolidation of control over content enabled cinema to take on some semblance of its modern aesthetic form suggests how intertwined are cinema's economic practice and film's ultimate form. By routinizing the content of films, the developing industry could devise its own distinct standards, including the clarity of the image, the rhythm of scenes, and the recurrence of motifs and formulas. All this allowed for a bond with audiences; such practices developed audience expectations, which were readily satisfied by future films. Porter's innovations are symptomatic of the Edison Company's emphasis on developing an attractive and abundant product with which to create and tap a potentially lucrative market. To develop the economic metaphor, the strategy to control presentation at the point of production recalls the centralization of authority that occurred in the reforms of Progressivism and in the rationalized modern factory.

Thus, to designate Porter without qualification as the genius who discovered film's natural language minimizes his institutional setting. Such a judgment also assumes that cinema is inherently narrative and that narrative film as he employed it and as it developed is objectively desirable. None of these assumptions adequately explains the place of Porter and his work in American film history. To imply that this genius dazzled his audience with his creative powers merely adopts the assumptions of other aesthetic histories (art or literature, for example) in considering the creator of a specific work as a transcendent genius who succeeded and survived because of his particular brilliance.

Indeed, the films of Edwin Porter are not the sum of motion picture entertainment in the first years of the twentieth century. By considering alternative modes of presentation we may see how the narrative methods that came to dominate American cinema were a matter of the choices made by audiences and producers. One form of presentation during this era was the illustrated lecture, which employed films in presenting some geographical, scientific, or, in the narrow terms of the day, anthropological spectacle. This practice had existed since the prehistory of the cinema. Eadward Muybridge employed this format for presenting his animals in motion. Though this practice was declining by 1903, it was still employed as a means of offering "safe" entertainment to audiences that disdained the vulgarity of more commercial film. It appealed to much the same elite class that would be familiar with Howells and the school of American authors known as naturalists. The "lecturer," who instructs audiences in the correct manner of apprehending what is on screen, recalls the naturalist narrator. That is, both the lecturer and the naturalist narrator intrude on their text to draw out the implications of their documentary presentation of the world. Both function as knowing experts who instruct their audiences while asserting that their presentations are simply the facts as they exist. In appealing to a specific class, the lecturer and the naturalist narrator assume the pose of the converted speaking to the converted, thus allowing for an elevated assertion of the peculiarity or unfitness of "others." Significantly, the distinction between the lecturer and the narrator is formal. The lecture, as it occurs external to the film, excessively highlights the flatness of that representation through its imposition of a three-dimensional device for mediation. The naturalist novel, however, garbs its narrator in the matter of the text. That is, it defines this device in words. As we shall see in considering the films of Porter and the dominant mode of presentation they illuminate, such disruption of realist conventions is antithetical to the forming of more complex narratives with the intention of making film a mass medium, as they strain the credulity of the apparatus by their inherent artifice. By 1908, the illustrated lecture was declining as a viable commercial mode of presentation, perhaps because the definition of the mass audience for film had become more inclusive and had eroded the demand for such material. This practice of the illustrated lecture still exists as a marginal aspect of late twentieth-century high culture.[4]

Another alternative practice with closer ties to the earlier one-shot actualities, called "Hale's Tours," proliferated from 1905 to 1912, just after the emergence and acceptance of the less intrusive narrative style used by Porter. These films featured sights, both natural and man-made, viewed within a simulated railroad car. Explains Raymond Fielding, "The stationary car provided a number of seats for its passengers, suitably inclined upward toward the rear to provide good sight lines. Through the open front, the audience viewed a motion picture which had been photographed from the cowcatcher of a moving train, and which was thrown onto a slightly inclined screen from a motion picture projector situated in a gallery slightly behind the car" ("Hale's Tours" 121). These pictures were augmented by whistles, bells and the rattling of the car, all to create the illusion of actually being on a train. Hale's Tours attempted to recreate the initial allure of the machine itself by introducing a range of profilmic elements to highlight the veracity of the apparatus. That this method of reinvigorating a prior state of presentation was short-lived confirms the choices of audiences in the prior century: now that the picture had been accepted as reality, audiences were ready for the greater resonance of narrative, for the "fictions of the real" trumpeted by William Dean Howells.

In general, Porter's films were well accepted. *The Great Train Robbery* was perhaps the largest-grossing film of the era of its creation, while *Life of an American Fireman* was a solid financial success.[5] This indicates that the audience exposed to these products enjoyed his work and found the form of these films intelligible and their content engaging. However, the fact of Porter's success, and his subsequent placement in film history, does not necessarily make a case for his primacy. The two films discussed are indicative of the increasingly common mode of presentation during the first decade of the twentieth century that either did or did not derive its methods from Porter. I do not wish to make a case for Porter's influence on the industry. Indeed, he was an employee for the Edison Company, and it remains possible that he merely did as he was told. However, since the films considered appealed to a wide range of Americans at the turn of the century, perhaps they are best approached for their ability to illuminate the bond between the audience and the film text.[6]

It is not difficult to trace Porter's methods and concerns back to Thomas Edison. The films considered here, the two generally considered the most pivotal in the development of the cinema's narrative form, were produced for the Edison Company. This is of particular note when one considers the emerging corporate structure of film production in early twentieth-century America. Without the support of the Edison Company, there would have been no mass production of prints and no widespread marketing and distribution of these films to various exhibitors. In this case, the "genius" of Porter would have been lost to the ages.

As an employee of the Edison Company, Porter was required to do two things: produce profits and express the concerns of the corporation. As stated in the previous chapter, the concerns of Edison and his corporation were both economic and ideological. While interested in a profit from his machine, Edison also believed that film's profitability relied to some degree on its continued assertion of its scientific-technical basis. Although the Wizard himself denied his role in the day-to-day functioning of his film production company, the considerable time and effort he put into litigation to assure his monopoly over its production indicates his interest. As Robert Sklar points out,

After the turn of the century, Edison inexorably consolidated his control over the products and personnel in the field. If middle-class reformers had realized how great an influence Edison wielded, they might have moderated their criticisms, for where could they have found an American industry run by a leader more admired, trusted, and indeed revered than Edison? But for his own good reasons Edison let it be known that he took no interest in day-to-day film-making activities. At the same time he was moving behind the scenes to subordinate his competitors, he carefully managed his public image so that he would appear to the public as a solitary, unworldly inventor, interested only in his continuing quest to link phonograph and cinema and attain sound motion pictures. (34)

Consistent with Edison's economic and aesthetic goals, the Edison Company filed and won a suit in the United States circuit court that virtually assured it a monopoly over the medium. This period of absolute domination lasted from approximately the end of July 1901 to March 1902. Charles Musser notes the limited types of film that became the rule during this period: "Taking advantage of its position the Company pursued an extremely conservative policy as it made films only within well-established genres, and relied primarily on news films and topicals" ("Early Cinema" 20). Part of the reason for such a limited approach was that producing such films was relatively inexpensive, but in all likelihood this business and production strategy was not overwhelmingly popular with patrons of the new medium. Eastman Kodak reported a decline in film sales during 1901 and 1902 (Musser, "Early Cinema" 20). The reason for this seems to lie in the types of films Edison was producing. Early films had increasingly shifted their content from moving pictures of the world to pictures of curiosities and viscerally exciting events; now, however, audiences had grown tired of these one-shot presentations. Again, while the form itself still posited the reality of its content, audiences were ready for more complex assertions. Audiences sought to be transfixed by the story itself, not just by the device of its presentation, a device that simply asserted the obvious. Since the image's reality was becoming increasingly self-evident, not that interesting in itself (as the declining popularity of trick films suggests), the next project of cinema in America was to produce complex narratives that told stories while not substantially undermining the illusion of the apparatus.

In 1902, with the dismissal of the patent suit that had produced its short-lived monopoly, the Edison Company produced four story films, all of which experimented with overlapping action as a means of asserting narrative continuity (Musser, *Emergence* 325). Culminating this cycle was *Life of an American Fireman*. The desires and intentions of the Edison Company emerge clearly from the short period when it had virtual control over the market: produce cheap films that take few aesthetic or ideological chances. Now, however, with competition reentering the industry, it was necessary to venture more widely in order to compete effectively.

As the cinema was gradually assimilated as a form of mass entertainment, the necessity of asserting its realist origins became less pressing and could assume a wider variety of compositional strategies. It could readily draw on other entertainment forms that more securely employed the fantastic. For example, among this cycle of story films in 1902 was a presentation of *Jack and the Beanstalk*. Still, the cinema's legacy as a putative scientific device remained. The most successful films were those that could blend conventions of melodrama with the tropes of realism. Thus, films such as *Life of an American Fireman* are exemplary in the way in which they address the paradoxical problem of developing films that both engage audiences and work within the inscribed codes of the cinema's technical basis. Indeed, this paradox recalls Howells's dilemma less than ten years before: how to produce narratives which do not substantially disrupt the cinema's powerful claims of mimetic representation.

Porter's strategy for solving this paradox in these two films is perhaps what endeared them to their contemporary audiences and to subsequent film scholars. He offers viewers the opportunity to have their sense of reality fixed by the terms of the image. For audiences of 1903, this desire had not substantially changed in the few years since the birth of the apparatus as a commercial form of entertainment. However, the means by which the film could satisfy this desire had altered. Porter anticipated this change of audience in a way that secured his place at Edison: he found a middle ground that employed many of the features found in realist literature, and produced hits.

In the two films under consideration, *The Great Train Robbery* (1903) and *Life of an American Fireman* (1903), we see a certain similarity of formal characteristics. Both films are composed of multiple shots, the former fourteen and the latter nine. Each of these shots is taken from a camera that maintains its distance from its subject throughout the shot. On the rare occasions where the camera does move, it does so in a pan or a tilt.[7] Each of these films possesses one close-up, but this shot does not employ a dolly; rather, the films cut to the stationary camera, which photographs its subject from a closer perspective.

Like naturalist literature, these early narratives seek out the implications of the realist ideology and further it. Each scene functions as a discrete unit of realist presentation, while a now-naturalized implicit human presence structures the film in a manner discernibly artificial.[8] That is, some logic of composition must control the sequence of scenes, but as in naturalist literature, the text suppresses the process of arriving at this logic in order to preserve its relative illusion of immanence.

These films' textual features reveal a worldview similar to that of Dreiser's novel. Early films and realist literature had sought to record the entirety of an event in order to allow the fixed observer to maintain his ideal plane of observation, thereby capturing its objective reality. In *Sister Carrie*, as well as in these two films by Porter, the notion of point of view is not quite as rigid as the "scientific" legacy of this mode of observation might suggest. Indeed, while it remains fixed from moment to moment, it is not necessarily constant throughout the narrative. Hence, Dreiser can seek out the fine points of the object world. Porter can insert a close-up, pan or tilt the camera, or film a scene from an angle other than directly in front of his object. This variety in point of view suggests relative fragmentation when compared with its more stable precedent, but it is not necessarily discontinuous. Continuity is largely a relative perceptual judgment and certainly not an absolute fact of the text. In these two films by Porter, as well as in *Sister Carrie*, we may infer specific strategies that have allowed the viewer to experience the presentation as a unified whole; judging from ultimate audience response in both cases these strategies were eventually adequate.

The process of objectifying the characters of the narrative is also a recurring feature in both these films and this novel. As I discussed, *Sister Carrie* is the sum of objectified humans and personified objects. In these films by Porter, the participants in the action barely qualify as characters in the traditional fictional sense. Though the technique of photographing close-ups appears in both films, it does not allow us to differentiate one character from another. The actors in these films are faceless and essentially reduced to simple plot function. They produce a range of behaviors, and in the terms of these films neither their faces nor their further motivations are considered. This is consistent with the intention of the apparatus itself. Developed to observe objectively animals and humans in motion, it is used for essentially the same purpose in these films. Behavior is the focus of early cinema, and that which is not clearly accessible to the camera is not represented on the screen.

These stories are, for the most part, tightly constructed around plot actions. That is, these films seem at least as concerned with *how* actions are accomplished as with *why* they are undertaken. Fittingly, then, activities that are not explicitly concerned with the narrative but that might indicate some further individual aspect of a character in the film do not appear. Indeed, these films, like the naturalist novel, shift the notion of realism toward its ultimate fragmentary and objectifying state. Historically, these two media continue to direct definitions of being toward the necessities of modern industrial life. That is, as Carrie's inner life is minimized and Porter's films concentrate on causal sequences of actions, these works emphasize the similarities between people and machines.

Indeed, as we look at the popular films of the first years of the twentieth century, their combination of a generally stationary camera and featureless figures in motion recall the methods formulated by industrial efficiency expert Frank Gilbreth from around 1912. Like the more famous Frederick Taylor, with whom he consulted, Gilbreth attempted to rationalize industrial production by employing the metaphor of the machine as the key to a system of organizing factory labor. Gilbreth sought to manipulate the factory's human cogs and gears to produce greater amounts of goods by reducing unnecessary movement on the shop floor. Unlike Taylor, whose preferred means of observing the workplace was his own eye,

> Gilbreth developed a new motion study technique, which he called micro-motion study. It involved filming a worker's operations against a cross-sectioned background while a chronometer recorded the time. By examining the film through a magnifying glass, Gilbreth could determine the times of each of the worker's motions to one-thousandth of a section. He could then compare methods and working conditions and synthesize the best elements into a method that would become the standard for that job. (Price 60)

If we consider the chronology of these early narratives in relation to Gilbreth's studies, the efficiency expert likely derived his use of the cinematic apparatus from a perception of its narrative conventions, which were clearly objectifying. This formal connection between the studies of Gilbreth and the early narratives of the commercial film industry suggests a similar reduction of "the human element" in the latter. It highlights how early cinema produces and reproduces the central metaphor of the modern factory system, which reduces humans to moveable parts in the machine of production.

The means we have of identifying the central figures in these two films, the firemen in *Life of an American Fireman* and the robbers in *The Great Train Robbery,* are their actions and their clothing. This use of clothing as a resonant aspect of characterization again recalls Dreiser's primary assumptions and concerns. In a world of mass production and commodified goods and experience, the material elements that garb a character have a meaning that suffices for the entire notion of a character's humanity. Porter's stories rely on the intelligibility of his characters' accoutrements. The robbers differentiate themselves from the telegraph operator in *The Great Train Robbery* by the fact that they wear Western hats and bedraggled clothing. In the ensuing scenes, as we watch them in a variety of activities, including skulking behind a water tower as they prepare to sneak onto the train or climbing across the moving train, we identify them by the objective facts of their appearance. These facts are, in sum, their clothing, as the camera never focuses on their faces. Similarly, in the opening scene of *Life of an American Fireman* we see a man sitting at a desk as a "dream bubble" appears to his left. We see a woman putting a child to bed within the bubble, as the man gets up from his desk and paces around the room. The only way we have of knowing the meaning of this scene is by the clothing of the man. He appears to be wearing the suit of a fireman, and indeed the subsequent events of the narrative suggest that this is the correct interpretation. In addition, in successive scenes, our way of identifying the participants in the film's plot activities is by their clothing and the other equipment that surrounds them.

Beyond these general similarities, both films incorporate a similar perception of what constitutes a narrative. Both employ a variety of scenes, each one a single shot, to construct the particular story they present. However, the temporal relationships between the various shots, as well as the method used in creating the transition from one scene to another, are generally different in these two films. *Life of an American Fireman* employs considerable temporal overlap in telling its story, and generally uses the technique of dissolving one scene into another. *The Great Train Robbery* presents a more chronologically sequential story and generally cuts from one scene to another.[9] A close examination of the specific narrative method of these two films, as well as a consideration of the ways in which these films refer to other media, reveals the likelihood that Porter's desire to produce a certain realism informed his aesthetic decisions. Because of this desire, he used techniques generally found in documentary films to make

The Great Train Robbery, a film that referred to the Western melodramas of dime novels and the actions found in Wild West shows, and which apparently borrowed title and incident from an 1896 stage play by Scott Marble.[10] In *Life of an American Fireman,* Porter allowed the documentary-like title of the film, as well as its seemingly "factual" subject matter, to assert its reality.

In order to deal specifically with the editorial strategies of the two films, it is necessary to provide a shot-by-shot description of them. Keeping to chronological order, let us first look at *Life of an American Fireman,* released in January of 1903.[11] The sequence of scenes which make up the narrative are as follows:

1. Long shot of a man asleep (presumably a fireman) in a chair in an office. At his left appears a balloon in which a woman puts a child to bed. The balloon dissolves, and the man begins to pace around the room. Dissolve to

2. Close-up of fire-alarm box. As it comes into view, a hand appears in the frame and pulls the lever that activates the alarm. Dissolve to

3. Long shot of men in a barracks. The pole at the center of the room suggests that this is a barracks at the fire station. Roughly simultaneously, the men jump from their beds and grab their clothes. They then slide down the pole. Eight men perform this action. Dissolve to

4. Long shot of the firehouse interior. The horses are already hitched to the fire engines, as six men slide down the pole in the center of the room. These men jump into these wagons and exit off screen to the right. Dissolve to

5. Long shot of the outside of the firehouse. The doors of the station fly open, and the engines emerge and exit to the right. Dissolve to

6. Long shot of a suburban street. The fire engines cross the screen from right to left, as a crowd of spectators watch the action (there are some jump cuts in this scene, but it is difficult to tell if they are the result of the film breaking and being spliced together in a way that mismatched the film ends or are an intentional means of shortening the time of the scene). Dissolve to

7. Long shot of engines racing down a street. There is a park in the background, and the vehicles pass before the camera from right to left. The camera then pans to reveal the front of a burning house. The camera then tilts upward to the top left window of the structure. Fade in to

8. Long shot of a room filled with smoke. A woman rises from the

bed and goes to the window. She then falls on the bed. A fireman enters through the door and then breaks the window. He lifts the woman with his arms and then carries her through the window. After a short time he reenters the room, picks up a child from the bed, and exits again through the window. Dissolve to

9. Long shot of the front of the house. A woman appears in the top left window. A fireman pounds on the front door and then enters the house. The other firemen place a ladder against the front of the house as others spray it with water. A fireman (presumably the one who entered through the door) emerges from the window with a woman, and descends. The woman arises from the ground, and gestures animatedly. The fireman climbs the ladder again, reenters the window, and emerges almost immediately with a child. He climbs down the ladder and delivers the child to the woman's embrace.[12]

The Great Train Robbery is somewhat longer than its predecessor, consisting of fourteen scenes of one shot each, thirteen of them long shots and the fourteenth a medium close-up.

1. A long shot of a train-station office. Two men with guns drawn, dressed in Western clothing that appears slightly worn, burst through a door into a room where a clerk (also denoted by his clothing) is sitting. A train appears through the rear window of the office, and a man in the window (the conductor?) hands the clerk a piece of paper. He departs, and one gunman hits the clerk on the head with the butt of his pistol. The intruders tie up the clerk and then depart. Cut to

2. A long shot of a water tank, as a train rolls into the frame. The outlaws (presumably) appear skulking beneath the water tower in the left corner of the frame. The train draws water, then the men come out from behind the tank and sneak onto the train. Cut to

3. A long shot of the inside of the train, in what looks like a mail car. Scenery rushes by in the background. The clerk goes about his business, sorting mail. He then starts, and frets around the car seemingly panicked. Two gunmen enter. There is a shootout, and the clerk gets shot. They rob the car, then leave. Cut to

4. A long shot of the top of the train. A man with a gun lies on top of it, and a second man enters the frame. A man emerges from the engineer's cab with a shovel, and wrestles with one of the gunmen. He is beaten, and thrown off the train. The other gunman enters the cab and makes the engineer stop the train; first a gunman fully vanishes

from the frame, seemingly down to the ground, and then the engineer begins to repeat the same process. The third gunman has not yet started down when the scene cuts to

5. A long shot of a gunman leaping off the train, with the engineer following him, followed by the third gunman. They follow the engineer to the joint between the two cars, and force him to uncouple them. Cut to

6. A long shot of the train cars. The robbers line up the passengers from the train. One passenger attempts to escape and is shot. The gunmen rob the passengers and then exit left. The camera remains on the passengers as they examine the fallen body of the dead man. Cut to

7. A long shot of the train. The bandits board the train and drive it away, as it exits to the left of the frame. Cut to

8. A long shot of the tracks. The front of the train enters the frame and then halts. The robbers jump from the train carrying money bags and run down a hill. The camera tilts down to follow them. Cut to

9. A long shot of a stream. The robbers enter the scene and cross it. The camera gradually pans after the last man to cross, and then beyond him to frame the four men riding away. Cut to

10. A long shot of the interior of the telegraph office, where the clerk remains tied up. He attempts to unbind his hands, and then collapses. A young girl enters, unties him, shakes him, and prays over him. He arises and runs from the office. Cut to

11. A long shot of a crowded dance hall, where people are engaged in a square dance. The dance stops, and then a man not in Western clothing is forced into the center of the crowd. The men in the crowd shoot at his feet as he dances to avoid the bullets; he then runs out of the door. They go back to dancing and then the clerk enters. He gestures frantically, and all the men run out of the room. Cut to

12. A long shot of the outdoors. A long procession of men on horseback enters the frame, presumably the bandits being chased by a posse. The third man (a robber) is shot. The last man (a lawman) stops to attend to him. Cut to

13. A long shot of the stream. The bandits return to the place where they stashed their money; now there are three. They begin taking money from their bags as the posse enters the frame. There is a shootout and all the robbers die. The posse recovers the money. Cut to

14. A medium-close-up of a man in western clothing shooting at the camera.[13]

Both these films assert the older representational strategies of the single-shot film by their general use of a stationary camera to record individual scenes. In addition, the type of activity recorded in a particular scene is often reminiscent in its style of the one-shot films that preceded them. That is, actions within shots are self-contained and have their own dramatic emphasis. In *Life of an American Fireman*, this includes movements like a man rescuing a woman or a child from a fire, a phalanx of fire engines riding down a street, or even firemen sliding down a pole and getting into their wagons. In *The Great Train Robbery*, these self-contained actions shot from a stationary camera include the robbing of a telegraph office, the holding-up of a mail car, the stopping of a train, and a shootout. Indeed, in one of the more curious scenes of this narrative, the scene in the dance hall when the outsider is forced to "dance" to avoid the bullets aimed at his feet, the action of the part is enhanced to increase the effect of the unit, but in a way that is mystifying in terms of the whole, as we never see this man outside of this one shot, nor does this activity have anything to do with the rest of the narrative.[14]

While maintaining the integrity and the realism of these component scenes, the films adopt a different editorial strategy in creating the whole. Through the difference in these strategies they assert their continuity, that is, the way in which they link the various parts to create their unified narratives. In *Life of an American Fireman*, Porter makes extensive use of the technique of temporal overlap, a method that explicitly refers to the preceding shot in the narrative. In addition, the primary method of moving from one scene to another is the dissolve. In *The Great Train Robbery* the sequence of actions does not place the same moment that occurs at the end of one scene at the beginning of the next. Rather, the chronology of the film apparently progresses.[15] In addition, the film makes extensive use of cutting and does not employ dissolves.

The transitions in *Life of an American Fireman* that invoke the preceding scene's final moment occur often. In scene 3 we see the firemen sleeping, apparently in the moment prior to the hand pulling the fire alarm in scene 2. In scene 4 we see the firemen sliding down the pole from the perspective of the firehouse interior, an action we have just seen from the perspective of the barracks in scene 3. In scene 5 the doors of the station open, and the fire engines emerge and exit left. In the preceding scene we viewed this action from the point of view of the firehouse interior. Scenes 6 and 7 employ settings that are similar and actions that correspond in a way that makes their relationship obvious. In scenes 8 and 9, however, the same action is viewed from two different perspectives, clearly repeating the same chronology, and the same woman performs essentially the same actions, as do the firemen in the scenes.

This temporal relationship between the various shots is obviously unreal, and in its blatant manipulation of the apparently natural properties of chronology, the film anticipates the modernist movement in various aesthetic modes, including literature and painting. Indeed, as it employs the technical properties of cinema to alter normative concepts of sequence and rhythm, it becomes a reminder of how deeply the modernist notion of fragmentation relies on the twentieth-century cult of technology that celebrates the power of the machine to alter nature. Thus, in its disruption of time as usually construed, the machine advertises its own ability to remake reality, much as the locomotive had or the automobile would. This method of overlap sacrifices the illusion that the camera is merely recording the world's events as they occurred. Even this remarkable machine cannot be in two places at the same time. In addition, the technique of dissolving one scene into another seems to bring into focus the artifice of the screen image, as it offers a relationship between events that seems clearly unnatural as it excessively enhances causality.

The challenge that presented itself to Porter was, how far can a filmmaker venture from the conventions of his medium? Porter not only reveals the transformative power of his machine but also elevates the continuity of the narrative itself over the concept of time's immanence. The method of *Life of an American Fireman* explicitly states the terms of its own continuity. The relationship between scenes is stated by actually having one scene blend into another. The use of temporal overlap sends the viewer back to the film's preceding action, thus making sure that the relationship between scenes is so direct that any viewer could easily comprehend it. Indeed, it obviates the need for the intrusive human lecturer to provide commentary to link the film's images.

The problem with this method is that it seems to sacrifice the illusion of realism—but only if we approach realism as a fixed concept. Indeed, this sacrifice does not appear: the illusion still comes through, implied through the construction of the film's individual scenes and their relationship to an earlier form of presentation. By altering the whole but maintaining the earlier definition of the representational integrity of the part, the film may adapt that definition and project it toward the further requirements of modern industrial life. Interestingly, this patently unreal method of bridging scenes had been established in other films with strong extratextual claims of verisimilitude but which combined actual and staged footage. David Levy notes,

> For his studio-produced fire rescue show Porter drew upon the methods he and other projectionist-showmen had employed in integrating or merging shorter lengths of footage, in a variety of styles, both genuine and staged, into longer more elaborate shows on the Spanish-American War, the Boer War, the McKinley assassination, the Martinique volcano tragedy and the coronation of Edward VII. . . . The result was a unique motion picture production that departed from the documentary rigor of the British as well as from Mélièsian plunges into fantasy. ("Edwin S. Porter" 226)

Like these other films noted by Levy, *Life of an American Fireman* asserts its images as being of the world through its use of various elements outside its strictly cinematic structure, even as its claims to documentary status are somewhat more specious. These claims include the use of a title that makes an explicit claim to a referent in the real world, as well as the resonance of that referent. By 1903, the American fire department had become, in the popular press and apparently in the popular imagination, a practical matter of pride (in the last thirty years of the nineteenth century the average fire loss in New York City had fallen from around five thousand dollars to around one thousand) and a symbol of the power of American technology and organizational acuity, the central elements of the Progressive political agenda. In the late nineteenth century, urban firefighting had been largely professionalized, as volunteer companies were replaced by centrally managed municipal forces. Charles Musser notes that this film actually employed four distinct fire companies in its presentation, two professional and two volunteer, as a means of bridging the gap between older and more modern forms of social organization. He also notes that the film's use of four different companies is perhaps more important in that "localism was superseded" (*Nickelodeon* 222–23). The number of fire companies is not readily apparent to a viewer. Indeed, to a filmgoer this was a visible assertion of an area in which Americans could claim a clear superiority over European cities. The public showing of firefighting skills and apparatus was a regular feature of late nineteenth- and early twentieth-century fairs and expositions. Thus, a film such as *Life of an American Fireman* merges the power of its technological form with its celebration of technical mastery in another field to create a spectacle. Indeed, when the film is considered as an expression of national pride, we may construe scenes 2, 3, and 4 as not simply the capturing on film of the routine actions of public servants. The close-up in scene 2 now reveals the innovations of the American alarm box, widely considered "the most advanced in the world." Scenes 3 and 4 show off the innovations in firehouse construction and harness design that make American firefighting notable (Teaford 241–45). Most urban Americans in 1903 not only had seen a fireman and had a sense of his general appearance and activity, they had also read with interest of his exploits and the precision of his equipment. This film does nothing to challenge the claims of its title in its presentation of dress or equipment. As a choice of subject matter, a story about a fireman easily asserts its realism as it elevates its objects from the mundane. This makes the content of this film particularly appropriate for an early narrative film. Since realism in this case need not absolutely rely on matters of structure, then certain compositional liberties may be taken. We see these liberties throughout the film's chronological sequence. The film can emphasize continuity and devise a means of solving a major problem of creating longer narrative films.

Scenes 8 and 9 extend this notion of continuity, that is, they further defy the strict notion of chronological sequence and repeat the same actions from different perspectives. Once again, we see that Porter considers the realism of his presentation a foregone aspect of its content, which frees the filmmaker to experiment with the narrative possibilities of the cinema. Unlike the earlier scenes, these two do not invoke the prior scene as a means of establishing sequence. Rather, here we see Porter using this documentary-like film to experiment with the presentation of simultaneous action. He attempts to define the apparatus as a machine that can transcend the binding physical realities of humans and be in two places at once, thus producing the ultimate recording device, one with the power of omniscience.

The success of Porter's strategy in using this structure for this film is asserted by subsequent critical response. Even a recent work like David Cook's *The History of Narrative Film* describes this work as "a documentary-like narrative about the activities of a fire engine company" (20). Gerald Mast notes that "the scenes of the fire brigade charging out of the firehouse and down the street were bits of stock footage. . . . The outdoor shots were clearly shot outside a real house" (20). A. R. Fulton describes this production as "constructed out of some fire-department scenes [Porter] found among the stock of the Edison Company together with scenes he shot expressly for his purpose" (32). The recurrence of comments that refer to the film's realism some seven decades after its release indicates the power of its illusion. Even these sophisticated viewers feel the need to refer the images of this film to matters outside it. Interestingly, none of these critics notes the unreality of its time frame or its use of a dream balloon in the first scene, a fact that indicates Porter's shrewdness in making his choices of form and content.

The Great Train Robbery, however, does not proclaim reality in the same manner as the preceding film. While *Life of an American Fireman* celebrates the present and future, this film joins a range of plays, dime novels, and romances that mythologize an idealized version of the American past in their celebration of a vision of the American West. Indeed, *The Great Train Robbery,* as much by its remarkable financial success as by its particular form and content, was instrumental in defining the Western genre that was to be so important for American cinema. The resonance of this genre reveals the terms in which the ideology of American exceptionalism frequently cloaks itself. This film appeared just a decade after Frederick Jackson Turner's announcement in "The Significance of the Frontier in American History," "And now, four centuries from the discovery of America, at the end of a hundred years of life under the Constitution, the frontier has gone, and with its going has closed the first period of American history" (28). Embedded in Turner's thesis was a mix of late-nineteenth century race-thinking and imperialism, and a dose of millennialism. Turner looks back on a period and place that perhaps never existed—or if it did exist did so for an historical minute—and declared it the bastion of "individualism, democracy, and nationalism" (26). In Turner's thesis was the effort to encode a usable past for a disrupted present. To its early twentieth-century audience, which was primarily urban and often not native-born, a film such as this had the power to dramatize with its technical immediacy the iconography of the West and, by implication, the historical legacy of Americans. It offers clear distinctions of good and bad and the role of a vigilant citizenry in guaranteeing the power of civilization. Indeed, in its latter assertion we can see the citizen-soldiers of the recent Spanish-American War as a referent of the film's posse. Westerns of this type proliferated, then, as antidotes to the stressful cultural processes of urbanization and economic consolidation. Writes Warren Susman on the popular function of the Turner thesis in early twentieth-century American life,

> The most characteristic use of the frontier in this period was the largely sentimental effort to retain what was considered to be the picturesque glamour and glory of the Old West. The announced disappearance of the frontier seemed to create an ever-growing market

for articles and stories of the American West and Frontier adventure. Even a cursory examination of such pieces listed year after year in the *Reader's Guide* indicates the enormous growth of this literature. The frontier had been, in Percy Boynton's word, "rediscovered." (30) [16]

Yet in certain ways this film is an ideological hybrid. While it evokes aspects of the frontier myth, its technological basis and the objectification of its characters are indeed modern. If the role of the frontier in early twentieth-century American life was, at least partially, to extoll the cult of individualism, this film does so in a mitigated way. It integrates appropriately corporate values in its presentation. Perhaps it is this synthesis that creates a portion of its mass appeal.

In light of its particular genre, this film had to find its own method of telling its story and asserting its materiality. One device was its catalogue description, which stated that it was a "faithful duplication of the genuine 'Hold-Ups' made famous by various outlaw bands of the far West" (in Levy, "Reconstituted Newsreels" 245). The ramifications of this assertion show up in the work itself.

As opposed to the documentary-like *Life of an American Fireman*, this film had little resonant realism based in its use of profilmic elements with which to maintain its illusion. Hence, in this case Porter had to take the chance of producing a narrative that did not tell the viewer as aggressively as its predecessor the proper manner of assimilating the film's narrative. That is, he adopted the style of making transitions from scene to scene employed in actuality films. This type of cutting gives the appearance of sequence and does not necessarily collapse the narrative into explicit causality, as dissolves seem to do. It assumes a more sophisticated audience, one aware that action does not dissolve into other actions, even in narrative reproductions. Though lap dissolves are still employed selectively today, they have long since ceased to be a primary means of bridging one scene with another.

Consistent with this method of joining scenes, the film does not generally impose temporal overlap from scene to scene. In one instance, the transition from scene 4 to scene 5, it does occur, as scene 5 begins with the first gunman jumping off the train and scene 4 ends with the engineer having already descended. This instance, however, does not indicate a dominant method, and its effectiveness is somewhat questionable, as the moment of overlap is far shorter and less consequential in terms of the plot than any in *Life of an American Fireman*.

For the most part, *The Great Train Robbery* has a fairly logical sense of chronology. The action moves in a way that does not explicitly require the viewer to suspend his notions of the laws of time as they function outside the film. Some critics, echoing the catalogue description, have noted that the scene where the clerk is found tied up in his office (scene 10) must occur simultaneously with the robbery and getaway.[17] This seems possible; however, it is not specifically implied by any of the film's elements, as are all occurrences of temporal overlap in the preceding film, nor is this interpretation required to make sense of the narrative. It is possible that the clerk was immobile for the duration of the robbery.

The film also makes use of the skewed angle shots often found in documentary films. Scenes like that of the robbers hiding behind the water tank (scene 2) or the scene where the engineer is forced to uncouple the train (scene 5) are shot from a camera position somewhat to the left of the traditional centered position.

The sum of these methods produced what the medium had been searching for, a fiction of the real. Despite this film's obvious fictionality, at the moment of its perception it has the ability to assert the possibility of its realism. Within a form that captured its audience the way film did (and does), a viewer's immediate response to a specific product was not necessarily based on knowledge outside the film itself. Hence, the trope of realism as it appears in such a medium has the power to affect its audience. As David Levy notes, "By 1903, the year in which Porter filmed his great classic, the *faithful duplication,* which is to say the application of newsreel styles to staged topical narratives referred to as reconstituted newsreels, reenactments and reproductions, had been reasonably well established by American producers" ("Reconstituted Newsreels" 245). *The Great Train Robbery* built on these conventions for asserting fact but applied them to material that was more clearly fiction.

It is interesting to consider the aesthetic choices made by Porter as to where to place the close-up in each of these films, when one considers the desire to produce the real that influenced each production. The close-up in *Life of an American Fireman,* appearing as it did in a film that was working within a genre that asserts its realism through its subject matter, appears as a key element within the narrative. It shows the hand that produces the action that triggers the film's entire train of events. The tightness of this close-up allows only a hand into the frame. As in the film generally, identification and character are not the emphases of the narrative. Rather, the film focuses on action and behavior. In keeping with this emphasis, as well as with the film's realism, a shot that reduces "character" to simple function is allowed within the narrative. It does not necessarily matter that the perspective of the shot is patently "unreal," since it creates the appropriate emphasis and does not erode the film's further claim to realism.

The close-up that appears in *The Great Train Robbery* (the man shooting at the camera) is not so tight as to cut off the identifying characteristic of its actor, his face. This perspective appears more "real" than its corresponding shot in the preceding film. This jibes with the film's formal strategy, its desire to apply methods of capturing reality to this obviously fictional film. However, in addition to using this more "real" perspective, the film also isolates this shot outside the closure of the narrative. The Edison Company shipped this one shot on a separate reel with the instruction that it could be placed either at the beginning or end of the film, recalling the older conventions of exhibition that placed editorial control over film programs in the hands of exhibitors. Such instructions suggest the tentativeness with which the industry moved toward consolidation in this area. However, these instructions make no sense in terms of the narrative as a whole. If it appears at the beginning of the film the viewer has no idea who this person is shooting at, nor does he know who it is who is doing the shooting. If it appears at the end, one wonders how this can be a member of the outlaw gang, as we have just seen them die. There are places to insert this shot where it does fit into the narrative, for example after scene 6, when the passenger gets shot, or after scene 3, when the mail-car clerk is killed. The choice to leave this close-up out of the sequence of shots that form the film's narrative, while including the tighter close-up of the hand within the narrative of *Life of an American Fireman,* again suggests the desire of Porter, and his parent company, to produce spectacles that seemed to reproduce the reality of the world. The less conventional shot, the close-up, may appear focally within the more "documentary" presentation, while in *The Great Train Robbery* the close-up recalls the earlier conventions of the exhibition of single-shot films.

The strategies employed in these films typified some of the methods used by early filmmakers to maintain the realism of cinema while presenting fictional narratives. Indeed, the year 1903 may be seen as a transitional year in the history of film form, as it defined the movement from one-shot vignettes and actualities to longer multi-shot story films and specified the form those more complex presentations would take.[18] In experimenting with this longer format, as Porter did in *The Great Train Robbery,* films often sacrificed the intelligibility of the autonomous film narrative for the normative realism of the relatively stationary camera and abrupt cut. For example, in the film version of *Uncle Tom's Cabin* (1903), fourteen different scenes from the novel are introduced by titles that refer to the scene's culminating event ("The Rescue of Eva," "The Auction of the St. Clare Slaves"), photographed by a centered stationary camera and joined by full cuts. While certain elements of the film strain credulity, such as the toy boats which appear in scene 5, titled the "Steamboat Race Between the *Robert E. Lee* and *Natchez*," *Uncle Tom's Cabin* attempts to valorize such scenes as realistic through its use of fixed perspective. To some degree this method sacrifices narrative continuity, though it does employ titles—it is the first film to do so—to ease the transitions between scenes. Indeed, its use of titles suggests the textual assimilation of the lecturer and provides a vital method with which silent cinema will ultimately assert its narrative continuity.

In films with explicit reference to actuality, such as *Life of an American Fireman,* more adventurous compositional strategies could be attempted. In the three-shot film *The Gay Shoe Clerk,* for example, the opening shot shows a setting that has the appearance of a shoe store. That is, it has stools, the movement of business, and a stock of shoes all within the frame. Two women enter, one young and one old. The second shot shows a close-up of the clerk fitting the young woman with shoes and documents her skirt gradually rising. The third shot is a long shot that finds the clerk rising to kiss her, and then being hit with an umbrella by the older woman. The close-up, which is integrated in the narrative action of the film in a manner similar to the way in which the hand pulling the alarm is central to *Life of an American Fireman,* may occur because of the other elements that assert the film's representational status.

Early narrative films also tend to close around events that effectively resolve the problems presented. In *Uncle Tom's Cabin* the tale is closed by the heavenly ascension of Tom and a vision of the emancipation of the slaves; in *The Gay Shoe Clerk* the sexual aggression of the clerk is ended by the woman beating him with an umbrella. In *Life of an American Fireman* and *The Great Train Robbery,* these problems of the narrative are expressed as a fire and a robbery, and are of the type that a twentieth-century American would rely on such burgeoning public organizations as the fire department or police department to control. Indeed, we see the official agency of the fire department and the quasi-official agency of the posse effectively performing their duty of protecting the public. The form in which these acts are presented asserts not only the realism of the events portrayed, but also the objectified and fragmented condition of the environment in which these events occur. These films present men without recognizable faces but whose clothes give them definition. They also present narratives that require the viewer to be aware that the world is composed of fragments that, though isolated in fact, may relate to one another to form a narrative whole. Without this awareness, a viewer has no reason to relate scene to scene. This fragmentation of worldview is a presupposition of these films, and indeed a seemingly correct one considering the audience's response to these two works. The fact that narrative became not the continuous running of a camera placed before an action, but a syncopated reconstitution of a story's activities implies that the legacy of Porter and Edison persists. Such a change suggests the power of cinema to assimilate and further the truisms of modern industrial life. As in Dreiser's novel, such a shift in narrative structure reveals the primacy of the concrete and the increasing disposition of producers and consumers of narratives to shift their definitions of the real toward the requirements of modern life. These texts redefine wholeness and being in a way that naturalizes the requirements of the twentieth century.

PART THREE

The Modern

SIX

D. W. Griffith's The Birth of a Nation:

Positivist History as a Compositional Method

Edwin Porter, like Dreiser, intuited that in a world where things attain primacy, narratives need not develop depths of human characterization. In such a world, people can be displayed as objects, and the materials that surround them will resonate with meaning. These things, then, should be sought out in their fine details by an increasingly mobile representational device. Porter's films develop the notion that complete film narratives can be structured by strategically combining essentially single-shot scenes. In the next phase of film narrative, indeed, during the period when the formal shift that begins the era of modern cinema occurs, narratives become the sum of radically subdivided scenes. This shift further fragments cinema form, yet realism persists as a stated intention of filmmakers and as a judgment by audiences, suggesting that this concept changes in relation to broad cultural transitions.

The filmmaker who has generally been acclaimed as the next major innovator of American cinema is D. W. Griffith. His career as a director began in 1908 when he first worked for the Biograph Company, and he directed for that organization until 1913. In this period he became known for his use of various innovative techniques, including creating scenes from a variety of shots, employing close-ups extensively, and lighting his films in unique ways. He also began to produce longer films: *Judith of Bethulia,* produced in 1913, was four reels long, twice the length of the usual Biograph film.[1] Though as Robert Sklar points out, "Edwin Porter preceded Griffith on almost every specific innovation" (53), Griffith's sense of how to employ selectively the range of techniques of the cinema in the creation of a film as a whole resulted in considerable notice from contemporary, as well as subsequent, audiences and critics.

The film that signaled Griffith's arrival as an influential innovator in American cinema was *The Birth of a Nation* (1915). *Birth,* arguably his most important film and certainly the one that has received the most attention, was based substantially on Thomas Dixon's racist and brutal novels, *The Clansman* (1905) and, to a lesser degree, *The Leopard's Spots* (1902). This is not to say that Griffith simply provided a visual translation of Dixon's novels or that the overall emphases of the film may be attributed to Dixon. While Dixon's novels were vastly popular and as thoroughly racist as Griffith's film, they lacked the kinetic power of *Birth*. Indeed, their narratives are distinctly Victorian in their reliance on melodramatic conventions of structure and tone. These novels provided Griffith with source material. He saw the cinematic potential of their basic plot and rewrote that plot to enhance its power in that medium. In effect, he reconceived Dixon's words and presented them as images of modernity.

As a result, critics and scholars have long been dazzled by this film's elaborate editing strategy, as well as by its epic sweep. Griffith structured his film by dividing each scene into innumerable shots, so that a single scene lasting five minutes or so may have fifty different editing splices in it. The film was first released in 1915, its world premiere taking place in Los Angeles. That text that was exhibited then is the one that still prevails, save for the deletion of 125 or so particularly racist shots which show, according to A. R. Fulton, "Negroes amuck in the Piedmont" (78). This edited version employs about fourteen hundred (more than ten times the average of that era), is twelve reels long, and runs for over two and a half hours.[2] Its overall expanse and method of composition were extremely influential in establishing the form and tone of American narrative cinema, as it paved the way for longer and more complexly edited films.

That these technical feats occurred in a work so venomously racist and politically reactionary disquiets me in that I have trouble separating these formal properties from the politics of the film as a whole. Film scholars and critics who have praised this film have reconciled its repulsive racist content with its innovative form, which they have generally judged as art, by separating them.[3] They generally note the fact *The Birth of a Nation* is a racist tract, and then go on to praise its method of presenting this vision. Garth Jowett can note the racism of its plot and then go on to state that, "the film nevertheless was a benchmark . . . in the development of American cinematic art" (103). Similarly, A. R. Fulton justifies its form while attempting to excuse its content: "Making allowances for the unfortunate bias in Griffith's interpretation of history, one can enjoy the immensity of its scope, the construction of its narrative, and its spectacular scenes" (89).

This practice of separating form from content strategically avoids a critical consideration of the ideological implications of the film's form.[4] Since our only means of apprehending the film's content is through its specific method of organization, the operation of extracting one from the other ought to be intellectually impossible. By dividing them, one also divides Griffith: on one hand there is Griffith the genius filmmaker, while on the other there is Griffith the racist storyteller. Critics who impose such a dual personality on Griffith allow themselves to ignore the politics of his formal innovations and may ultimately apologize for them through their elevation of his "art."

Griffith chose a method of composition for *The Birth of a Nation* that he believed appropriate for telling his story of black inferiority, the dangers of miscegenation, and the errors of Reconstruction; that is, the method suited the way he wanted these things perceived. Griffith forms its narrative in a manner that specifically conveys the "facts" of black inferiority and of slavery as natural. In doing so he draws on widely accepted assertions by respected intellectuals, not simply those of the popular but suspect Thomas Dixon. Indeed, one prominent theory of the period, most visibly espoused by Nathaniel Southgate Shaler, a professor and dean of the Lawrence School of Science at Harvard, was that of African-American retrogression. In this theory, having been loosed from the civilizing constraints of slavery, blacks were in the process of reverting to their ancestral condition, which in Shaler's view was barbarism. Shaler, a relative moderate in that he spoke out against lynching, was among a group of "scientists," including evolutionary scientists and social scientists (notably anthropologists), who gave intellectual credibility to extreme race theories. They accomplished this by offering assertions that, with their veneer of scientific reputation and method, could be taken to "prove" the fixed (biological) condition of black inferiority.

Yet, even among moderates who eschewed the Shaler theory and other extreme versions of the argument for black subjugation, figures as politically active and well known as Edgar Gardner Murphy, an Episcopalian priest and noted author of books and articles preaching paternalist solutions to the race problem, and Atticus Greene Haygood, a noted Methodist minister and president of Emory University for over a decade in the 1870s and 1880s, there was broad agreement on African-American inferiority.[5] By the time Griffith began working on this film in 1913 and 1914 the debate over the place of African Americans in United States culture seemed, to most whites with a racist disposition, fairly settled. The American system of de jure and de facto segregation was securely in place in both the South and the North. Not incidentally, large-scale disfranchisement of the black voter had also occurred in the South. In the federal government, Woodrow Wilson was in the process of segregating all branches of the federal service. Griffith, then, simply reproduced common racist assumptions that were well within the mainstream of late-nineteenth and early-twentieth century white American thought.[6] By drawing on such assumptions Griffith, in the manner of Howells, Dreiser, and Porter, practices the realist tendency of reifying a vision of a particular historical moment and devising explanations that "prove" its inevitability and ultimate intransigence.

Griffith did not use the range of techniques used by those filmmakers who preceded him, or even those he himself had employed at Biograph: the film uses very little camera movement within particular shots and no dolly shots. Griffith's practice of dramatically composing scenes from multiple fragmentary shots was his means to an end; it was a method of structuring the information he wished to present without appearing to emphasize technique. As Charles Musser states of the early cinema, "It was an inventive period with each director using a range of strategies which, taken as a whole, was less than the sum total of those being used" (4). Griffith, then, was not the figure who devised the next step in film art, the one that further revealed cinema's natural language. Rather, he devised a specific formal method that was interwoven with his content.

Griffith's notion of realism and the content of his assertions illustrate the way in which this concept has shifted in cultural function over the three or so decades traced in this study. In the late nineteenth century, as social chaos seemed to threaten the continuous process of American social life, realism was employed as a strategy for containing disruption. Howells and Edison assert a specific worldview that allows for minimal change and optimum continuity. With the realists' strategy of containment in place, the naturalists could assert, scientistically, the organic fact of social truths. That is, Dreiser and Porter show the nature of social being in a manner which argues that social life as it is expresses the hard facts of the world. As Howells and Edison had devised strategies for the assimilation of their realism, Porter and Dreiser assert the further necessity of accepting these "facts." Griffith's definition of realism again asserts the conserving intention of the ideology of that worldview and method of composition, which derived from a positivist conception of the real. Indeed, Griffith takes the Progressive strategies of containment and encourages them toward reaction. As Howells and Edison had carefully posited the need to fix a definition of social order based on the top-down conception of managerial preeminence, and Dreiser and Porter had more forcefully asserted the fact of the positivist reduction in their elevating of the resonant powers of objects, Griffith now declares that the nature of reality is the world as it has been, and that this condition is self-evident and immutable. Since change violates this doctrine, it is both unnatural and "unreal." Because black Americans were slaves and dominated by whites, then this is the fact of the world. His film seeks to prove the eternal truth of this condition by showing the error of attempting to alter a "fact."

Considering Griffith in terms of the cultural movement of modernism makes sense from the perspective of chronology and in light of his specific method. When *The Birth of a Nation* was released in 1915, the Armory Show had already trumpeted the arrival of modernism in America. Ezra Pound's first two books of poetry had appeared in 1913 and 1914; in 1915 he was involved in the journal that polemicized for modernism, *Blast*. Gertrude Stein's *Three Lives* and *Tender Buttons* had been published, and Pablo Picasso had been introduced to the American public. Though there is no evidence that Griffith was influenced by these occurrences, much of his method suggests the works of these figures of the avant-garde: its radical fracture, its idealizing of direct impression, even its emphasis on history. Indeed, Griffith's notion of his text as a dynamo whose energy can heal the present by reconstituting it from the fibers of the past echoes Pound's mission for modernist poetry. As Frank Lentricchia explains, "One directive of Pound's 'make it new' is 'make it old'" (208). This impulse toward reaction pervades the modernist movement and informs Griffith's film. Indeed we may group Griffith in Jackson Lears's category of "anti-modern modernist," with figures as diverse as Henry Adams and T. S. Eliot (*No Place* 300–312).

Like Porter, Griffith employs a variety of profilmic methods to assert the realism of his presentation. He dresses his characters in appropriate costumes, and the famous historical figures who appear in the film, such as Abraham Lincoln and Generals Grant and Lee, resemble their counterparts outside it. The well-known historical events the film depicts, such as the battle of Atlanta, Sherman's march to the sea, and Lincoln's assassination, all have outcomes that jibe with the popular perception of those events. We are not asked to believe that the South won the Civil War, or that Lincoln shot Booth at Ford's Theater. By using reproductions of these well-known events, the film draws its audience into its illusion of realism. It establishes itself as a trustworthy document by relying on the viewer's knowledge of these and other actual events. The film primarily proceeds from scene to scene in the same manner as *The Great Train Robbery,* using both the abrupt cuts that became popular in the actuality narratives of the previous decade and a progressive chronology (that is, the film does not go back in time from scene to scene as events over its sprawling chronology—over two centuries—move forward).[7]

The relationship between *The Great Train Robbery* and *The Birth of a Nation* suggests that Griffith intended audiences to perceive his film as a revelation of the factual truth of the events it portrays.[8] As Porter's compositional method asserted the realism of a film that had only a very broad grounding in fact, so Griffith employed many of these same techniques as particular devices within a range of possibilities proclaiming the reality of his film.

Griffith repeatedly signals the ties between his text and history as a means of asserting its truth. At four points in the film he provides documentation to imply that the events of the film occurred in fact. In addition, the titles that open the second part of the film proclaim, "This is an historical presentation of the Civil War and Reconstruction period, and is not meant to reflect on any race or people today." In the same sequence of titles he goes on to quote selectively and extensively from Woodrow Wilson's *History of the American People.* Wilson's words support the perspective of the film as a whole, and the viewer receives the doubly effective jolt of historical documentation and presidential prestige.[9]

Just as those who sought to produce fictions of the real adopted the formal characteristics of the positivists' scientific method to produce a fictional scientism, so Griffith employs the cinematic trope of realism to present a philosophy of history as "fact," requiring only a neutral device to recapture and reproduce it as it truly exists. Griffith views history as the process of assuring continuity, rather than the process of noting change. Hence, in the structures of his film the success of human action is severely limited by its relationship to his theory: his figures are ultimately pawns of his idea of history, as the inevitability of reaction is assured by his theory of what must be. *The Birth of a Nation* asserts the biological necessity of whites dominating blacks and forms its narrative to show that history must, finally, be ordered by this fact. In linking assumptions of biology with apparent historical inevitability, Griffith reproduces a motivating ideology both for those materially involved in the restoration of white rule in the South, as well as those who explained that restoration subsequently, that is, historians of Reconstruction and its aftermath. In the former case, this theory catalysed action and also served as an expedient for rationalizing policies that benefited a certain group. As Joel Williamson explains in his study of Reconstruction in South Carolina, "A central theme of native white thought was that Negroes should be subordinated to whites whenever and wherever contact between the races occurred. Emancipation hardly altered this attitude. The subordination of the freedmen had obvious economic advantages for whites of all stations, but in the minds of the dominant group it also had higher purposes. Most important, it was God's way" (*After Slavery* 245). Thus, we see Redemption, the term applied by white Southerners to the restoration of lily-white rule in their region, as a political strategy that was appropriately titled; that is, it was often pursued with a fervor akin to that of a religious crusade.

This vision of history as an inevitable linking of biological fact with social condition provides the impetus for Griffith's philosophy of composition. The film's narrative centers on two families, the Northern Stonemans and the Southern Camerons. In general, the members of these families are dominated by the impulses of history. However, in each family there exists one figure who attempts to master these forces: Austin Stoneman and Ben Cameron. The former, based on the historical figure Thaddeus Stevens, is one of *Birth's* forces of evil, attempting to elevate blacks to equality with whites. The latter is heroic even in defeat, but ultimately triumphant as the leader of the Ku Klux Klan. The film shows the irrationality of the former and the rationality of the latter. In its terms it asserts its "right" ending; the conversion of Stoneman and the elevation of Cameron is historically inevitable. These characters, then, dramatize Griffith's vision of history. In this vision lies the rationale for Griffith's formal method: he is able to divide his film into minute affective elements because his characters are not responsible for their actions. Rather, their movements succeed or fail based on their relationship to Griffith's grand scheme of reaction and racial dominance.

The full legitimation for the twisted vision of *Birth*, and Dixon's *The Clansman*, beyond its relationship to the legacy of the restoration of white racial hegemony in the 1870s, occurs in the writings of many of the preeminent American historians of the first decades of the twentieth century. In historical terms, we may see this theory developing academic respectability and even authority as part of the Progressive disposition to minimize disruptive social elements. That is, the prevalence of racism, both northern and southern, meant that African-American participation in a full range of cultural activities would meet with significant resistance. Among conservative-minded intellectuals, a belief in the tenets of that racism, as well as a disposition to use their powers to promote order, contributed to their further explanations for white domination. We may also locate this explanation as part of the broader ideological disposition to employ positivist methodology as a means of explaining the correctness of a particular, visible model of social organization.

Historians who were central in developing an explanation of Reconstruction that termed its results just and inevitable included, most notably, John Burgess and William Dunning at Columbia University. Indeed, the particular vision of Reconstruction asserted by Griffith is generally described as that of the "Dunning School." Dunning offered the interpretation that "to stand the social pyramid on its apex was not the surest way to restore the shattered equilibrium in the South. The enfranchisement of the freedmen and their enthronement in political power was as reckless a species of statecraft as that which marked 'the blind hysterics of the Celt' in 1789–95" (*Essays* 250–51). Eric Foner's recent recapitulation of the view of Reconstruction held by Dunning and his many influential followers (a perspective with which Foner profoundly disagrees) reads like a plot synopsis of Griffith's film and its literary sources in Thomas Dixon:

When the Civil War ended, the white South genuinely accepted the reality of military defeat, stood ready to do justice to the emancipated slaves, and desired above all a quick re-integration into the fabric of national life. Before his death, Abraham Lincoln had embarked on a course of sectional reconciliation, and during Presidential Reconstruction (1865–1867) his successor, Andrew Johnson, attempted to carry out Lincoln's magnanimous policies. Johnson's efforts were opposed by the Radical Republicans in Congress. Motivated by an irrational hatred of Southern "rebels" and a desire to consolidate their party's national ascendancy, the Radicals in 1867 swept aside the Southern governments Johnson had established and fastened black suffrage upon the defeated South. There followed the sordid period of Congressional or Radical Reconstruction (1867–77), an era of corruption presided over by unscrupulous "carpetbaggers" from the North, unprincipled Southern white "scalawags," and ignorant freedmen. After much needless suffering, the South's white community banded together to overthrow these governments and restore "home rule" (a euphemism for white supremacy). All told, Reconstruction was the darkest saga in American history. (*Reconstruction* xix–xx) [10]

The desire for reaction implicitly and explicitly embedded in this theory of Reconstruction is masked, for both the reader and such writers as Dunning and Burgess, by claims that history is a "science" and that the "objective" historian simply allows the facts to tell themselves. We can see these claims repeatedly employed by Burgess, Dunning, and Griffith. Through Dunning and Burgess, we can trace the ideal of objective history in the United States and its appeal to authority and conservation of the status quo. The figure who is seen, correctly or incorrectly, at the head of this movement, is the German historian Leopold Von Ranke.[11]

In the late nineteenth and early twentieth centuries, the American academy modernized and divided into disciplines along the lines of the German model of higher education. At the center of this model was the idea of the professional scholar engaged in active research; his object was nothing less than "truth" and, as it had been for the literary realists, his method was "objective." When the American Historical Association was formed in 1884, its goal was professionalization. Though the terms of this goal were somewhat vague, the early leaders of the movement to professionalize historians largely agreed that the discipline should be defined by methodological standards. As in Howells's literary realism, however, the historian was required to balance somehow the dictates of morality with those of impartiality. In this case, as with Howells, morality largely functioned as an abiding agreement to assist in preserving the existing social order. Thus, if an historian dissented from the truisms of the day he was not simply immoral but also lacking objectivity—and therefore unprofessional and out of a job. This practice was often enforced by university administrators, who relied on wealthy donors for the capital necessary to the well-being of their institutions.[12]

At Columbia, the German model was precisely followed. Burgess studied with Ranke in Germany in the years immediately after the Civil War, before returning to the United States in 1873. At Columbia from 1876 until 1912, he presided over the development of the credo of "scientific" history in America. Burgess wrote, "We seek to teach the student how to get hold of an historic fact, how to distinguish fact from fiction, how to divest it as far as possible of coloring or exaggeration" ("Methods" 219). In his writings he expresses his belief that the historian should efface himself in order to allow the facts to tell the story. Of course, such a retelling is impossible, but the act of attempting such a division of subject and object likely results in the perpetuation of dominant beliefs. This "objective" method confirms the solidity and relative immutability of empirically verifiable materials as it limits the role of an active interpreter who may advocate change. In the writings of Burgess, a friend and teacher of Theodore Roosevelt, we see this propensity toward reaction. Burgess employs his "science" to offer a view of race that cites the biological dominance of those of "Teutonic origins."[13] Not surprisingly, his work *The Civil War and the Constitution, 1859–1865* (1902) treats the period much as Dunning does. The intellectual bond between the men was not purely methodological; they also shared a range of assumptions regarding the inferiority of blacks. Writes Burgess, "It is the white man's mission, his duty to hold the reins of political power in his own hands for the civilization of the world and the welfare of mankind" (*Reconstruction* viii–ix).

In associating Burgess and Dunning with Roosevelt, it is possible to take the ideology of race that these historians developed and asserted and see the implications of those ideas in material occurrences of the first decade of the century. As an element of his own racial dispositions and as a political gesture that would win him general approval among white voters, Roosevelt, despite once having invited Booker T. Washington to lunch in the White House, presided over policies that further estranged African Americans from the center of American life. He did nothing to intrude on the general practice of legal segregation and disfranchisement that was becoming routinized in the South. Indeed, in his desire to break the Democratic hold on the South, he was instrumental in making his party a purely white one in that region, so that it could attain some power regionally and a majority in the Congress. Similarly, he made, as Joel Williamson notes, "many white and very few black appointments in the South" (*Crucible of Race* 352). In a more general sense, we may see Roosevelt's belief in the primacy of the Anglo-Saxon and the rightful and constructive role of that "race" as abetting his support for United States imperialism, wherever it should lead— China, the Philippines, Santo Domingo, Colombia. In noting the role of the genteel and "objective" racism of figures such as Dunning, Burgess, and Roosevelt, we may see the full historical power of a film such as *Birth*.[14]

The Dunning and Burgess school of thought regarding race and Reconstruction illustrates the ways in which the reactionary orthodoxy of the historian's profession was upheld. As racists and practitioners of a method with no reflexive element, they unquestionably represented the consensus of America at the turn of the century and defied dissenters to rebut their "facts." This consensus blossomed with the assistance of the burgeoning social sciences—of which history was one—which generally employed their methods to affirm the prejudices of its practioners. The growth of American imperialism also provided a further cultural impetus toward viewing those who deviated from an Anglo-Saxon norm as inferior. The higher cause of Burgess and Dunning, then, was the reconciliation of North and South, as well as the justification of white superiority. Thus, as Peter Novick writes, "Through some give-and-take, a nationalist and racist historiographical consensus was achieved on the 'middle period' of the nineteenth century" (77).

Griffith, then, employs the medium of film to reproduce these assumptions regarding the nature of the past and the idea of race. In doing so he uses this vision of history-as-fact as a basis for both the content *and* the form of his film. Thus, in this perspective Griffith is allowed to deny his responsibility for the racism of his film, much as Dunning and Burgess, among others, denied the racism of their historical narratives, hiding behind the justification of "historical objectivity."

By situating Griffith within the context of respectable opinion, we may see the film as a means of confirming that opinion for the majority of Americans who were disposed to devise elaborate rationales to justify racial segregation. Indeed, when located within the history of American cinema, *The Birth of a Nation* signals the fruition of the motion picture as a respectable mode of entertainment for the middle class. That is, through its specific marketing strategies, exhibition in respectable theaters, and aesthetic intricacy, the film was instrumental in making cinema a thoroughly respectable medium. Explains Richard Koszarski, "It was the first feature to attract vast crowds to theater box offices, and it did so while offering an experience that was technically and artistically in the vanguard of 1915 production standards. . . . *The Birth of a Nation* should never be thought of as just a movie, however. Rather, it was the first great film event, the first film to force its way into the national consciousness" (320). As Roy Rosensweig has claimed, "The exhibition of *The Birth of a Nation* sealed the marriage of middle-class audiences and movies" (211). In effect, the film's relationship to dominant modes of thought allowed Griffith to produce an extremely polemical film without any overt polemic. He achieves this effect by using events that in the view of his audience are discernibly "historical"—which can also be defined as objective (the process) and factual (the result). A viewer of this film who accepts the seeing-is-believing trope of realism would have no way of disproving any of its "facts" in the way that the film itself proves them. That is, while there exists empirical evidence that Lee surrendered to Grant at Appomattox, it is impossible, through historical research, to prove that Silas Lynch (a fictional mulatto villain in the film) was not a personification of evil. In effect, the film's fiction may become, in the viewer's mind, inextricable from its assertions of fact because he or she approaches it from the dominant philosophical frame of positivism. Since the viewer sees the fact of what is taking place on the screen and can verify parts of the presentation, the tendency may be to verify the whole.

This tendency may be counteracted by a concerted effort on the part of the viewer to deal critically with the film's form and content. In fact, various viewers have approached it in this manner since its release. When *The Birth of a Nation* was first shown in 1915, various organizations picketed it, and it is probable that countless others found it repugnant.[15] This response has recurred in the years since, suggesting that one who goes into the film will not necessarily become a racist. Still, the film did reflect and confirm dominant beliefs. It is likely that in 1915 more viewers used this film to verify their racial predispositions than confronted its worldview by resisting its potentially engrossing presentation. Indeed, in anecdotal responses, the judgment of the mayor of Worcester, Massachusetts, George Wright, seems typical: "It is the greatest thing I have ever seen in the way of a moving picture" (in Rosensweig 211).

For Griffith, then, the guise of objectivity "proved" the efficacy of his beliefs. The conflation of social life with science was a central element of positivist philosophy and a major impulse in the professionalization of the social sciences in the early twentieth century. Griffith employs cinema in a manner consonant with its origins to represent this reduction. Indeed, at the core of Griffith's "history" is the impulse to "prove" that blacks are biologically inferior to whites and therefore need be dominated by them. In opposition to this fact, which in the terms of the film results in an inevitable and correct social order, are those who deny or evade these facts for one reason or another. The film seeks to prove their error and display their conversion.

The film's opening title declares its intent in an assertive tone but in a way that misrepresents its argument: "We do not fear censorship, for we have no wish to offend with improprieties or obscenities, but we do demand as a right the liberty to show the dark side of wrong that we may illuminate the bright side of virtue—the same liberty that is conceded to the art of the written word—that art to which we owe the Bible and the works of Shakespeare." This title was added after its initial showings in order to address the calls for its suppression with a plea for understanding and good will. In effect, Griffith masks his idea of fact in the rhetoric of high art and free expression.[16] However, Griffith's vision of the past as an absolute erodes the very ideals he asserts. The film inserts itself into the national myth by invoking the keyword "liberty" and by placing itself in the canon with the Bible and Shakespeare. In keeping with the film's aspirations as entertainment for the middle class, as well as its connection to the judgments of professional social scientists, this statement announces the film's place in Western culture and thereby provides it with a legitimacy that transcends temporal disputes.

In the opening scenes, it continues to claim its "objectivity" and historical validity by presenting a title that states, "The bringing of the African to America planted the first seed of disunion." Appearing immediately afterward is a hunched black man with no shirt on, parading before a white man who is elevated on a stage and dressed in eighteenth-century minister's clothing. Though within the film as a whole the racism that marks this scene is obvious, as an introductory statement of Griffith's sentiments it is fairly mild. Indeed, it seems merely to state the "facts." Had no slaves been imported to America, then it is possible that there would have been no Civil War. The minister, who in retrospect we know as a symbol of racism and paternalism, seems to express concern.

The next scene is similarly "neutral" and historical, as the title proclaims: "The abolitionists of the nineteenth century demanding the freeing of the slaves." The scene is then of a meeting house and a church pulpit, where a white minister preaches and then points to two black men at his side, one of whom he pats on the head. Next the camera finds a rotund white woman in the audience who nods her approval. Another white man then walks a black child through the parishioners. The two are then framed by a circle vignette.[17] Finally a collection plate is passed.

Griffith shrewdly begins his polemic by first misrepresenting its content and then giving it a bland tone. He specifically invokes history to proclaim the neutrality of his vision. That is, by providing a chronology that suggests a full explanation of the events of antebellum and postbellum race relations, Griffith situates himself as a voice of rationality. The subtext of these two scenes is the racial inferiority of people of color. Griffith gives us two situations where "kindly" paternalism is pictured. As we come to see, this film asserts as its center the error of attempting to overturn biological essence with abstract social practice. Hence, Griffith designs his history to base its inevitability in material—that is, biological—fact. His presentation refers to the regional argument for slavery, "that God had made black people precisely to be slaves, and it was the genius of the white Southerners to recognize this fact" (Williamson, *Crucible* 22).

The first figure introduced by name is the patriarch of the Stoneman family, Austin. The title states, "In 1860 a great parliamentary leader, whom we shall call Austin Stoneman, was rising to power in the National House of Representatives." This is the first specific date that the film provides, and in doing so it places this nonexistent figure in the historical frame it has already invoked. Further, by stating that "we shall call" him Austin Stoneman, as opposed to asserting that this is actually his name, the film seeks to establish this figure's existence even if he fails to appear in any other texts of the period. (This fictional character is based on the congressional leader of the period, Thaddeus Stevens.) He is both involved in the family drama and seeking historical effect. One of the three major villains of the work, he is the only one without black blood. Stoneman's crime is his attempt to recast reality according to the idea of equality. That is, he seeks to elevate blacks to equality with whites. He does so under the spell cast by his mulatto mistress, a union the film defines as unnatural and therefore likely to produce disaster.

By using a figure who refers to the historical figure of Stevens but who is named Stoneman, Griffith can indict the specific activities that occurred during Radical Reconstruction, as well as develop an elaborate rationale of the deep and depraved character flaws that would produce such an "unnatural" view of race. The actor who plays Stoneman, Ralph Lewis, does bear a resemblance to the photographs of the congressman and wears a rather obvious wig. Stevens himself wore a hairpiece to cover baldness caused by a childhood disease; in the film, Griffith makes the wig another odd vanity and a further symbol of this figure's inability to accept the natural order of things. Of course, the most unnatural thing about Stoneman is his relationship with his housekeeper. In his second appearance in the film, after we have met the other central family of the narrative, the Camerons, Stoneman's irrational impulse toward blacks is defined as sexual desire. The title states: "The great leader's weakness that is a blight to a nation." Then, Stoneman and Lydia, his mulatto housekeeper, are shown in the Victorian equivalent of intimacy, with the scene ending with Stoneman's arms around her. Both Dixon and Griffith defended their presentation of Stoneman's relationship with his housekeeper by explaining that such a relationship did exist between Stevens and his housekeeper, Lydia Smith (Schickel 189; Dixon 76).[18]

As opposed to the intraracial unions of the film, of which there are many, Griffith treats interracial longing as a simple case of depravity, whether it be a case of white men seeking black women or black men seeking white women (in Griffith's universe women do not covet men). Indeed, as we trace the two distinct narrative lines that form this film, we may see that

on one hand there is a line of ruin emanating from Stoneman and his co-
horts, and on the other a line of redemption defined by those who follow
their purer instincts. In *New People,* his study of interraciality and its mythology, Joel Williamson describes the ideological impulse that fuels Dixon
and Griffith's obsession. According to Williamson, prior to the nineteenth
century, it was relatively common for African-American women to have
children by white men, though there was a distinction between the upper
South (from North Carolina and northward and westward) and the lower.
In the former, "mulattoes appeared very early in the colonial period and in
relatively large numbers. In the upper South mulattoes in the mass, having
sprung from the lower orders, were generally treated by the white elite as
if they were black". In the lower South,

> mulattoes built their numbers slowly but continuously in the eigh-
> teenth and nineteenth centuries. . . . An important number were born
> of well-to-do white fathers and were recognized and sponsored by
> their fathers, sometimes as slaves, sometimes as free. . . . In the upper
> South, whites came to regard the lightest of free mulattoes as often
> dissolute and difficult people. In the lower South, before the 1850s the
> white elite seemed to value them in important ways.
>
> Free mulattoes of the more affluent sort in the lower South were
> treated by influential whites as a third class, an acceptable and some-
> times valuable intermediate element between black and white, slave
> and free. (14–15)

In the 1850s, however, on the eve of the Civil War, such acceptance in
the lower South succumbed to the ideology of race that was employed to
argue for the necessity of continuing the increasingly beleagured institution of slavery. After the war, the arguments for returning African Americans, if not to the status of chattel, then at least to that of young children,
centered around the supposed unfortunate social effects of allowing black
people to exist without the direct oversight of civilizing whites. One prominent—indeed the central—explanation for such oversight was the belief
that African-American men would be unable to resist their overwhelming
desire to rape white Southern women. Nell Irvin Painter explains,

> Sex was the whip that white supremacists used to reinforce white soli-
> darity, probably the only whip that would cut deeply enough to keep
> poor whites in line. Political slogans that spoke straightforwardly of
> property or wealth (which not all whites held) had failed to rally
> whites en masse. . . . The sexually charged rhetoric of "social equality"

invited all white men to protect their property in women and share in the maintenance of all sorts of political power (including the economic and political, which disproportionately benefitted the better-off) in the name of protecting the sexuality of white womenhood. (49)

Purer impulses, made all the more sanitary through their contrast with those that are clearly defined as impure, are typified by the "traditional" Southern family that serves to oppose the Northern Stonemans. As *Birth* begins, the Camerons live in genteel antebellum splendor in Piedmont, South Carolina. After we have met Austin Stoneman in Washington and his family in Pennsylvania, the film acquaints its viewers with the Camerons, who are defined by their association with the past. That is, in this film about returning to the necessary conditions of the past as completely as possible, the Camerons are introduced "In the Southland. Piedmont, South Carolina, the home of the Camerons, where life runs in a quaint way that is to be no more."

In the scene that follows, an establishing long shot of Piedmont frames the Camerons' columned house on the right, horses and carriage before it and a church in the background. The juxtaposition of home, religion, and a form of transportation that was in eclipse by 1915 elevates the Camerons and their way of life. The title itself expresses a sense of longing for the past, as it laments that this way of life "is to be no more." Of course, the life suggested here is the fictional idyll of the antebellum Southern planter.[19]

In the next scene, Ben Cameron appears for the first time. Ben is the essence of nobility in this film and consequently its hero. The only Cameron brother to survive the war, he marries Stoneman's daughter Elsie and founds the Ku Klux Klan. Unlike the Stoneman family, where we are first introduced to the family patriarch, here we first encounter the family heir. His inheritance is suggested by the ensuing shot, framed as if seen by Cameron himself, of two black children falling off the back of a wagon, then being spanked and put back on the wagon by their father. Ben reacts by laughing condescendingly.

The series of relationships suggested by this shot reveal the racial politics of the film: black children are the responsibility of black parents, and black parents are the responsibility of white masters. The de jure condition of slavery need not exist for this responsibility to apply; rather, it is a fact of nature that transcends legalisms. Considered with the opening shots of blacks in the care of white ministers, it is difficult to miss Griffith's assertion of the childlike nature of African Americans.

In this first treatment of the South, Griffith reestablishes the natural state of race relations with frequency. Within the context of the film we may see the metaphoric treatment of this state in the scene where a hand introducing kittens intrudes upon a close-up of puppies. Griffith suggests that the natural relations between blacks and whites is as inevitable as those between cats and dogs. The title then blankly states "Hostilities," before revealing the actual skirmish. The fusing of assumed biology and social practice emerges as one of the compositional strategies of the film, as Griffith's editing method effectively parallels them. Since the film fragments its structure, its logic of continuity defines its conceptual center.

Soon after Griffith introduces the Camerons, the Stoneman brothers visit Piedmont. As Ben Cameron and his brother Tod usher the Stonemans around the plantation, we are given a series of obligatory shots of slaves working the cotton fields, which culminate in a large close-up of a cotton blossom, symbol of the glory of plantation life. Subsequently, we see the slave quarters, where happy slaves dance for their visitors and then wave them a smiling and fond good-bye.

The Birth of a Nation treats the Civil War not simply as an example of all wars, as one Griffith biographer has stated, "at once huge, heroic, pathetic, wasteful, harrowing, cruel, degrading and horrifying" (Williams 69–70). Rather, though Griffith views this war as all of these things, he does so because of the rationale that creates it. Griffith is not so much opposed to war as he is opposed to conflicts that attempt to disrupt biologically correct relationships and the science of history. The film defines the cause of war not as Southern intransigence but as Northern hegemony. The first explicit mention of the coming conflict is cast in a cause-and-effect relationship that defines the North as the reason for conflict. In the scene immediately following the happy slaves dancing for the Cameron and Stoneman heirs, a title declares "The Gathering Storm. The power of the sovereign states, established when Lord Cornwallis surrendered to the individual colonies in 1781, is threatened by the new administration." The imposition of the year 1781 once again defines history as the persistence of correct relationships and not their disruption. Indeed, the possible change in status between the states and the federal government is treated here as analogous to the possible shift in power between slaves and masters. The autonomy of the states in relation to Washington is a fixed and correct relationship that shall not be disrupted, except by a party clearly in error. Two scenes later, that other organ of objective fact, the newspaper, is pictured with a headline that reads: "If the North carries the election, the South will secede."

Since war is the result of this attempt to overturn the natural relation between the states and the federal government, and between blacks and whites, it occurs as a cataclysmic event that utterly dominates the two families pictured, save for the evil Austin Stoneman. It becomes a force within a world gone awry, the result of change that triggers not progress but anarchy and atavistic violence. If for Griffith history is order and inevitability, the entire event of the Civil War is the impulse of antihistory. It replaces "science" with irrationality. Thus, its effects are patently immoral, as good is eradicated by the evil unleashed by Stoneman and others afflicted by "weakness."

As history is redemptive and irrationality destructive, the manner in which Griffith photographs his battle scenes defines their irrational status. These scenes offer action in the larger sense, uncontrolled by any rational impulse. We see the representation of battle in all its disorder, often shot by a camera situated high above the action. In addition, there are rarely figures in this scene who are recognizable to a viewer. When we do see Stonemans or Camerons, they are diminished by the compositional strategy. When we locate the young Duke Stoneman and Tod Cameron, they are within a battle that has already been established with a panoramic shot of the event. Only after having established the "fact" of the skirmish does the camera find these recurring characters, thus diminishing their importance by locating them as incidental to the larger scale of activity. That is, in such an upheaval all suffer equally. The title reminds us that "War claims its bitter, useless sacrifice." Having shot Duke, Tod seems to apologize before being shot himself.

In following the film's portrayal of this war as an act of irrationality based on an unnatural idea, we can see the ultimate acts of heroism within the film as possessing elements of futility. Ben Cameron, in one battle scene, first succors a fallen enemy and then, after being wounded himself, picks up the flag of the Confederacy and carries it into the Union trenches where he rams it down a cannon before he falls. A conflict where such heroism fails to accomplish victory must be wrong. This is confirmed by the ensuing title's proclamation: "The North victorious."

The first part of the film ends with the assassination of Abraham Lincoln and the response of the elder Doctor Cameron: "Our last friend is gone." John Wilkes Booth unleashes the further forces of irrationality with his act. The idea that inappropriate violence begets chaos echoes the film's representation of the Civil War itself. Indeed, the assassination of Lincoln signals a chaos and desolation that will require the forces of history to correct. Thus, at the beginning of the film's second part, "Reconstruction," its titles make the film's most blatant statement of its accuracy as history, as they go on to quote extensively and with acknowledgment from Woodrow Wilson's *History of the American People*.

> The policy of congressional leaders wrought . . . a veritable overthrow of civilization in the South . . . in their determination to "put the white South under the heel of the black South." . . .
>
> The white men were roused by a mere instinct of self preservation . . . until at last there had sprung into existence a great Ku Klux Klan, a veritable empire of the South, to protect the Southern country.

The coupling of black rule and the overthrow of civilization again defines the historical/biological view of the film. In Griffith's mind, one results necessarily in the other. Similarly, the Ku Klux Klan is typified as a spasm of reaction to an unnatural imposition. In Griffith's view, the KKK embodies the rationality of history righting itself.

The framing of the violence and chaos of *The Birth of a Nation*'s second part with an explicit historical voice provides a sense of history as a device to contain this upheaval. Wilson's authoritative voice, in ways the ultimate paternal ideal of rational historian and political leader, seems to promise that truth will conquer and provides a reassuring backdrop to the scenes prior to the emergence of the Klan.

In the opening scenes of part 2, Stoneman finally becomes the embodiment of evil he has threatened to become throughout the film. Griffith expresses this menace through his rapid introduction of both Lydia, the symbol of Stoneman's weakness, and Silas Lynch, the effect of this affliction. Lynch, titled the "mulatto leader of the blacks," bows to Stoneman only to be reproached: " 'Don't scrape to me. You are the equal of any man here.' " In case this title failed to outrage the audience sufficiently, Griffith essentially repeats it after two more scenes: "The great Radical [Stoneman] delivers his edict that the blacks shall be raised to full equality with the whites." Griffith goes on to further build on this idea as he provides a leisurely shot of a placard at the "Southern Union League rally":

"Equality"

Equal Rights	"40 acres and mule"
Equal Politics	for every colored citizen
Equal Marriage	

In the event that the first two propositions listed were not sufficiently inflammatory, Griffith turns to biological ideas of race to fix his point.

In his treatment of Lincoln's assassination, we can see Griffith reproducing historical views that were common to racial radicals of the period from
1890 to around the time of the film. In the mythology that grew out of the
need to justify the return of absolute white dominance to the South, the
framers of Radical Reconstruction, including Thaddeus Stevens, are cast
as demons in a melodrama. In contrast, Lincoln, who had been the scourge
of the South just a few decades before, became, for the purpose of extreme
contrast, lionized as the voice of moderation, "the great conciliator."

Part 2 of the film dramatizes the results of idealism about race and offers
the film's extremes of violence and sexuality. This portion of the film shows
the nefariousness of Reconstruction, as Lynch, taking his cues from Stoneman, stirs up the once happy slaves. In an early scene, he induces them
to stop working, leaving them to dance idly. This scene recalls the earlier
one where slaves owned by the Camerons danced to entertain the visiting
Stonemans and their masters. In the social upheaval of Reconstruction, the
innate propensity of blacks toward sloth is unchecked by a "good" white
master: Lynch's misrule leads this flock astray.

But Lynch, because of the legacy of his black blood, cannot initiate
the action he apparently commands. As we see in the opening scenes of
this part, Lynch would be passive if not for the perverse egalitarianism
of Stoneman, which we know is based in his sexual impulses. In Griffith's
further merging of biology and history, the symbols of miscegenation—
those who display their mixed parentage—serve as the film's other two
principal villains. Because Lydia and Lynch also have some white blood,
the turbulence of their biology makes them particularly dangerous. They
possess the desire to dominate without the means. But when enabled by
Stoneman, they do so unwisely. Lydia and Silas symbolize the unrestrained
desires of weak whites and further incite anarchy. It is the province of the
forces of history, then, not simply to quell Lynch and Lydia, but also to
quell Stoneman's desires. When the Klan does arise to dominate the film,
it is precisely to avert interracial sex. The Klan appears as a force that will
assure the genealogical purity of both races and therefore the dominance
of Caucasians.

The presentation of the characters of Silas Lynch and Lydia as prime
forces of disruption draws on the mythology of the mulatto that developed
after 1850 and that became enmeshed in the postbellum racial hysteria. The
African-American woman served as a temptress for the white male, but if
a white man succumbed, he was clearly engaging in a sin of grand proportion. Indeed, one commentator wrote, apparently not atypically, that
the ravages of the Civil War were "the judgment of the almighty because

the human and brute blood have mingled to the degree it has in the slave states" (in Williamson, *Crucible* 448). Within the racial ideology of the late nineteenth and early twentieth centuries, a visible mulatto possessed the wiles of whites and the moral degeneracy of African Americans. Race thinking created such a bizarre mystique around the products of black and white sexuality that in one popular conception mulattoes were thought to be a distinct genetic species and incapable of reproduction. Apparently deriving from the writings of Charles White in the late eighteenth century, this conception had led to the term mulatto, which derived from the word mule, and it had currency until E. Franklin Frazier finally disproved it "to the satisfaction of most scholars" in 1939 (Williamson, *New People* 123).[20]

As the portion of the film where the redemptive action of the Klan occurs, part 2 includes its most dramatic scenes. It also displays, in the terms of the film, the more outrageous actions of blacks and the more heroic actions of whites. It is in the second part that we may view how Griffith's vision of history as an objective march of inevitabilities provides a rationale for the radical subdivision of scenes into many shots.

From its first scenes, *The Birth of a Nation* reveals its formal innovation, as it structures these coherent units of action through the use of many shots of differing perspective, including everything from long shots to close-ups. This subdivision of action provides Griffith with a means of defining appropriate rhythms and emphases for the story he wishes to tell. That is, like Dreiser in his reverence for objects, Griffith gives mobility to his narrative device in order to picture the intricacies of the world of things and thus reproduce their common meanings. For example, in the important scene at the film's beginning where Ben Cameron shows the Stonemans around the plantation, a scene is composed of a long shot of cotton fields with black field hands picking cotton, then a semi-close-up of them, and finally a close-up. Next, Ben, his younger sister, Phil Stoneman, and Margaret Cameron enter a long shot of the fields. Then a three-quarter shot of the group appears in which Phil shows a picture of his sister to Margaret, and Ben shows a cotton blossom to Margaret and Phil. The next shot is a full close-up of the cotton blossom. The two close-ups in this scene provide its points of emphasis. The picking hands produce the cotton blossom, and the cotton blossom is the metaphoric flower of Southern culture—like its women.

By making his camera mobile, Griffith can contextualize slavery in nostalgia and emphasize its glorious product, its flowers and its women. He has, in effect, found a visual method for the ideal of reaction, the myth of the lost cause. The sequence of these shots clearly has an emphasis, but it has no distinct point of origin. That is, since there is no specific mechanism by which the filmmaker appears in the film, this sequence seems to run on the momentum of its own logic. Tom Gunning terms this method Griffith's "narrator system," which he defines "as a sort of interiorized film lecturer" who "comments on the action of the film through the form of the film itself" (*D. W. Griffith* 176). Similarly, this sequence is by no means a matter of the psychology or consciousness of the figures pictured.[21] We do not see the meaning of the cotton blossom in terms of Ben Stoneman, but only in terms of itself. That is, it is an object of history, and it takes on resonance through its historically inscribed meanings. In effect, we can say that the cotton flower is the idea of the lost cause and the center of the Dunning "scientific" interpretation of the Civil War and Reconstruction.

In such a compositional method, autonomous action by specific individuals is severely circumscribed. That is, since form dominates content in this case (as form defines what we will know as important and the means by which it will become important) and because figures within the film cannot generate form, they tend to be asserted as figures of pure action, governed by laws of action and reaction beyond their control. These laws are inscribed in Griffith's historical vision, a vision that operates within the objectivist ideals of the first generation of professional historians in the United States, historians like Burgess and Dunning who believed equally in their own objectivity and the biological limits of those of "inferior races." In his racially determined *Foundations of Political Science* (1890), Burgess defines politics according to his notion of race and thus elevates those of Teutonic origins: "Teutonic political genius stamps the Teutonic nations as the political nations *par excellence,* and authorizes them, in the economy of the world, to assume the leadership in the establishment and the administration of states" (40). He goes on to explain the need to fix this political hierarchy by each nation maintaining racial purity: "The prime policy, therefore, of each of these [modern constitutional] states should be to attain proper physical boundaries and to render its population ethnically homogenous. In other words, the policy in modern political organization should be to follow the indications of nature and aid the ethnical impulses of conscious development" (41).

Griffith offers his disintegrated affective form as a means of showing the dynamic power of history itself. For Griffith, that power can only go backward toward the essential truths that Burgess and Dunning assert. Hence, his historically powered text produces inert truths, but attaining these truths relies on an objectivist vision of history as a system of laws and inevitabilities that are outside the powers of either its actors or its recorders to alter. Fittingly, then, as the film's second part is about the outrages leading to the inevitable dominance of the white race, its scenes generally become longer and more complexly edited. In these longer scenes, the invisible hand of Griffith becomes objectified as the power of historical reaction in order to animate the necessary disruption that leads to order. That is, the film moves frantically only to arrive at a place in the past—which Griffith defines as the eternal present. *The Birth of a Nation's* second part displays great cinematic motion, but traverses less historical time than its first half.

The agent who emerges to drive the narrative and, in Griffith's view, history, back to where it belongs, is Ben Cameron. He emerges to offer a view that is the opposite of Austin Stoneman's. As Austin Stoneman is evil for the paradox he creates—the paradox of biologically inferior people being responsible for themselves and others—Cameron rises to heroism for his ability to resolve the film's historical paradoxes and effectively define the birth of a nation. This resolution lies in the reassertion of white power through the agency of the Ku Klux Klan and the subsequent agreement among whites that blacks are inferior and require domination. If the tragedy of the film is the anarchy wrought by basing action on something other than biological truth, Ben Cameron's explicit recognition of this truth empowers him. He becomes a means by which history can reassert its inherent logic, and he derives his force from his recognition of its laws.

Within the film, the idea of the Ku Klux Klan occurs to Ben as he watches children play. He sees white children scaring black children by hiding under a sheet. The title reads: "The inspiration." Then Ben rises in an exclamation. The next title reads,

The result.
The Ku Klux Klan, the organization that saved the South from the anarchy of black rule, but not without the shedding of more blood than at Gettysburg, according to Judge Tourgee of the Carpetbaggers.

Despite Griffith's citation of Tourgee, a federal judge who presided over the prosecution of many Klansmen,[22] Griffith's portrayal of the Klan violence characterizes it not as anarchic and senseless in the manner of the Civil War, but as heroic and ultimately redemptive. This redemption draws its current from its recognition of the "facts" of the world. Ben's idea for the

KKK, while deeply indebted to dramatic conventions, emerges from his observation of a racist truism that in Griffith's film is inscribed as fact: that blacks are superstitious and easily frightened. The KKK, then, achieves its power not through its brutality, but through its use of symbols. In the first scene in which the Klan shows its power, it does so simply by appearing in its costumes. Immediately, two blacks—"The negro disturber and barn burner"—shake and run away in fright.

Griffith's portrayal of the rise of the Klan in South Carolina takes considerable historical liberties. The Klan, as a vigilante organization devoted to terrorism, originated in Tennessee in 1867 and its first Grand Wizard was Nathan Bedford Forrest, a Tennessean. The events that Griffith portrays seem to refer to the Klan riots in York County, South Carolina, in 1871, as well as to the Klan overtaking of polling places in that general region during the elections of 1868. However, the figure of Ben Cameron is modelled after Dixon's uncle, Colonel Leroy McAfee, to whom *The Clansman* was dedicated. Apparently, to enlarge the scope of his tribute to his uncle, Dixon joined references to the most visible Klan leader (Forrest) and its greatest military actions (in the South Carolina piedmont), and named MacAfee as their point of reference. One may question why neither Dixon nor Griffith resituates McAfee in his native Cleveland County, North Carolina, providing Cameron with a point of reference akin to those for Lydia Brown and Stoneman, but in 1871 many of the central figures in the Cleveland County Klan, including McAfee, were arrested, and that chapter ultimately dissolved as a result of the dissension caused by Klansmen informing on one another. Writes Allen Trelease, "In general Klan demoralization was so great that its activities came to a halt in North Carolina by the beginning of 1872" (348). Such an inauspicious ending would seem to have little inspirational power to spawn "the birth of a nation."

Within the logic of the film, then, the Klan's existence results only from the chaos of black rule. As a force of order, it only responds to violence, it never initiates it. The title tells us: "Lynch's supporters draw first blood against the Ku Klux." Similarly, the Klan executes the black man Gus only after he has illicitly pursued the innocent Flora and "forced" her to jump to her death to avoid him. This highly dramatic scene of Gus's pursuit and Flora's suicide is one of the most complexly edited in the film, as it draws on the biological depravity of Gus, which is aroused by the socially deviant conditions of Reconstruction. As Gus is a symbol of biology run amuck, it is only fitting that he be eradicated by the Klan. In the title that precedes the Klan's throwing of Gus's body onto Lynch's porch, the title tells us, "The answer to the blacks and carpetbaggers."

Similarly, the final scene of the film also features a white woman who is sexually threatened by a man of color. This time, Elsie Stoneman is sought by Silas Lynch. Since Lynch is empowered by Elsie's father, and even Austin does not approve of this union, Lynch's designs ultimately prove even to Austin Stoneman that the races must be separate. On such proof is based the agreement among whites that can lead to the birth of a nation.[23] This agreement is precisely the intention of the reigning group of historians at the turn of the century.

Formally, the unleashing of the atavistic forces of Reconstruction and the redemptive forces of the Klan further fragments the work. Indeed, as the form increasingly subdivides scenes into multiple shots we see the dynamism of Griffith's vision of history as a vortex of reaction. This contrasts with the four scenes that he defines within the work as "historical facsimiles" and documents from historical sources. Griffith pictures Lincoln signing the proclamation calling for volunteers to serve in the Civil War and documents it by citing Nicolay and Hay's *Lincoln, a History*.[24] Griffith shows us Grant and Lee at Appomattox signing the papers that seal the defeat of the South, "after Col. Horace Porter in *Campaigning with Grant*." The film portrays Lincoln's assassination in Ford's Theater and again cites Nicolay and Hay, and it shows us the South Carolina House of Representatives in 1871, "after photograph by The Columbia *State*." In contrast to the direction of the film as a whole, these four scenes depict events that figure in the South's ultimate subjugation. Also discordant with the film as a whole is the fact that these "historical facsimiles" show us history as still and inert. That is, they are static tableaux captured in film, not cinematic in the dynamic way of the film as a whole.

It is true these four instances provide further grist for Griffith's claim that *The Birth of a Nation* was factual. Wrote Griffith in defense of his film, "[It is] based upon the authenticated history of the period covering the action of our plot" ("Reply" 78). However, the content of these scenes and their form places them outside the film's idealized vision of history as a rational force. Griffith supersedes this earlier mode of stage and photographic realism with his new device of scientific truth.

These four points finally are undone both formally and historically by the rise of the Klan. Indeed, the final scene of the film, in which the Klan reconquers the South, signifies the film's climax both in form and content, as it lasts some three hundred shots and includes three distinct lines of action, among which Griffith crosscuts. This dynamic editing asserts the kinetic power of historically correct actions to shape the world. It is a virtuoso formal performance, but one in which the performer has been displaced. As Tom Gunning explains, "The cut masters the action through interruption, terminating it at a point of intensity. In other words, instead of a shot being a simple container for an action, a means of recording and presenting it, it intervenes and structures it, overriding its natural unfolding. The placement to the cut discloses its own force—its ability to assert itself as a manufacturer of meaning" (*D. W. Griffith* 205). Since Griffith's cuts are defined by his historical vision, he has effectively transformed the subjective hand of the filmmaker into the objective force of history. He has enlarged upon the realm of the manager in the industrial workplace and employed his tools for discovering objective laws in the interest of revealing the necessity of stasis.

In doing so he grafts his own vision of objectivity and historical inevitability onto Edison's naive belief in the realism of his new medium, the cinema. Wrote Griffith in 1915 shortly after the release of *Birth:*

Imagine a public library of the near future, for instance. There will be long rows of boxes or pillars, properly classified and indexed, of course. At each box a push button and before each box a seat. Suppose you wish to "read up" on a certain episode in Napoleon's life. Instead of consulting all the authorities, wading laboriously through a host of books, and ending bewildered, without a clear idea of exactly what did happen and confused at every point by conflicting opinions of what did happen, you will merely seat yourself at a properly adjusted window, in a scientifically prepared room, press the button, and actually see what happened. ("Some Prophecies" 35)

Griffith believes in the fact and truth of the cinema image in the manner of its earliest practitioners, but he further enlists his apparatus with the power to contain the verities of the ages. In effect, he disingenuously asserts the immanence not only of this highly structured film, but of all cinema. He asserts its objectivity in a manner that makes it a device for education, an education that is as presumably true as *The Birth of a Nation.*

This vision of history as a series of given truths that may instruct the ages again recalls William Dunning, who explains: "The province of history is to ascertain and present in their causal sequence such phenomena as exerted an unmistakable influence on the development of men in social and political life" (*Truth in History* 4). For Dunning, the objectivity of his profession requires that the historian repress explicit judgments of past historical error, but his absolutism—based in his ideas of history-as-science and science-as-progress—dictates such polarities of right and wrong. The result of such tortured reasoning is a historical text that represses its textuality and hides its judgments behind its assertions of truth and objectivity. Griffith's positivist stance also dictates an illusory division between subject and object that results in a similarly deceptive assertion of factuality and truth. The form of the medium enables this stance, as the apparatus's roots as an instrument of nineteenth-century science result in a perspective that virtually reproduces what Hayden White calls "the Rankean conception of the 'innocent eye' of the historian" (53).

This "innocent eye"—Griffith's camera—ultimately finds the former enemies, Phil Stoneman and Ben Cameron, united to defend their "Aryan birthright." This is done under the power of the Klan, which creates the stasis necessary for the film's retreat into private consummation, the marriages of Phil Stoneman and Margaret Cameron and of Ben Cameron and Elsie Stoneman. In a title that is preceded by the Klan menacing blacks, we are left with: "The aftermath. At the sea's edge, the double honeymoon." For Griffith, history having run its course, the need for public action is eliminated: the fruition of history is its eradication. Indeed, this culminates as the very essence of reaction and recapitulates a focal idea in the reactionary aspect of aesthetic modernism. As Pound and Eliot declare that what is essential in the past must be resurrected to produce an eternal order, Griffith employs history to effect a similar stasis.

Griffith relies on his audience's predisposition to believe in the reality of the image, on their dominant belief in the positivist dogma of the time, and above all on their willingness to have their racism verified as fact. The film was a remarkable success and continues to be shown. Subsequently, the form that Griffith developed became a recurring one in American cinema. It established the epic as a possible type of presentation, as well as the popularity of this dynamic method of editing. Though his specific strategy has never been precisely reproduced, elements of his style have often been incorporated in later films. As Richard Koszarski notes, "*The Birth of a Nation* had an unprecedented effect on the cinema's economic, aesthetic, technological, and cultural development. While other films may have matched it in one category, no other work in film history achieved an impact so broad and so deep. . . . It was the first film to force its way into the national consciousness" (320).

Critics still apologize for its content, employing strategies that baffle, as they freely separate form from content or claim that Griffith was no racist. Such apologies avert confronting the fact that this form was specifically employed to legitimize barbarism with its unreflective assertions—which were broadly based in dominant American ideologies.

As an historical event, *The Birth of a Nation* has both symbolic and specific effects. As a symbol, it serves as the culmination of efforts by whites virtually to ban African Americans from American politics, to restrict access to viable forms of education and economic power, and to make separate virtually all public facilities. As this film was shown to Woodrow Wilson, his administration, under the leadership of such avowed white supremacists as Josephus Daniels, William McAdoo, and Albert Burleson, was making federal service yet another area of racial exclusion. It presages the publication and popular success of Madison Grant's *The Passing of a Great Race* (1916) and the extreme nativism that culminated in the restriction of immigrants in 1924.

As a direct result of this film, the long dormant Ku Klux Klan reemerged in 1915, under the leadership of William J. Simmons. This later Klan reflected the broader social anxieties of its age and pitted itself against all people and things construed as un-American: Catholics, Jews, foreigners. After World War I it became a major political and social force, particularly in the Midwest. While it is difficult to lay these historical events entirely at the feet of D. W. Griffith, it is possible to see them as a suggestion of the film's immense power. That power is related to its art, but by no means is its art distinct from its social impact.

SEVEN

Ernest Hemingway's In Our Time

and the Objectification of Experience

Ernest Hemingway, revealing his realist's myopia, proclaimed in a much-cited quote: "All modern American literature comes from one book by Mark Twain called *Huckleberry Finn*." In tracing the line of his aesthetic form back to one of the pioneers of literary realism, Hemingway makes explicit what might be readily apparent to any reader of his early major works, including *In Our Time, The Sun Also Rises,* and *A Farewell to Arms:* that these volumes culminate the first phase of the realistic movement in American letters. In them, Hemingway pushes language virtually into the realm of the concrete, as he only sparingly employs words with abstract referents, minimizes authorial comment, and reduces character to simple function. These works all but follow Howells's vision of the novel, while they revere objects in a manner recalling Dreiser. They also feature the radical fragmentation of character found in the films of Griffith after 1915. Yet, for all their radical technique, they form the basis of the cult of Hemingway, suggesting that he touched a cultural nerve that continues to vibrate some six decades after the first of these works was published.

In Our Time was first published in virtually its present form in 1925. Though this was some ten years after Griffith's film, its specific formal antecedents can be traced at least as far back as Gertrude Stein's *Three Lives,* published in 1909 but written in 1905. Stein's work tells of three women who never meet one another. Though one could concoct some thematic unity for this work's content, its available coherence rests primarily in its radical restructuring of linguistic and novelistic convention. Stein severely limits her choice of words, repeating whole phrases many times in each story. She also shows a fondness for nouns and a complementary minimalist sense of description.[1]

Hemingway's work also evokes Sherwood Anderson's primarily realistic *Winesburg, Ohio* (1919). Like Hemingway, Anderson stresses the concrete properties of language in order to push words toward becoming the things they represent. Also like Hemingway, Anderson disrupts the conventional realist notion of cause and effect to fragment his novel into a series of vignettes. At the heart of each of these fragments lies a tale of emotional disruption, which Anderson tells with some understatement. Though Anderson's method has similarities to Stein's, it is far less severe and considerably more accessible to a wide audience. Hemingway's method falls somewhere in between these two in its employment of high-modernist devices.

The third figure who specifically defines the tradition on which Hemingway built and which he popularized is the poet Ezra Pound. Pound's idea of Imagism, poems evoking immediate, concrete images that resonate and engage their readers to respond but not necessarily to reflect, was important to Hemingway's prose style. In 1920, Pound published his poetic sequence *Hugh Selwyn Mauberly* and the first of *The Cantos*. While both emplot strategies of radical fragmentation and the idealization of the word as a producer of virtually concrete images, it is the former that more distinctly connects to Hemingway. *Mauberly* chronicles the cultural decline of the twentieth-century West through a series of vignettes that achieve power through their apparent simplicity of structure and the acuity of their choice of words. They also look back upon an idealized classical age that Pound would reproduce through the politics of his aesthetic.[2]

Grouping Hemingway with these other writers makes sense not simply from the perspective of compositional similarities; it also finds justification in his biography. The young Hemingway was well acquainted with Stein, Pound, and Anderson. All three helped him in devising his compositional ideals and in establishing his affiliation with the modernist movement. Anderson encouraged him to leave Chicago for Paris in 1921 and provided letters of introduction to Stein and Pound, among others. Stein and Pound fully initiated him into the modernist movement, preaching to him at length on the transcendence and significance of art and the neccessity of spare and accurate prose.

Through Pound we may also connect Hemingway to the modernist poet T. S. Eliot. Like Pound, Eliot believed that the power of language could transcend time and culture. Eliot termed the linguistic structure he refined into a method for evoking this transcendent response "the objective correlative." By this he meant "that when the external facts, which must terminate in a sensory experience, are given, the emotion is immediately evoked" (124–25). Like Pound, Eliot was a political reactionary who decried the great leveling he found in modern Anglo-American culture. Eliot later found refuge in Catholicism, a faith he embraced with obeisance and which he employed as a shield against the onslaught of vulgarity. Pound's own later refuge was in Mussolini's Fascism, though his brand of authoritarianism was not the same as Il Duce's. Rather, he saw in the dictatorship of the Italian leader the prospect of exacting fidelity to his principles of aesthetics and social organization, a fidelity that the ideas themselves would never elicit. Though the other modernist proselytizer I have included, Gertrude Stein (a student of William James's at Harvard), is not so easily classified as Eliot and Pound, she was, like these male poets, a self-avowed elitist and aesthete.[3]

By noting, however briefly, the reactionary politics of these figures, I wish to introduce the problematic of the politics of modernism. Certainly writers as diverse as John Dos Passos, William Carlos Williams, and Josephine Herbst have attempted to use modernist precepts as a structuring device for what they believed was their politically radical method of expression. Still, these writers seem dwarfed by the ranks of those in the avant-garde of the first four decades of the twentieth century who have been either backward looking or simply devoted to the cause of preserving the social and political status quo. We may also wonder whether the compositional method these avowed leftists used was one that, finally, ill-served their political intentions. To put it bluntly, do the textual devices generally associated with literary modernism finally promote reaction or conservatism? I would propose that modernism need not be tied to authoritarianism but that it easily can be. Its radical fragmentation is often employed as a representation of contemporary disorder, a disorder to which modernists generally propose some textual resolution. In the works of Pound and Eliot, that resolution takes the form of a strong charismatic leader or faith in authority. In the early works of Dos Passos, that resolution is the raised social consciousness of the reader. The former inscribe docility and the cult of art; the latter promotes activism and, explicitly, the social possibilities of disruptive texts. I place Hemingway in the former group as a popularizer of the reductive manner of Pound and Eliot's vision, for reasons I will subsequently outline. Suffice it to say, at this point, that the idea of the transcendent, transhistorical literary referent is difficult to locate as an explicit commentary on social life.[4]

By the time *The Birth of a Nation* premiered in 1915, the idea of creating a narrative by juxtaposing a sequence of related elements—recurring characters and themes within relatively autonomous parts—was a feature of the growing modernist movement. While Griffith's work was the first of its type, a work that created a truly complex narrative by using an editing strategy that radically subdivided the film's various scenes, Hemingway is a later figure in the generation of writers who created narrative wholes by relating various compositional fragments. In bridging the chronology between Griffith and Hemingway, we see that the philosophy of language that informs Hemingway's modernism does not necessarily result from his war experiences, which is the reigning explanation of what caused him to question abstractions.[5] Rather, his concrete prose builds upon the realist tradition in American letters, although it does not reproduce it with absolute fidelity. In his early works, Hemingway's prose seems designed to raise questions about the naive documentary impulse of Howellsian realism and conventional American naturalism; yet these questions do not fundamentally undermine the positivist basis of these other representational strategies. His prose, by means of a pseudo-concrete style, attempts to translate the relatively static observational apparatus of these methods into something more dynamic, more appropriately modern. In this vein, Hemingway's method and his place in literary history is quite like Griffith's in cinema history in that he comprehends the plasticity of his medium and shapes it to produce a higher affective reality for the technological age. In doing so, he relates to his predecessors much as Griffith does to earlier narrative film.

Though his fiction effaces its author in the extreme, Hemingway felt comfortable entering his "nonfiction" works and making his own personality their explicit focus.[6] This practice echoes the strategies of Edwin Porter for assuring that the realistic illusion of a given work would prevail. That is, like Porter, Hemingway felt comfortable breaking the conventions of realism in works that referred explicitly to a world beyond the text, while in writing labeled as fiction he generally maintained his fidelity to the objective ideal. In books he defines as journalism, such as *Death in the Afternoon* and *The Green Hills of Africa*, Hemingway's voice is rambling and self-referential, while in his fiction his method of composition excludes the author from the text and concentrates on the empirically verifiable "data" of the world.

In *Death in the Afternoon*, Hemingway explicitly places himself in this tradition by discussing his early difficulties as a novelist, as well as his intentions as a writer:

> I was trying to write then and I found the greatest difficulty . . . was to put down what really happened in action. . . . In writing for a news-

paper you told what happened and, with one trick and another, you communicated the emotion aided by the element of timeliness which gives a certain emotion to any account of something that has happened that day; but the real thing, the sequence of motion and fact which made the emotion and which would be as valid in a year or in ten years, or with luck and if you stated it purely enough, always, was beyond me and I was working very hard to try to get it. (2)

Throughout Hemingway's writings about his aesthetic, he elaborates on the components of this statement. He insists that a writer's success depends on his or her ability to capture the thing itself—which was the artists's transcendent truth and not the journalist's temporal fact—and that the result of perfect representation is a reader's specific emotional response. He wrote in *Men at War*, "A writer's job is to tell the truth. His standard of fidelity to the truth should be so high that his invention, out of his experience, should produce a truer account than anything factual can be" (xv). In *Green Hills of Africa* he similarly insisted on the timelessness of his aesthetically pure rendering of events, while in *A Moveable Feast* he wrote of how the act of writing truly was akin to living the experience itself, telling of how at the end of a day composing *In Our Time* "I did not want to leave the river" (76). When he detailed the impact of such fidelity to the essence of an experience on a given reader, he invariably reiterated that such writing produced a specific emotional response: "the good and bad, the ecstasy, the remorse and sorrow . . ." ("Old Newsman Writes" 26); or he devised what he called "the gooseflesh test" to make sure that a piece would have the desired visceral impact ("A Letter" 11).

It is significant at this point to note the conflation of the idea of transcendent truth and the temporal materiality of fact. I would say that Hemingway, in truly modern fashion, tries to invest his specific concrete details with the qualities of timelessness. That is, he inscribes a notion of the perpetual meaning and significance of a particular event as embedded in the reduced description of its material aspects. To produce this putative timelessness, he tends to remove references to time, sometimes to place, and generally to broader historical context. Thus, by making his specific compositional terms float in chronology and circumstance, Hemingway asserts transcendence.[7] While admitting a certain logic in this equation, it is important to consider the idea of historicity as Hemingway employs it in this theory. The assumption at work here is of a world where data pervade the atmosphere; where the preponderance of information makes history, defined as a totality of the past, either unknowable, due to its sheer bulk, or irrelevant, due to the deluge of information that appears anew each moment. If the world in modernity is truly too complex to fathom as a whole, then it is the province of the artist, as Eliot said, to make us feel more than we understand. In this model, then, the author appropriately selects data to produce certain visceral responses. Hemingway's prose style reveals an acceptance of these presumptions, creating the hybrid form—always linguistic, but aspiring to be the concrete object itself—Pound referred to as a "prose kinema." This notion of an author reproducing a reality already there affirms the worldview central to the form of realism. Hemingway seeks to record and represent a timeless and absolute reality by employing methods closely related to those William Dean Howells had so ardently argued for over four decades before the publication of *Death in the Afternoon* (1932). Just as Howells had placed the author in the role of observing the world objectively and carefully, so Hemingway believed that an author of fiction should not intrude on the text itself but should observe the elements of the world from a distanced position and then select the appropriate elements for their universality.

The theory of composition that Hemingway espouses effectively separates subject from object in the text. Oddly, (since its theoretical precepts result from a renunciation of historicity) this theory summons Griffith's (and Ranke's) practice for attaining historical fact. The common elements of these compositional structures coalesce around the idea that events exude specific meanings and that intrepetive structures should be effaced to the point of virtual nonexistence. Further, in this effacement, both methods assume that the act of interpretation ceases to exist and that the authorial imperative is simply to make available the essence of an event or object. Since there is generally no (explicit) author in this form, nor a dramatized narrator who interprets the actions that occur in his fiction, the reader is left with a mass of apparently objective details. There is no presence to take issue with, since the author is invisible within the text. This method, then, purports to record the world as it is and offers it as an immanent vision of the world-in-fact. The author who employs this method, because of its precepts of composition as well as its philosophy of the world, cannot problematize this vision; he simply presents it to the reader as the fact of the world as it is, was, and always will be, and as a politically potent plea for social continuity.

This is not to say that all reflexive forms are necessarily politically enabling. Indeed, depending on the terms of a specific compositional strategy, these general effects may occur in varying degrees. What I can say about Hemingway and Griffith is that both express well-inscribed cultural truths, wrapped in an immanent package; their works, if read *with* the general strategies suggested by the texts themselves, have the power to make us feel good by showing us that what we had uncritically assumed was in fact the correct way to view a body of circumstances, such as the relationship between men and women portrayed in Hemingway or that between whites and African Americans in Griffith. This is not to suggest that *In Our Time* devotes itself to gender relationships in the way that *The Birth of a Nation* concerns itself with race. While I have discussed Griffith's racial views at length, in *In Our Time,* it seems safe to say, women occur as an encumbrance and indeed a lesser class of humans in a world dominated by men and masculine values, even if this work does not focus polemically on the relationships between men and women. In stories such as "The Doctor and the Doctor's Wife," "The End of Something," and "Out of Season," women appear as explicit annoyances. They disrupt distinctly masculine activities, such as fighting and fishing. Other tales, such as "The Three-Day Blow," "The Battler," and "Cross-Country Snow," tell of males bonding, happy in their exclusive society and threatened by the women who are not there. Arguably, every story contains some sexist assertion. It seems vital, therefore, to consider these texts by Hemingway and Griffith in relation to the social strivings of the "New Woman" and the "New Negro" of the 1920s. In that light, *The Birth of a Nation* and *In Our Time* become forces for stasis, part of the persistence of inequalities based on truisms about innate character and abilities. At the date of *In Our Time*'s publication, William Chafe tells us, despite the publicly prominent image of the emancipated flapper, women's work opportunities had actually declined, as the number of women employed in the professions had shrunk significantly since the turn of the century, and would continue to wane for some fifty years (48–111).

If we consider Hemingway's modernism in relation to that of Pound and Eliot, we can see that the manner in which the distinctive, aesthetically radical methods of modernism may be adapted to the cause of political conservatism or outright reaction. By joining a reductive philosophy of language with the overriding strategy of narrative disjunction, modernist writers produce a world of circumscribed possibilities. That is, both Pound and Eliot use words to elevate their vision of the past as the hope of the future. This strategy echoes the realist concept of a world already made, but rather than hypostatize the present, Pound and Eliot, in ways like Griffith, define an ideal of the past as the condition to strive toward and ask readers to trust them as guides to the future of the aestheticized past. For Pound and Eliot, history is not simply a reified aspect of the past. It is also the imposition of their knowing leadership, which will result, in their millennial visions, in a transcendent and static moment. Thus, their audience must accept them as priests of high art and cultural regeneration.

Hemingway is far more worldly and less distinctly backward looking than his mentors, though perhaps equally authoritarian. He seeks not the ideal state of the past but the uncovering, by the writer, of the true laws of physical cause and emotional response. Hemingway's project is more modest than that of Pound and Eliot: he seeks only to limit definitions of being and to define certain specific behaviors—which he divorces from their social context—as correct. But in its relative modesty, Hemingway's worldview has greater power to influence a broad audience. Hemingway, then, popularized the modernist aesthetic by divorcing it from its more extreme expressions and intentions. Indeed, in the scale of things, his motivations appear as conservative and not reactionary. As a popularizer, he links his expression with a range of related contemporary cultural expressions, at the same time making his luminous public persona the emblem of his literary expression. The name Hemingway became a brand name that could be used to sell books and other goods, particularly objects that "meant" masculinity: beer, hunting and fishing equipment, exotic travel, and "men's" magazines (Raeburn 138). Indeed, in a fitting amalgam of his connection to all of these products, *Argosy* magazine referred to him as "the world's greatest writer and authority on hunting, fishing, drinking, and other manly occupations" (in Raeburn 152). This fame was both intentional and fortuitous. As John Raeburn explains, "His public reputation was created by a dynamic relationship between his advertisements of his personality and the mass media's exploitation of it" (10). But Hemingway's eminence as a figure of popular culture also stems from his aesthetic: the writer and the icon are one thing. The figure means what his heroes come to mean: the elevation of the reductive, the caricature of masculinity, and the power of the image above the abstraction of the word. It is a tribute to his aesthetic that far more people know what the image of Hemingway means than have ever read his books.[8]

The philosophy with which Hemingway organizes his fictional works reveals a belief in the notion that man is a machine who can be fully apprehended by his actions. If the essence of his fiction is to record "the sequence of motion and fact," then an observer is relatively uninterested in immobile objects or in those processes that are not readily observable by the eye. This perception of man places Hemingway's fiction within the canon of the behaviorist theory of composition that Howells had implied in his early discussions of the methods and goals of realism, as well as in the theoretical domain of the industrial scientific managers of his era. Howells never stated explicitly the manner in which these visually unavailable processes were to be transmitted, but suggested in his discussion that they would be produced and reproduced in reified form through the actions described in the text. Hemingway, however, explicitly defines his method of communicating these invisible processes. He defines the "real thing" as not merely "the sequence of motion and fact," but rather "the sequence of motion and fact which *made the emotion*." This statement confirms what Howells left implicit. Hemingway believed that an emotional response was not a subjective reaction to a specific event (an event being assimilated and acted upon by a subject). His theory claims that emotion lies not in the individual but in the event itself. It is as if every occurrence includes in its deep structure a template for the correct reaction to it, and the reader of this verbal representation of an event will apprehend this code and respond appropriately. Hence he assumes, in behaviorist fashion, that man is governed by rigid laws of stimulus and response and never intelligently analyzes experience, but merely receives its impulses passively and responds as he must.

This notion of the predictability and inevitability of human behavior places Hemingway in the philosophical company of the pioneer of behaviorist psychology, John B. Watson—as well as of Griffith.[9] Hemingway's mechanistic definition of humans recalls Watson's reductive claim in his preface to his work of 1919, *Psychology from the Standpoint of a Behaviorist:* "the reader will find no discussion of consciousness, and no reference to such terms as sensation, attention, will, image and the like" (xii). In Hemingway's early works these terms are largely unrepresented. Rather, Hemingway, like Watson, asserts that a particular set of stimuli produces a specific behavioral response. Within the logic of his composition, Hemingway also argues that these actions result in a similarly inevitable emotional reaction. Watson's definition of emotion well fits Hemingway's conception: "a hereditary "pattern reaction" involving profound changes of the bodily mechanism as a whole, but particularly of the visceral and glandular systems. By pattern reaction we mean that the separate details of response appear with some constancy, with some regularity and in approximately the same sequential order each time the exciting stimulus is presented" (225).

By locating a homology between this most visible and respected literary figure and a pioneer in the shaping of modern psychology, it is possible to see the pervasiveness of certain assumptions regarding the nature of being. In the previous chapter, I elaborated the historical occurrence by which the concept of history as a narrative that plots change was preempted by the idea of history as that which tells us why certain repressive practices are scientifically correct. Similarly, in this chapter we see a related "scientific" ideal at work. Hemingway inscribes individuals in a universe where a science of cause and effect regulates their actions. Included in this equation are his readers, whose specific buttons he attempts to push for a particular emotional response. In this model, then, psychology as the exploration of the multiple mysteries of the human mind becomes subsumed by the idea of the psyche as a dynamo that produces behavior. Further, in this mechanistic model, behavior becomes not simply something that can be reductively comprehended, but also something that may be controlled.

Hemingway's and Watson's idea of psychology refers back to the late nineteenth-century definition of that discipline as it developed its intellectual boundaries and its status as a distinct field of study. In the American academy as it existed after 1875, the relatively new field of psychology was increasingly at odds with its institutional companion, moral philosophy. The basis of this disjunction was the rising tendency of psychologists to claim the status of scientists, or at least the potential to become scientists. Indeed, within this claim and in the other means by which psychology differentiated itself from the abstractions of moral philosophy, it is possible to view the emergence of this discipline as resulting from, and promulgating, some of the dominant ideological assumptions of twentieth-century American life. In 1883, the first American laboratory for experimental research in psychology was established by Granville Stanley Hall at Johns Hopkins University. In 1890 we find even William James, whose writings evocatively index the connection between philosophy and psychology, offering analysis that anticipates behaviorism. In his two-volume *Principles of Psychology,* James describes emotions, although not without some self-criticism and reservation, as "the resultant of a sum of elements." James refines his notion of the material basis of specific psychological response: "Each element is caused by a physiological process of a sort already well known. The elements are all organic changes, and each of them is the reflex effect of the exciting object" (453).[10] In 1892, Hall founded the American Psychological Association to further "the advancement of psychology as a science" (in O'Donnell 3). Still, despite Hall's efforts, the discipline retained its ties to philosophy. Thus, a disciplinary imperative to cut those ties and make psychology distinct and scientific remained during the first decade of the twentieth century. The effort proceeded by gradually making the study of the mind the study of observable actions. The culmination of this effort was the emergence of Watson's behaviorism in 1913. On the way to Watson, however, we also find psychology lending its science to the problem of managing the industrial workplace, through the establishment of industrial psychology.[11]

Clearly Hemingway's theory of response was well supported by the young social science of psychology, a discipline that was also based on the positivists' conception of the real and that based its method on the same type of careful observation as grounded realist literature and "scientific" history. But behaviorism is, at least initially, more of an effect than a cause. Behaviorism burgeoned both in the discipline of psychology and in American culture at large in the twenties. Hemingway popularized and was popularized by its credo. But the power of this reductive definition of humanity stems from the ideology and implementation in the industrial workplace of "scientific" management, eventually codified as "Taylorization," which grew in the last years of the nineteenth century and the first decade of the twentieth. Indeed, scientific management presaged many elements of the modernist aesthetic with its method of radically subdividing the production process into the smallest rational parts, its mechanistic perception of human capabilities, its rigid belief in the precepts of science, and its ability to reproduce those tenets.[12]

Hemingway's politically quieting intellectual frame refers not only to Watson and Frederick Taylor, but to figures such as Walter Dill Scott and Hugo Munsterberg who, in devising the subfield of industrial psychology, studied workers specifically to modify them psychologically, to make them both more productive and more docile. Indeed, at the intersection of Taylor and Watson stands the emerging discipline of industrial psychology. In 1901, as part of the general movement of psychologists to assert their discipline's concrete status as an applied field, Walter Dill Scott, a professor at Northwestern, addressed a group from the advertising industry to inform them of the uses of psychology. Scott's work culminated in two volumes on this topic, in 1903 and 1908, and in broader treatises on managing the psychology of the market and workplace, after 1911. In addition to Scott's writings, the other major force in the establishment of this area of study and application was Hugo Munsterberg, a colleague of James at Harvard, whose *Psychology and Industrial Efficiency* appeared in 1913. Wrote Munsterberg advocating the use of his skills in the factory, "The millowner must learn to use the mental energies of his laborers in the same way that the farmer knows how to use the properties of his soil" (in Mankin 11). Like Progressivism in general, industrial psychology also resorted to the rhetoric of a greater good and the efficiency wrought by its science, but its primary goals were to ensconce its own managers as experts and to use its influence to further minimize the power of workers. Indeed, Watson's formulations broaden many of the Progressive precepts of management, as behaviorism replaces the ideal of industrial management with that of social control.[13]

In its defining of humans by their behavior and in its methodologies that attempt to inscribe certain repeated actions, the goal of Watson's method is to produce a docile social entity that can be managed through the reductions of behaviorism. Hemingway's modernism complements these other cultural movements in employing the same reductions and vision of authority. He also provides this ideological formation with the affective power of art. If one considers the limited range of his language and the circumscribed reactions of his characters to extreme situations, the idea of managed responses comes readily to mind. For example, in the story "The Battler," ex-boxer Ad Francis's disturbed mental state is described repeatedly with the singular term "crazy." Further, the explanation for his craziness is that his ex-wife "just went off and never come back" (61). The treatment for his threatening behavior is a tap on the skull. Nick's response to all of this is to remain impassive. This story fails to divulge much about Ad, his friend Bugs, or Nick. What we do get is a reduced description of a complex condition and the absence of any character sufficiently curious to elicit a more satisfying explanation. Also missing, of course—and this cuts to the heart of the Hemingway aesthetic—is any narration to tell us more about the event recounted. Readers of such a tale, and *In Our Time* is composed of similarly minimalist tales, may feel some visceral response to the description of a tap on the skull or the menacing behavior of Ad, but given the form of the story, this may be all that is immediately forthcoming. If one wonders what it means in somewhat more considered terms, but still accepts its basic assertions of form and content, then the truisms of mass culture regarding the simplicity of the human machine may come to mind.

Hemingway's determinism also places him in the philosophical realm of Dreiser. Dreiser's *Sister Carrie* reveals a world of human objects and personified things that make moot the distinction between the animate and the inanimate. In this realm, Carrie's life experiences are commodified in a manner that makes their meaning a product of the experience and not a result of her human response to these events. In this novel's view, an individual's actions merely refer to those of other humans, and cease to have any uniqueness or to express a specific idea of self. As a result, one responds to the occurrences of the world as those occurrences dictate. Individuals are not responsible for making the events of their lives meaningful; rather, they simply respond to various stimuli as they must.

Dreiser persistently argues for the correctness of this worldview through an interposed narrator who intrudes on the novel's narrative. Hemingway, on the other hand, radically reduces the narrator's explicit function. While there is clearly an intelligence that determines the shape of the stories, Hemingway collapses form into content and creates works that explain the narrative they present by the simple revelation of plot events. Hemingway presents these activities as if they were universally meaningful and resonant. This method is perhaps the purest enactment, to this time, of Howells's theory of the novel. The events are "little acted upon, and the characters speak for themselves" (as Howells wrote in praise of another novel). While Howells, in his fiction, tentatively experimented with this form of exposition, which offers the reader the appearance of unmediated action, Hemingway virtually creates such an illusion. The result of such an emphasis is the fulfillment of the authoritarian implications of the Howellsian vision. Hemingway becomes the author as social expert, who relies so fully on the precepts of positivist science that he may cease to appear at all. His works take on the appearance of the concrete representation of a world already made.

In Our Time illustrates Hemingway's philosophy in the relationship it presents between the parts of the work and its coherence as a whole, as well as in the formal structure of its individual components. This work is not a traditional novel. As it was published in 1925, it is as a sequence of sixteen short vignettes, referred to as chapters in the text and numbered from 1 to 15 with the closing sketch unnumbered and titled "L'Envoi." Between every two vignettes there is a short story; fifteen appear in all.[14]

Though *In Our Time* is not a conventional novel, it was arranged carefully by its author to appear as a unified mass and not merely a collection of various writings. Hemingway documents this intention in a letter to Edmund Wilson in early 1925:

I've finished the book of 14 stories with a chapter of *in our time* between each story [sic]—that is the way they were meant to go—to give a picture of the whole between examining it in detail. Like looking with your eyes at something, say a passing coastline, and the looking at it with 15x binoculars. Or rather, maybe looking at it, then going and living in it—and then coming out and looking at it again. . . . I think that you would like it, it has a pretty good unity. (*Selected Letters* 128)

The unity Hemingway claimed exists on a variety of levels. The style of these stories is remarkably consistent. All but two ("The Revolutionist" and "My Old Man") are narrated from a third-person point of view that relates their actions with a sparseness of language. The two that employ the first person reveal a similar relation to the actions they detail. There is also a character who, though not ever-present, recurs in seven of the fifteen stories, as well as in one chapter. Further, the chapters focus on war scenes seven times (five refer to World War I and two to the Greco-Turkish War) and bullfighting six, while two relate tales of criminals in the United States. As noted, these vignettes recur at regular intervals between each short story and its successor and never exceed a page.

The obvious way to read this work for unity is to assume that Nick Adams is its main character in the sense of the traditional fictional protagonist and start from there. He is indeed the work's central character, but the task of defining his place is not so simple. His role is no more that of the "protagonist" than this is a typical novel bound by the conventions that define that form.

Nick Adams appears in the first five short stories of the book, and then appears for the sixth time in the next chapter, chapter 6. This is the only time in the work that the action of the stories and that of the chapters converges in any obvious manner. He then recedes for the next six chapters and six stories to return in "Cross Country Snow." He is removed again in the next story, "My Old Man," and then reappears in the two "Big Two-Hearted River" segments. In all he appears in seven of the work's fifteen stories, giving him a rate of appearance of slightly less than 50 percent. He also appears in chapter 6, which asserts his presence, however ephemeral, in this phase of the book.

Nick's centrality is further posited by the placement of the stories in which he figures. One of the unsettling aspects of *In Our Time* is the disruption of one's expectations of the text. When approaching the work, the first character named, in "Indian Camp," is Nick, and he dominates the first five stories of this work. One begins to expect a novel or a more unified collection on the order of *Winesburg, Ohio*.[15] The means by which Hemingway continues to create these expectations of the work as a whole are scattered throughout its beginning section.

As the reader begins the 1925 version of this sequence of stories, chapter 1 describes a scene that is ostensibly from World War I, as it names the region of Champagne. The setting is established by noting the presence of the lieutenant and by having the narrator end the vignette with the statement, "That was when I was a kitchen corporal" (13). While establishing a sense of place, the sketch names no characters. "I" is never identified, nor is the lieutenant given a description other than his rank. The reference to "that was" also places the narrator subsequent to the event described. The effect of this lack of identification and this reference to a time passed is perhaps to leave readers groping for the meaning of the text as they begin the initial short story of the sequence.

The character Nick is named in the second paragraph of "Indian Camp," the collection's second short story, and the other figures given specific references are characterized by their relationship to Nick: "[Nick's] father" and "Uncle George." ("The Indians" remain the plural noun throughout the initial paragraphs, and are then identified only in the most indistinct manner as "an Indian lady," or "the young Indian," or the "young Indian woman.") In the third paragraph the narrator further creates the impression of Nick's centrality by briefly breaking his objective plane of observation and noting that "Nick heard the oarlocks of the other boat" (15). In the story's central event, the doctor's delivering a baby, the narrator notes, "Nick watched his father's hands," "he was looking away," and "Nick did not watch" (17).

With these textual assertions, readers may, if they have a fixed idea of what constitutes a novel, go on to chapter 2 to test the theory that this is indeed a book about Nick Adams and that these vignettes are simply another perspective on his experience. This sketch again describes a scene from a war, but this time it is of the Greco-Turkish War, and again it names no characters. The scene recounted is told from a strictly observational perspective and describes a mass procession of Greeks driven from their homes by battle.

There is nothing in this vignette to disprove the reader's notion that the unity of *In Our Time* centers on the character Nick Adams's role as protagonist. Though he has not been identified in these italicized portions of the text, neither has any other character. If we approach this work as possessing a specific unity, then to this point Nick seems to endow it with coherence.

"The Doctor and the Doctor's Wife" presents a point of view similar to that of "Indian Camp." (That is, Nick's importance as the center of meaning reveals itself through various textual assertions.) Although the events of this story—the disagreement of the doctor and Dick Boulton and the doctor's wife's reaction to that disagreement—have ended by the time it introduces Nick, his appearance asserts that he is a vital character in the text and that it is only the effect these events will have on Nick that makes them important.

Again no proper names are stated in chapter 3, as another war scene is described, this time of Mons, Belgium. In the next story, "The End of Something," Nick is again the first character named. This story tells of Nick and his girlfriend Marjorie fishing for trout; they argue and seem to end their relationship. At the end of the story another character, Bill, is introduced. Once again Nick is the center of this narrative, as he is the only character who appears in its entire scheme of events, and again the narrator breaks his plane of observation to note that, "[Nick] felt Bill coming up to the fire" (35).

Chapter 4 again names none of its characters, and describes a scene of waiting for battle, possibly in the same locale as chapter 3, in a highly exaggerated tone.[16] The scene is consistent with those of the prior chapters, yet this chapter is distinct from the other writing in the book in its stilted use of modifiers, as it uses the words "absolutely" and "frightfully" twice in its single paragraph. This change of tone is so radical and absurd, as it occurs in a work that has been previously defined by its terseness, that the effect is to assert not that another voice is reporting the scene, but rather that the same voice that has dominated the text to this point is adopting a tone of parody.

The effect of such a tale may be to highlight that which is distinctive in the voice predominant in the other stories. Through the garrulousness of the narrator of chapter 4, the controlled voice in the Nick stories appears in clear contrast. The association between that measured voice and Nick is so strong that some critics have defined Nick as the virtual narrator of the stories in which he appears.[17] Of course, associating Nick with the narration of these stories is technically incorrect: his stories occur in the third person; but in this conflation critics are able to make sense out of these most elliptical pieces in a critically fashionable way: through biographical analysis. Thus, Nick become a virtual Hemingway and Hemingway becomes a virtual Nick. Through this equation we see the identification of the particular terms of Hemingway's celebrity fusing with the terms of the tale itself, creating a mythos of the writing and a popular legend of the writer.

Yet this most publicity-conscious writer deplored biographies of living writers and resisted the entreaties of potential biographers, often stymieing them with threats that he would refuse permission to quote from his published materials. Though in the cases of Philip Young and Charles Fenton he "challenged, and responding to financial pleas, relented and allowed Fenton, as well as Young to quote from his work" (Mellow 575), his mission seems to have been to make their work as difficult as possible. This ambivalence is difficult to swallow considering his enormous public performance but comprehensible in relation to his aesthetic of strength through silence. It is far easier to understand this reluctance as a desire to continue to manage the specific terms of his display. Indeed, in this paradox of spartan texts and personal prolixity emerges a metaphor of exchange appropriate to the twenties, where consumer goods, rather than capital production, became the focal point of the U.S. economy. In such a situation, the necessity of creating greater demand for products is paramount. When the product is literary, biography is particualarly important because the popular image of the commodity (the author as public persona) has the power to alter the way in which consumers (reader/buyers of Hemingway's fiction) conceive of and use the thing itself. Such promotional activity is necessary in an era of burgeoning production and limited buying power. Indeed, this economic condition well describes the twenties: while real wages grew by around 30 percent, industrial production rose by two-thirds. The culmination of this disparity was the the depression of the 1930s (Shannon 95–102). Hemingway wished to avoid a comparable deflation of his capital and attempted to maintain his image (value) by managing it carefully.[18]

In the next stories, the narration returns to the voice that is most characteristically Hemingwayesque. Further, the work apparently becomes chronologically coherent: "The Three-Day Blow" seems to take place immediately after "The End of Something," as the characters who act in it are Bill and Nick, and they refer to Nick's termination of his relationship with Marjorie. Again Nick is central to this narrative, as it is his past life that causes these characters to ruminate and his is the recurring character. In addition, here the narrator breaks his "objective" plane in the most radical manner yet, as he notes that "All [Nick] *knew* was that he had once had Marjorie and that he had lost her" (47). This statement of Nick's knowledge is the most baldly interpretive assertion yet to appear in the work. While the narrator has rarely broken the plane of observation in this work, when he has, he has noted some sensory activity, Nick feeling or hearing. In this case he affirms the content of Nick's mind.

Chapter 5 and "The Battler" continue in this vein. This chapter describes a war scene in a way similar to that of the other chapters and, though it mentions no place, is set in Athens in 1922.[19] It names no participants in the actions it describes. "The Battler" again places Nick at the center of its story and again reveals its narrative by addressing the question of what happened, while leaving the question of why it happened unasked.

In chapter 6, for the first time, the vignette names a character, stating in its first sentence, "Nick sat against the wall of the church where they had dragged him to be clear of machine-gun fire in the street" (63). It also mentions Rinaldi and is set in Italy during World War I. With our "evidence" to this point, the correct way to read this novel seems to be as a story of Nick Adams's maturation. In each story he seems to grow somewhat older, though the chronology of the stories is irregular. The chapters have named no characters prior to this point, but upon reading chapter 6 it seems reasonable to assume that the unnamed figure who generates these vignettes is Nick, and the reason that he writes these chapters in the first person and the stories in the third is to indicate his estrangement from these events, which occurred prior to his military career. This explanation also accounts for the occasional liberties the narrator takes in asserting Nick's subjective responses.

The only problematic element of this interpretive strategy is that while the stories could be construed as moving chronologically forward, to assume this of the chapters requires that one not notice that they are of two different wars and shift back and forth between them. Chapters 1, 3, 4, and 6 are of World War I, while 2 and 5 take place in Turkey and Greece. The events in the former take place in 1918, those in the latter in 1922. Knowing this, one cannot unify the first part of the book by assuming a progressive chronology. But these distinctions are suppressed by Hemingway as a specific strategy of composition. There are no dates in these sections and often no place-names. Indeed, this repression of context seems to work, as almost all of those who reviewed this volume in 1925 paid little attention to this disruption of chronology and, in general, did not note the references to different wars. For example, Paul Rosenfeld in the *New Republic* commented that these vignettes "bring dangerously close instantaneous pictures of the War . . . the naked, the mean, the comic brute in the human frame" (in Stephens 9–10). The reviewer in the New York *Sun* called these sketches "youth's defense against rawness" (in Reynolds 15).

By ignoring the context to which these scenes refer, these reviewers show how well Hemingway's strategies make the case for the transcendence of his vision. In moving from journalism to fiction, Hemingway sought to alter his role from that of a recorder of the temporally significant to that of a medium for timeless truth. In removing virtually all reference to context in these chapters, we see the author's strategy to essentialize the concept of war. That is, Hemingway inserts one war or another as the remote arena for his sketches because his aesthetic vision relies on the absence of difference. Apparently, this also holds true for reviewers smitten with the art of this book, who also assert that a war is a war is a war. If one does not notice this disruption of chronology, a placing of Nick as the work's protagonist is relatively easy. But if one does notice it, our sequential reading strategy is disrupted, and we must begin to theorize another.

The idea of timelessness at work here suggests a notion of cause and effect derived from a distinct idea of science. That is, phenomena (such as war) are isolated in order to see their essential properties and their observable and ultimately predictable relationships to other phenomena. War is that which disrupts human life but is finally that which separates ordinary people from the extraordinary. It is the condition that reveals Nick's courage, his emotional control. Indeed, in the celebration of restraint that marks this book, a reader's means of identifying with its protagonist might be to affect his attitudes. Thus, war produces an appropriate emotional distancing. In chapter 6 Nick is shot in the spine, but at the end of the vignette we find him "smiling sweetly" (63).

Once again we see the fusion of form and content in the interest of a vision of appropriate behavior. This behavior is not the response to danger that one would assume comes readily and usually, that is, extreme fear and the tendency to seek safety. In *In Our Time* the expressed response to compromising situations is the famous Hemingway cliché of "grace under pressure." By asserting the nobility of such an attitude, the work defines the goal of Nick—and all who would be Nick—as mastery over one's natural inclinations. While I am generally loathe to use the term "human nature" for its essentializing qualities, I think it is safe to say that it takes a great deal of control over one's raw impulses not to run from a stampeding bull (chapter 12) and not to express revulsion at the sight of a mass execution (chapter 5). This predominant attitude emanates both from the stories themselves and from the manner in which they are told: spare, concrete, unemotional. In both these textual elements we see related hegemonic assertions. On one hand, Hemingway asserts the efficacy of the masculine, in its denial of emotions and its emphasis on action; on the other, he shows us the desirability or inevitability of humans dominating nature.

To comprehend the particular modernity of this text, we need only consider how easily these two impulses synthesize into one in the creation of the modern industrial economy, where means-end logic pervades all aspects of production, from the particular direction of research and development to the organization of the workplace. Indeed, the logic at work here defines a technology of response based on a reductive model of scientific process, or a technology of affect. Hemingway seems to reproduce textually focal ideological assumptions of the period around the turn of the century. As Stanley Aronowitz explains of maturing capitalist economies,

> By the late nineteenth century, industrial production depended on scientifically based technologies; the craft traditions, of which early manufacturing was merely a form of rationalization, were themselves subordinated to the new technology; the motive force of production, energy, was no longer mechanical . . . but became electrical, the principle of which derived from "pure research"; engineering replaced artisanal knowledge in designing the mode of transformation of raw materials into end products; in turn, the intellectual foundation of engineering became physics and chemistry, which themselves were institutionalized into large laboratories sponsored by and controlled by the state and large corporations. Thus, science itself no longer is only a hegemonic ideology of the new social order and its industrial age, but becomes integrated into the practices and discourses of production. The interchangability of science and technology is, of course, either denied or ignored by most philosophers and scientists, but their growing convergence extends beyond the workplace. As scientific discourse permeates state and civil society, scientific culture spills over beyond the laboratory. (9)

I would argue that one of the places into which it spills is literary and cinematic production. In *In Our Time* the stripped-down aesthetic seems specifically designed to view the actions narrated in relation to the question, "What does an individual action produce?".

After chapter 6, the reader turns the page expecting that the form of the work has become apparent, and that the successive stories will reveal a new dimension of Nick Adams. This next story, "A Very Short Story," suggests the error of this interpretation of the work's structure and the possible failure of this method of reading it. In this tale no male character is named, and a story of a figure referred to as "he" and his wartime lover, Luz, emerges. Since we do not know that this figure is not Nick ("he" has no name to prove this) and the setting seems to refer to chapter 6, this interpretation of the novel's structure is possibly correct, but it is somewhat puzzling as to why this is the first story in the book that fails to name Nick.

Chapter 7 again tells of a war scene and, like 1 through 5, names no characters. In the next story, "Soldier's Home," the puzzlement of the previous narrative becomes outright confusion, as a new protagonist is introduced. This figure, Harold Krebs, has just come home from the war and is experiencing the trauma of readjusting to life in a small western community. Though the content seems appropriate for Nick and the form of the story is consistent with those that have preceded it, its presentation of a new main character is problematic.

In the ensuing four stories, Nick remains absent from the text: he also fails to appear in any of its chapters. Further, the content of these chapters shifts from war scenes to bullfighting, with two scenes of American violence thrown in. The chronology continues to be erratic; they range from 1917 in chapter 7 to 1924 in chapter 14 to 1918 in chapter 15.

At this point, it is necessary to reconsider the meaning of Hemingway's claim of unity and find an explanation for the persistent impression that these various components somehow function as an ensemble to create a coherent impression of the work. To do this we must go back to the author's philosophy of composition. Hemingway believed that an author should record the factual events of the world by dehumanizing his perspective, becoming an objective viewing apparatus. He would then select from among these events to reproduce these true and empirically verifiable facts in textual form, by putting them into a language that did not create its own reality but reflected the realities of the world. Hence, in this model neither language nor author transmutes these facts, both simply express it objectively.

Hemingway's philosophy of composition is very similar to Griffith's in that the novelist also considers himself a neutral recording device whose goal is to capture the fact of the world. As Griffith believed that the "facts" of history exist suspended in time as absolutes that require no analytical intelligence to recover or to interpret them selectively, so Hemingway has a similar perception of the "facts" of the world. He also denies his human role in shaping these units of hard truth and declares himself, in the manner of the ideal cinematic apparatus, simply a recording device. Hemingway concerns himself with occurrences that he asserts maintain a timeless emotional truth and thus transcend human intervention and chronological frame. While Griffith offers us his objectivist's "history,"

Hemingway speaks to the growing cultural definition of psychology—that is, behaviorism.

Hemingway's method of composition and theory of language place him squarely in the positivist tradition, which abstracts the observer from the observed, the event from its process of being assimilated, and ultimately subject from object. Since the experience is a fact and its representation the goal, the assumption of this theory is that an event is inherently meaningful, even without a human intelligence acting upon it. Indeed, this philosophy is the ultimate conservative approach to the world, since it does not hold any individual responsible for determining the meaning of a specific event but leaves that meaning implied and subject to the reader's own unproblematized cultural assumptions.[20] It is quite possible that the meaning that is plugged in is the widely accepted one (if any meaning is inserted at all). This may leave readers in the position of either accepting the meaninglessness of the sequence of activities portrayed or inserting their own meanings into the narrative. The problem with this formula is that it may not lead readers toward their own conclusions but only give the appearance of doing so. Once again we see the realist form creating the illusion of subjective choice, while it powerfully inscribes its narrow cultural definitions of being and the world. Hemingway takes images and settings out of the popular American culture, such as formulaic love stories or tales of adolescent angst, and represents them in his stripped-down linguistic manner that concentrates primarily on the actions of the narrative. He relies on the resonance of these actions because, in a culture that commodifies language and images through various forms of mass media (the movies, popular magazines and fiction), the meaning of these narratives is so conventionalized it is not worth restating. He at least seems to assume that it is not necessary to make explicit the meaning of his writings.[21]

Hemingway's assumption that these narratives of "motion and fact" will produce the real thing that made *the* emotion comes through in his form. There seems little other means of arriving at the end he claims to desire if one does not rely on culturally received images. His use of the article "the" to describe the desired affective response implies that he is not interested in producing just any emotion, but a specific one. This worldview that places emotion in an event, and not in its assimilation by a human observer, also makes rigid the available categories of emotional response. Indeed, this formula recalls John B. Watson's idea of the relationship between a given stimulus and a patterned response: "The movements which result from a tap on the patellar tendon, or from stroking the feet are simple responses which are studied both in physiology and medicine. In psychology our study, too, is sometimes concerned with simple responses of these types, but more often with several complex responses taking place simultaneously" (11). Hemingway inscribes language as having a power akin to Watson's tap on the knee. The word is indistinguishable from the materiality it represents. Further, in his formula, language is cut adrift from culture and becomes not simply the thing it represents, but a thing with a meaning that transcends time and place. Thus, his disruption of chronology in the chapters reveals only that, as Henry Ford once said, "history is bunk," as actions always produce the same emotional fact of response. Hemingway collapses matter, action, and time into his concept of "the right word": one feels the word, which *is* the timeless reality. This reduction also informs the aesthetic of his fellow modernists Pound and Eliot, in the former's Imagism and the latter's objective correlative.

Hemingway explained the means by which a reader may comprehend the correct emotional response to a narrative by stating, it "may be racial experience. I think that is quite possible" ("Monologue" 15). This confusion of the terms *race* and *culture* occurred frequently during the late nineteenth and early twentieth centuries (as seen in my discussion of Griffith and the racist precepts of "scientific" history). Indeed, the conflation of race and culture provided a foundation for the racist theories that marked the early scholarship in the emerging fields of sociology and anthropology.[22] Drawing on the positivist conception of the real, these disciplines sought to explain the cultural fact of a particular moment by using the observational technique of the sciences. Then, in keeping with their scientific method, scholars often concocted theories as to why the fact that they had observed was immutable. In searching for an encompassing explanation, they often looked to the natural sciences, particularly genetics. Hence, to them these facts were not simply the observations of a particular point in time, subject to the biases of the observer and his method, but absolute realities. John Watson was among those who confused these terms, stating that emotional reactions "are inherited modes of action" (255). Hemingway apparently agreed with Watson.

By "racial experience" one guesses that Hemingway means an amalgam of understanding based on the innate comprehension of all experience that is somehow passed down genetically. It seems doubtful that any author writing in a cultural/linguistic context can reasonably make such a claim, since it denies the historical nature of his writing and the historically and culturally produced responses it both sought and received. A more probable, though certainly less sweeping, explanation is that the experience he refers to is cultural, and indeed cultural in a very narrow historical and chronological sense.

Keeping in mind Hemingway's philosophy of composition, it is important to remember that his faith in his science of representation makes the event the fact, and estranges subject from object. In this perception, experience is generally treated as a noun. Individuals do not experience events. Rather, experiences are a fact of the past: hardened entities that are not subject to an individual's interpretation or modification. Hemingway is not writing the story of Nick Adams experiencing the world as he matures. Rather, he is telling us about the *experiences that happened* to Nick Adams.

Because experiences of various forms are the "main characters" of this work, who they happen to has less importance than their occurrence. Nick can be written out of the novel and replaced by Harold Krebs because the important thing is what happened. Indeed, when we meet Harold Krebs in "Soldier's Home," having already been baffled by the disappearance of the character who seemed to be at the center of the work, we are further confused by the fact that the story told is one that could easily have placed Nick at its center. Since at this point in the sequence we are virtually convinced that this is the story of Nick's process of maturation, and in chapter 6 this character has been placed in the war in Europe, his homecoming in the work's seventh story seems logically to follow. However, when we do read a story of a soldier's return, it is of a soldier other than Nick.

This philosophy commodifies experience into a thing, rather than defining it as an aspect of an individual's life that is uniquely felt and experienced by that person. These hardened units of fact do not belong in any specific context and therefore allow for a fragmenting of worldview. Their meaning has nothing to do with context, since each action theoretically contains in its structure its own template for meaning. These units of experience are simply means of producing specific effects and therefore have no integrity or specific place in the life or memory of a particular character. These stories might have occurred on subsequent days, weeks, or years; the context provides few distinct clues.

This disjunction in chronology, which marks this work throughout, is symptomatic of the work's reading of modernity. Neil Larsen's *Modernism and Hegemony* defines the modernist epoch in terms that illuminate Hemingway's particular historical mediation: modernism is "the inversion . . . of a historically objective crisis in representation affecting the construction of what are initially social and political identities." As modernist texts potentially pose questions of *their own* connection to the things and events they reproduce, they do so in a manner that situates such interrogation in the apparently apolitical real of aesthetics. Thus, they have the potential to displace the historical referent of such texts into the discourse of art, or art criticism. Larsen sees this crisis as stemming from "the tendency of capital in its real abstraction to break free from certain political— and in this sense representational—relations," becoming a "superordinate social agency with no fixed political or cultural subjectivity." Indeed, in a mature capitalist society, as capital becomes an increasingly abstract concept, the terms by which one is economically subjugated become increasingly difficult to articulate. In this formulation, a human awareness, however explicit or implicit, of an extraordinary power beyond the subjective with the power to shape events by its own logic creates not only a "crisis in representation" but also "a crisis in agency" (xxiv).

As the modernist text retreats from its own representational crisis to re-emerge as the aesthetic object, it takes explicit historical occurrences and, by removing them from the various contexts that provide them with meaning, commodifies them as "information" and/or aestheticizes them as "art." This analysis evokes a major area of contention in Marxist interpretation of the modernist text. For Theodor Adorno, this retreat held the promise of autonomous art capable, through its retreat, of retaining a residual idealist utopianism that could not be found in the materiality of the twentieth century. For Georg Lukács, this retreat was the decadence of modernism and its inability to either represent the complexity of social relations or to influence its readers in a significant concrete way. My tendency, in the case of Hemingway, is to see how one might read against the text to produce Adorno's perception, but as a reader interested in the historicity of Hemingway's formulation, I see this aestheticization of the historical referent as reproducing the very effective cultural formula for social ennui found in a range of social productions. Indeed, in the reception of Hemingway (and this includes the range of responses over the last seventy or so years) there seems a remarkable tendency to accept his very obvious method of unmooring the signifier from the historically signified. Thus, his aestheticizing strategy seems generally to accomplish its goal.[23]

This irregular chronological sequence suggests that, when viewed with the intention of extricating this work from its historical camouflage, the unity that Hemingway spoke of is, in fact, disunity. This fragmentation of time and character is allowed, even required, by his behaviorist philosophy, which dictates that the world can be understood by perceiving its events and that every event is its own explanation. This theory of humans makes them captives of stimuli which produce predictable responses and allows Hemingway to focus on the fact of the event itself. Hence, the book fractures even more markedly after the disappearance of Nick.

This removal appears a willed gesture to impose an alternative, but thoroughly modern, rationality on this work. The question of how to represent a complex character slides from focus and reemerges as a question of how to reify response into a thing itself. By focusing on the plasticity of the objects represented, Hemingway is able to reduce the idea of humanity in a manner that reproduces that codified and publicized by Frederick Taylor in his reorganization of the industrial workplace. Hemingway's Nick, like Taylor's assembly-line operatives, is assumed as a depthless projection of specific functions that are vital to the job at hand. Taylor also assumes the plasticity of his represented objects, workers, and inscribes them, like Hemingway's characters, in a system of production that divorces their activities from any knowledge of the world that falls beyond his system. This system presupposes, as Martha Banta notes, "that the best workers for the industrial shop are strong of body and like patient animals" (7).

Taylor's methods of industrial organization were implemented at the Midvale Steel Company in Pennsylvania, where he worked as a manager, as early as 1883 when he was promoted to chief engineer. By the first years of the twentieth century Taylor was associated with the imperatives of the Progressive movement. His theory for reorganizing the industrial workplace reproduced the broader ideological formations of the Progressive social managers. Explains Daniel Nelson,

> He attempted to strengthen the position of the traditional firm by substituting scientific management for the seeming disorder and unrest associated with the first factory system.
>
> Taylor's mechanism for achieving this end inadvertently provided his most important link with the progressives. After 1901 [the year Theodore Roosevelt became president] the essential figure in the implementation of scientific management was the "expert," the skilled independent systematizer. . . . Until at least 1907, however, Taylor was oblivious to the similarities between his approach to factory reform and the ideas of the businessmen, scientists, engineers, lawyers, and journalists who agonized over the "distended" character of American society. Their answer to the disorganization and inefficiency so apparent in labor-management conflict, big business chicanery, and

machine politics, like Taylor's answer to the defects of the factory system, was to elevate a cadre of technicians to positions of power. . . .
Appropriately, it was progressives of this type who recognized the
reform implications of Taylor's message and projected him into the
public spotlight. (169)

In 1910, lawyer and later Supreme Court Justice Louis Brandeis invoked
Taylor's name and method at an Interstate Commerce Committee rate
hearing. Brandeis, representing a trade association of eastern railroad ship-
pers, attempted to rebut the railroad's request for a rate increase by arguing
that implementing Taylor's methods would increase efficiency and negate
the need for such an increase. Brandeis's arguments paved the way for Taylor's broad celebrity. But it was in the years after 1911, when an abridged
version of his theories, *The Principles of Scientific Management*, appeared
in serial form in the popular Progressive journal, *The American Magazine*,
that the rationalization of the production process in Taylor's general terms
became a broad managerial imperative. Indeed, some have argued that this
method dominated American industry through the 1970s.[24] Perhaps even
more significant is the way Taylorism captured the popular imagination in
the years immediately following the publication of this series, as Taylor and
his theories became widely cited and celebrated.

The system of industrial management widely known as Taylorization
was designed to reduce factory work to a sequence of simple tasks done
by workers whose movements were dictated by a manager. This manager
employed time-motion studies to define the minimum amount of time
and movement a task should take and to assist him in determining what
should constitute a day's work. This method differed from earlier models
of production in removing all authority from the worker and foreman on
the shop floor. Now, all decisions were made from above. Explains David
Montgomery,

> The essence of scientific management was systematic separation of the
> mental component of commodity production from the manual. The
> function of thinking and deciding were what management sought to
> wrest from the worker, so that the manual efforts of wage earners
> might be directed in detail by those of "superior intelligence." Frank
> Gilbreth [another efficiency expert and a sometime associate of Tay-
> lor's] contended that work guided by his instructions would be "ideal
> for a man who had no leaning toward brain work." (*Fall of the House
> of Labor* 252)

The worker thus was employed as a movable part in the machine of production. In the Taylorized factory, work was regimented and thoroughly
alienated.

In the Taylor method we can see the culmination of the goals of top-
down organization that formed the center of the Progressive concept of
reform. These include the concentration of power in a class of experts who
observe carefully the material realities of the world and surmise the laws
of behavior through their scientific method, the disempowering of all but
an elite class to make decisions or even to participate in the process by
which decisions are made, and the ultimate reduction of individuals to a
simple idea of their behavior. Indeed, behaviorism is the transformation
of Taylorism into "psychology." Watson's writings perform precisely the
same reduction as Taylor's and theorize it to a more generalized social
end. As Samuel Haber tells us of the ultimate ramifications of Taylorism in
the Progressive movement, "the Taylorites stepped out of the factory and
projected a role for scientific management in the nation at large" (xi).

In Our Time's reductions and fragmentation tell a story of Taylorization,
as it abstracts behavior from the individual performing it and gradually
amasses a reproducible entity, a body of actions and responses, but not a
human being attached to them. The stories after Chapter 6—"A Very Short
Story," "Soldier's Home," "The Revolutionist"—tell of characters who
might be Nick but are not named. In "Mr. and Mrs. Elliot," "Cat in the
Rain," and "Out of Season," we once again see characters who explicitly
are not Nick. In the first of these, the event recounted is not one that Nick
might have taken part in, though the embedded judgments of normative
behavior fit well within the implied vision of Nick. In the next two, though
these stories do not specifically call up Nick's experience, the parallel to
the themes of "The End of Something" and "Three-Day Blow" emerges,
which had told of Nick's separation from his girlfriend. Similarly, "My Old
Man" tells of a boy's admiration of his jockey father and his ultimate dis-
illusionment upon finding that his father has fixed races. This focus on the
father-son relationship refers back to the work's first two stories.

The story between "Out of Season" and "My Old Man" is "Cross-
Country Snow," which tells of Nick's activities while skiing in Switzerland
with his male companion. Given the sequence of events Nick has engaged
in throughout the novel, one assumes that this tale takes place after he
leaves the war and before he returns home. The tale also has the effect of
reestablishing Nick's centrality.

Like *The Birth of a Nation, In Our Time* objectifies experience and, through its arrangement, declares that what happens to one character is as important or meaningful as what happens to another. We are led into Nick's narrative and then introduced to parallel situations asserting that there is nothing unique about Nick or his experience. Rather, what has happened to Nick has happened to others, and what has happened to others might have happened to Nick. To note another group, "The Three-Day Blow" is similar to "Cross-Country Snow" and "Out of Season"; they all elevate the bonding of males with one another and somehow make this fraternity a plausible response to the condition of women. Indeed, in "Out of Season" the problem of the narrative is that the male has included his wife in the apparently masculine ritual of fishing. In the other two stories, activities that Hemingway asserts as specifically masculine—hunting and skiing—become celebrations of men together in the act of excluding women. This collection acquires its unity by relating various tales about unrelated people, a strategy seemingly designed to produce disunity. Yet the stories tell of incidents that refer to each other and of characters that act as another might have acted, or did act. Had Nick married Marjorie he might have been in the plot of "Out of Season." Had Nick's father been a jockey in Paris, then, given the lack of character, he exhibits in "The Doctor and The Doctor's Wife," he might have behaved like Butler in "My Old Man." One experience refers to another, and since, in Hemingway's philosophy, a man is as he does, and since many humans do similar things, then the world is composed of interchangeable characters with interchangeable lives.

In his essay "An American Tragedy, or the Promise of American Life," Walter Benn Michaels details the logic of the apparently paradoxical relationship between the idea of the individual and concepts of class in the late nineteenth and early twentieth centuries. In Michaels's argument, these terms are reconciled in the overriding notion of the singular and correct system, which provides a basis for individuals to affiliate with a higher ideal and not with a social entity. Thus, "hostility to the group finds expression as enthusiasm for the organization" (73). Nick's particular behaviors become identifiable through their connection to others who exhibit related actions or their contrast with those who do not. But the efficacy of these desirable actions, within the logic of the book, lies not in their relationship to other character's actions—which would make them imitative and not individual at all—but in their adherence to higher laws of system. Indeed, to attain these objective behaviors becomes the act of having become realized as a particular person. As Michaels explains the ramifications of Taylorism, "Scientific management makes it possible for the worker to experience satisfaction or dissatisfaction with his performance. It makes it possible . . . for him to know what it means to do his best and so be able to tell whether or not he has done it" (84–85). Nick becomes the beacon of two-fisted Americanism by having become an individual through his exhibition of reproducible, and reproduced, behaviors. That Nick exhibits such behaviors suggests the terms by which he can be an individual yet have no particular depth.

The last two stories of the collection are the two parts of "Big Two-Hearted River." These stories both refer to the same event in Nick's life, a fishing trip he took alone, and span two separate days. The stories are strategically set off from each other by a chapter, after the end of the first day. It appears that the intention of the division of these two parts is once again to make the assertion that the units of Nick's experience are not tied uniquely to his character but are free-floating facts of the world. Hence, their continuity relies not on the reappearance of their central character but rather on their recounting of related experiences. The actions of these stories tell of Nick meticulously controlling the activities of his fishing excursion, and then detail his movements with precision. The text suggests that Nick's extreme care in his actions is due to a desire to assert control over his life and gradually to come to terms with the events of the past. The stories tell us that "he felt he had left everything behind, the need for thinking, the need to write, other needs. It was all back of him" (134); that "his mind was starting to work. He knew he could choke it because he was tired enough" (142); and that "he did not want to rush his sensations any" (151).

The trauma that it seems logical for Nick to be struggling with is the war. The terms of the stories imply that Nick's experience was of considerable impact, and since we know from chapter 6 that he was in the war, then it seems reasonable to assume that this is what has disrupted his life. Of course, in keeping with the book's overall philosophy, these stories refer not only to Nick's experience but to that of Harold Krebs and of the unnamed male characters in "A Very Short Story" and "The Revolutionist." The two parts of "Big Two-Hearted River" are the most explicitly related stories of *In Our Time*. When considered as a single tale, they are also the book's longest. Here Nick fleetingly shows us his powers to resist becoming a mass of unmanaged impulses. He accomplishes this through a mastery of his actions, a posture that finds Nick experiencing a feeling (control) "appropriate to the emotion that has been imitated" (Michaels 86). As Michaels explains, in regard to a different narrative, "Emotion here is no longer regarded as an expression of individuality"; it becomes its "chief threat." "And by the same token, standardization—the attempt as [Weir] Mitchell puts it 'to produce complete identity of product'—becomes the great technology of passion" (86).

Rather than seeking solace in nature, Nick attempts to dominate it, through both fishing and psychic repression. He engages in a patently masculine activity in a manner where every discomfort is a direct threat to his masculinity. Arguably, the story is about the need to dominate impulses that are culturally defined as weak or feminine. This not only accounts for the moments of psychic repression I have noted; it also includes the denial of physical sensations as well. Thus, in the beginning of the story, though he is "tired and very hot" (136), he keeps walking; later, though "the water was a rising cold shock" (148), we have no statements of hesistancy. When he feels faint, he similarly resists giving in to the feeling, though he eventually does sit down (149). Nancy Hartsock finds such assertions endemic in a capitalist patriarchy. She writes, "In the community structured by masculine eros, bodies and their desires are given no legitimate place. The body and its desires are treated as loathsome, even inhuman, things that must be overcome if a man is to remain powerful and free. To meet the cultural standards of masculinity, individuals must separate themselves and conquer the feelings and desires of the body" (177–78). Nick engages in acts of denial that define well-embedded cultural practices of gender-based domination. This denial is expressed in a manner that complements these explicit assertions.

Throughout the work, Hemingway's philosophy allows Nick never to develop complex intellectual or emotional responses to the events he observes or in which he partakes. Since every act is its own explanation, there seems little to reflect upon. The *sense* that *In Our Time* is a coherent work is enough for most readers. Indeed, reviewers of the work generally commented in some way upon its cohesion. Its philosophy dictates that it should be accepted, not challenged or analyzed, since in Hemingway's view it is a factual reenactment of "the real thing" itself and therefore not subject to intellectual consideration. Rather, it is designed to strike an emotional chord, as the event would have done if the reader had apprehended it first-hand. Therefore, we are to trust the writer's observations.

Hemingway's philosophy has him trying to use language in a manner that denies its function as an instrument of thought and reflection. This philosophy of language and its corresponding view of the world asserts the man-is-machine perception of humanity in perhaps the most emphatic

tone of any of the works considered in this study. Hemingway's behav-
ioristic reduction pervades his work on every level, from the theory that
produces the words on a particular page to the construction of the sequence that constitutes *In Our Time*. It constantly entreats us to accept the
world as it appears as though it were a "fact" and offers us the ideological
obviousness of our unchallenged cultural assumptions.

Hemingway's barely adorned prose, existing as it does with little subordination and few modifiers, effectively vanquishes the authorial presence
in the way that Howells entreated realists to do. Indeed, there is neither
an authorial voice nor an insistent narrator arguing for the correctness of
this worldview as in *Sister Carrie*, nor a less polemic narrator suggesting to
us the way that this book *should* be read, as in Howells's fiction. There is
only a narrator who presents the "sequence of motion and fact" and who
assumes that the "facts" he presents are so resoundingly obvious that no
further argument is necessary. Since there is nothing or no one to argue
with—no bellicose narrator as in Dreiser nor a mildly insistent one as in
Howells—then the reader may be spirited along on the text's rapidly moving re-presentation of actions. Neither the language of the text nor the
structure of the work as a whole explicitly requires reflection. Though its
self-referential aspect may be found, this is a possible reading and not a
popular one.

Ultimately, Hemingway's career was a monument to the dual possibilities of American society: he received both critical success and general
adulation (and the latter's resultant riches). Hemingway struck the anti-
intellectual chord of American society, and he continued playing it for
decades. The interesting matter is that his works sold—and sell—well,
even though most readers will admit they lack the usual drama of popular
novels. "Big Two-Hearted River" is an example of this. For twenty or so
years this tale was read as the story of a fishing trip and a fairly prosaic one
at that.[25] It was not until Malcolm Cowley offered his explanation in 1944,
and Philip Young elaborated on it in 1952, that readers were "sure" of its
meaning. Writes Young, "Clearly, 'Big Two-Hearted River' presents a picture of a sick man, and of a man who is escaping from whatever has made
him sick" (47).[26] While Young's explanation is plausible, and its dominance
over the interpretive possibilities offered in academia perhaps justified, the
remarkable thing is that prior to Young's fixing this story's meaning it was
still well read and well known. In a 1926 review in the *Nation*, Allen Tate
praises this story for its barrenness. "Most typical of Mr. Hemingway's precise economical method is the story 'Big Two-Hearted River,' where the

time is one evening to the next afternoon and the single character a trout fisherman who makes his camp-fire, sleeps all night, gets up and catches a few trout, then starts home; that is all" (in Stephens 14). Hemingway was perhaps not communicating the emotion but rather lulling his readers with his "realism," providing them the unproblematized assumptions of the facts of the world that dominate his prose. As Hugh Kenner says, "If the book was so little understood for so long, one may ask why it was so respected" (150). The answer seems to lie in its appropriate assumptions regarding the nature of humanity and its expression of those beliefs in a prose style and a philosophy of composition that was finely attuned to those assumptions. Its integration of form and content perhaps make it a fully realized work of art, but it is one with a worldview both relevant to its cultural circumstances and disturbing in its presentation of them.

EIGHT

Epilogue: Realism in

the Late Twentieth Century

Since one purpose of this book has been to situate the aesthetic of American realism in its late nineteenth- and early twentieth-century cultural context, one might assume that realism was so strongly tied to that particular historical situation that its life ended with the erosion of the specific circumstances that it at first elucidated and that nurtured it. But this denies the adaptive element of the aesthetic that this study has attempted to note, as well as the residual conditions of culture that refer to historical continuities easily found in the last century. Indeed, in moving from the single-shot films of the late nineteenth century to the kinetic form of Griffith and from the realism of Howells to that of Hemingway, I have taken pains to show the ways in which the realist aesthetic has defined and responded to broad historical movements. Realism is an aesthetic and cultural strategy that employs positivist precepts of the real; as such, it serves as a means of co-opting change in order to conserve to the degree possible the outlines of an existing order. In writing an historical study, I intended to reveal an element of the process of cultural production that seeks to affirm the rationality of such conserving goals. In looking at the historical moment when America industrialized, I dwell on the period when the now-common means of defining the real passed from the realm of controversial assertion to "common sense."

I employ the term *common sense* in the sense given it by Antonio Gramsci:

Every philosophical current leaves behind a sedimentation of "common sense": that is the document of its historical effectiveness. Common sense is not something rigid and immobile, but is continually transforming itself, enriching itself with scientific ideas which have entered ordinary life. "Common sense" is the folklore of philosophy, and is always half-way between folklore properly speaking and the philosophy, science, and economics of the specialists. "Common sense" creates the folklore of the future, that is, as a relatively rigid phase of popular knowledge at a given place and time. (326 n. 5)

In the mass dissemination and acceptance of the textual terms of realism, we may view an aspect of the process by which the definition of the real wedded to the terms of Progressivism and corporate liberalism has passed from the realm of the philosophical to that of common sense and has come to stand for reality itself. Thus, in the late twentieth century the inevitability of *what is* becomes a cultural truism and the perpetually vexing question, did it *really* happen, passes as a critical response to texts that exhibit the core elements of realism.

Realism of the type described in this study persists. Works of fiction that rely on a distanced narration primarily recounting the objective circumstances of the world can be readily found. Writers such as Raymond Carver, Ann Beattie, Philip Roth, Jay McInerny, and a range of others compose novels that fall well within the dictates of the Howellsian method. Indeed, John Updike, in a 1987 *New Yorker* essay, finds a contemporary resurgence of a realism related to Howells's as a result of the exhaustion of "the modernist vein of formal experimentation" (88). Updike also notes Howells's interest in "domestic morality and sexual politics" (88—subjects that often define the center of his own novels); thus, he implicitly includes himself in the body of writers who compose within the Howellsian tradition. I would not argue that works of realism are dominant, only that they effectively compete to define the terms of the contemporary novel and suggest that certain strains of the historical epoch defined in this study refuse to vanish.

In the contemporary world of commercial film, the line that harks back to the fragmentary aesthetic of fact articulated by Griffith in *The Birth of a Nation* is all the more apparent. The institutional practice of the film industry long ago ensconced the affective methods of rapid editing and action-based narratives as norms. Indeed, as one looks at the contemporary film industry, the aesthetic (and politics) of Rambo and Dirty Harry easily trace back to those of Griffith.

Given that the last seventy or so years have seen the decline of the novel's role as a popular medium, and that in the same period the commercial cinema has in many ways become more reliant on known formulas, it seems more remarkable that the mode of realism traced in this study remains a factor in American literature than that it recurs in commercial films. Perhaps this disparity in my expectations refers to the cultural domain of each medium in the late twentieth century. If literary realism's obsession with the visually available had a role in the naturalization of the reified image as reality itself, then it played an even more prominent role in the cultural diminishing of the novel by media that could offer iconic images: film and television. Although one of the strategies of the realist novel is to attempt to materialize language so that the word virtually becomes the thing itself, the properties of language leave such a transformation impossible. Even the most transparent of print media, the contemporary newspaper, finds its role eclipsed by televised news.

The late twentieth-century novel thus finds itself as a form that requires of its readers a devotion and method of concentration that is unique. The novel has moved to the margins of mass culture. In some ways this movement has been liberating, as the novel's reduced economic and cultural status has allowed some novelists and some publishers to experiment with a range of expressive forms and resonant subjects. Yet, even in an age of experimental fiction, the realist mode, defined in much the same way that William Dean Howells defined it a century ago, is alive.

To consider the further implications of this study, I would like to characterize two contemporary cultural events, one in each medium. To look at the status of the Howellsian project, I will consider two critical efforts by highly visible authors to revivify the dictates of Howells's realism: John Gardner's *On Moral Fiction* (1978) and Tom Wolfe's "Stalking the Billion-Footed Beast" (1989).[1] To look at the present aesthetic and reception of realistic cinema, I will examine the debate on Oliver Stone's fact-based drama *JFK* (1991). That these cases are not as parallel as those outlined in the body of this study makes sense in that the cultural role of each medium has changed so greatly. That they are parallel at all defines the legacy of realism.

In 1978, John Gardner's *On Moral Fiction* raised a furor in the realm of the academy and among the learned magazine-reading public. Indeed, this reaction occurred in many of the same places where Howells's critical writings had provoked a similar response almost a full century before. Gardner's treatise amounted to a polemic against most of his literary contemporaries, dismissing various writers as "unsatisfying" (88), "self-indulgen[t]" (91), and possessed of "inflated reputations" (94). The list of those whom Gardner castigates includes Norman Mailer, Saul Bellow, Joan Didion, John Updike, and others who figure prominently in the late twentieth-century world of American letters. Gardner's collection of essays not only dismissed a wide range of writers; he also articulated a program by which American fiction could be redeemed. Writes Gardner, "The traditional view is that true art is moral: it seeks to improve life, not debase it. . . . That art which tends towards destruction, the art of nihilists, cynics, and merdistes is not properly art at all. Art is essentially serious and beneficial, a game played against chaos and death, against entropy" (5–6). In defining true art as that which seeks explicitly the spiritual uplift of its audience, Gardner also takes aim at the critics who have neglected their duty to promote and sanction such art. He criticizes them for focusing excessively on trivia, including "technique" and matters that overemphasize the role of the intellect in writing and reading (8–10).

The echoes of Howells's critical precepts resound throughout Gardner's writings. Both figures put forth a narrow definition of an author's moral mission as central to his or her cultural role. Both define this notion of morality didactically: for Howells, it is the act of elevating the essential goodness of American life and the positive truths of human existence; for Gardner, it is the proper assertion of "traditional values, such as honesty, marital fidelity, work, and moral courage" (42). This emphasis on the role of fiction to assert morality also leads to agreement in matters of technique. Both writers feel that the artist must use language as a transparent device for capturing the truths of nature. Both also define the true artist's method of composition as that which uses his text to find these universal truths. In each case, only bad art and bad artists impose temporal observations upon available transcendent truths.

Some eleven years after Gardner's creed, in *Harper's Magazine* of November 1989, Tom Wolfe issued what he called "a literary manifesto for the new social novel." Wolfe called on authors to cast out the pretensions of the avant-garde and go about chronicling the realities of everyday American life, "not to leave the rude beast, the material, also known as the life around us, to the journalists" (55). He argued that even if America does not necessarily need such literature, American novelists do (56). Wolfe's vision of the materials and methods of art follows Howells's to the extent that he proselytizes for the social novel and the writer who minimizes his or her self-consciousness. Wolfe, whose own nonfiction prose self-consciously called into question the journalist's guise of objectivity, now asks that novelists adopt the empiricism he cast out. Unlike Howells and Gardner, Wolfe does avoid the high-toned terms of mission and morality, but his fixed idea of good art and his sense of the process of writing and reading novels makes realism desirable and a worthy challenge for any writer.

Despite areas of departure from Howells and from each other—Wolfe dismisses Gardner and Gardner ignores Wolfe—in general Gardner and Wolfe attempt to resuscitate the realist project. But neither invokes Howells's name or the particular designs of American realism. Instead, both prominently employ the figure of Tolstoy. Gardner uses Tolstoy to define the high mission of art: to create "a world ruled . . . by moral choice, a world where every man's ambition was to be Christlike" (26). For Wolfe, Tolstoy exhibits the worthwhile representation of "hearts at war with the structure of society" (51). Howells also invokes Tolstoy prominently, praising him both for his morality and for his technique. He says that Tolstoy's words never "contravene the Sermon on the Mount" and that his characters' "lives are pictured with fidelity" (312). Oddly, then, Tolstoy becomes the patron saint of American realism.

The resumption of the realist project in the late twentieth century may be viewed as nostalgia. Both Gardner and Wolfe exhibit strong urges to employ literature not as a force of accommodation in the manner of Howells but as a force of reaction that would resituate the novel in its former place of cultural prominence. Because the age of realism is in decline, its assertion in relatively unmodified terms is strikingly nostalgic. For these contemporary realists, the emergence of mass media dominated by images has never taken place. The novel still serves them as the primary site of cultural instruction and documentation. In their myopia, Wolfe and Gardner cast out Howells from their tradition because of his shifting literary reputation. As they assert the transcendent value of realist prose, they also must find the line of their historical origin leading to a writer whose status is unquestioned in the western literary canon. Thus, Howells's problematic reputation in the late twentieth-century world of American letters ill-qualifies him for their tradition. Yet, in rejecting Howells these writers show their adherence to his strategies of asserting the temporal as transcendent. Realism, in this view, becomes a mode for the ages, a true art above all others.

The persistence of American literary realism and these treatises that would place it prominently within a conservative idea of American culture suggests that the historical line from the organization of the industrial economy in the late nineteenth century to that of the postindustrial economy of the late twentieth is readily drawn. Howellsian realism expressed the mystifying existence of a world already made according to the dictates of class-specific concepts of means-end rationality. Gardner and Wolfe restate the terms of that rationality even as the power of literature wanes. As the importance of the industrial workplace diminishes in American economic life, its organizational terms of efficiency and "expertise" are stretched to government, the service sector, and business bureaucracy. Indeed, the role of contemporary realism may be to avert the potentially liberating result of economic restructuring. Both Gardner and Wolfe tend toward the contemporary conventions of political conservatism and seek to employ existing cultural hierarchies as pillars of stasis.

The response to Wolfe and Gardner was generally negative, though in most cases there is evidence that respondents were put on the defensive. Gardner was harangued for his logical flaws and mean-spirited lambasting of his contemporaries. Indeed, some critics noted that those he readily dismissed, such as Philip Roth and Saul Bellow, would apparently fit into his category of moral fiction writers.[2] Wolfe was rebutted in similar terms for ignoring or diminishing existing realists as well as for his apparent naive empiricism.[3] For the purposes of this study, a notable aspect of these responses is their number and ardor, suggesting the power of the Howellsian legacy even as it fades.

In December 1991 Oliver Stone's historically based film *JFK* was released. The film tells the story of the assassination of John F. Kennedy in Dallas in 1962 by following the investigation of New Orleans district attorney and conspiracy maven James Garrison. The film shows its viewers the process of Garrison's conspiracy unfolding. In this view, the assassination becomes a murky and highly involved plot of the CIA, the Mafia, high levels of the military, and Lyndon Johnson. At the end of the film, Garrison, played by Kevin Costner, declaims for some forty minutes on the nature and meaning of this conspiracy. "What is the future where a President can be assassinated under conspicuously suspicious circumstances?" he asks.

In many ways, the film recalls *The Birth of a Nation*. It resituates historical facts within an overarching structure of high drama. It also employs a kinetic editing style and the dimensions of the epic. Despite these similarities, the two works, released some seventy-six years apart, possess several vital differences. Griffith's work took the elements of an increasingly dominant historical narrative of Reconstruction and placed them in the still young medium of film, employing a specific technique that was at the time virtually unknown. He announced his film as history and employed explicit documentation on the screen from reputable historical sources, including books written by the current president of the United States and an esteemed former secretary of state. Stone's film employs as its model a narrative that has yet to pass from speculation to history.[4] Indeed, besides

Jim Garrison there are relatively few, though they are quite devoted, who would argue that Stone's thesis is more than intriguing. Even Stone, who is not usually accused of possessing a subtle intellect, has said, "The artist's obligations are to interpret history and reinterpret it as he sees fit. . . . Film-makers make myths" (Ansen, "Interview" 49). In various interviews Stone has argued not for his film's indisputable factuality, as Griffith did, but for its adherence to interpretive possibility.

JFK as a cultural production of the late twentieth century works within a tradition of fact-based narrative that, within the medium of cinema, ex-tends back virtually to its beginnings, and the reception of the film sug-gests that cinema retains much of the power of its scientific roots, though I would argue that this power is also diminishing. Indeed, many of the respondents and reviewers avoid treating it as a document and directly ad-dress its interpretive strategies. For example, in the *National Review,* Tom Bethell, as part of a longer memoir of his days in Garrison's office, despite suspicions of the sanity of both Garrison and Stone, finds himself "sus-picious . . . of the Warren Commission's lone gunman theory" (50). He concludes, "It does strike me that if the Vietnam War is fair game for re-visionism, so is the Kennedy assassination. Just so long as we remember that Clay Shaw and I had nothing to do with it" (50). In the *Nation,* Alex-ander Cockburn pointedly illuminates the historical presumptions and the sources that form the heart of Stone's narrative. In treating the film as sub-jective expression, both Bethell and Cockburn astutely recognize its status and power, as do Stewart Klawans and Andrew Kopkind in their responses in *Nation.* Both of these commentators focus on Stone's facility in struc-turing and asserting his point of view while recognizing the necessity of subjective intention in such a text.

In locating the film's assumptions and rationale, these writers neither misread the medium nor the particular object. The view of Bethell and others illuminates the possibility of a relatively sophisticated approach to films in general and to those employing historical referents in particular. This is in contrast to the manner in which *The Birth of a Nation* was received in 1915. Wrote one reviewer, "*The Birth of a Nation* has been criticized and attempts have been made to suppress it. If history should be suppressed in schools for children, *The Birth of a Nation* should be supressed in a theater of thinking people. The picture is vindicated by historical facts" (McIntosh 36). This approach to the film is echoed in various journals, as the film is lauded for its "picture of conditions in the South" (W. S. Bush 26) and its point of view justified by its use of "reported facts" (Vance 23). The comparison between the ways commentators approach these two films reveals at least some contemporary intellectual disposition to demystify the realist text.

Problematic, however, was the broader reception of *JFK*, which had disturbing elements of hysteria. Various reviewers, including David Ansen in *Newsweek* and Stanley Kauffmann in the *New Republic*, took issue with Stone's *right* to make a film such as this. The movie, writes Ansen, "puts the critic—and the audience—in a strange, indeed, absurd position: we are asked not only to pass judgment on its virtues as an entertainment but to hand down a judgment on history" (50). He goes on to note that the film is "quasi-documentary in style . . . so that you can't always tell what's real footage and what's not, never mind what's true and what's not" (50). Similarly, Kauffmann questions Stone's use of the representational powers of the medium.

> Cinematically, *JFK* is almost a complete success. . . . But is it fitting that the very power of the film should serve questionable history? The customary acceptance of historical inaccuracy in art works—in Shakespeare, Schiller, Shaw, for instance—is slight defense here. Or to take a film example: few historians would endorse the values, or all the details in John Ford westerns, but to everyone save the mentally unbalanced, Ford's values and details are the lineaments of an American romance, and contemporary application is slight. Viewers of *JFK*, however, might find themselves shaken in their views of government, society, the media. Certainly this disruption might be salutary for us— if it were more soundly based. (Review 28)

Each of these critics posits a response that expresses a peculiar lack of sophistication, whether actual or feigned. In my view, the cultural problem of early cinema was its general power to implicate its inexperienced viewers in a signifying system that produced and reproduced the ideological assertions of positivism and corporate liberalism. In the late twentieth century, the prospect of disrupting the legacy of that system lies in an awareness of its specific history and modes of assertion. This awareness derives from an exercise of critical insight. Yet, here are the practiced viewers of cinema entranced by the medium in a manner that recalls the reviewers of Griffith's film. For Kauffmann and Ansen, the fact-based film seems to provoke a discomforting intellectual dissonance. At the center of this intellectual disquiet lies certain viewers' need for clear categories of fact and fiction, with fact defined as what we cannot question and fiction as what we cannot believe. This split denies the interpretive dimension of the historical text and the historical dimension of fiction. Such a split takes us back to the intellectual currents of the late nineteenth and early twentieth centuries. This lack of critical insight leads me to question these reviewers' manner of apprehending any text in this medium. Indeed, without going deeply into the logic of Kauffmann's John Ford–Oliver Stone contrast, I must say, having lived through the epoch of Ronald Reagan, I find Ford at least as dangerous as Stone. But I also find that what I bring to the text mitigates that danger since I am always, on some level, aware that this medium, despite its apparent objectivity, is driven by subjective device. All viewers should repeat the incantation of an advertisement for a forgotten slasher film: it's only a movie.

While the response to the writers Gardner and Wolfe was largely confined to the world of letters—academic journals and limited circulation magazines—the flap over *JFK* occurred in the larger culture. There were a number of pieces in major media discussing Stone's crimes against history, including one by Tom Wicker in the *New York Times*, an interview with Jack Valenti on network television, a piece by Bill Moyers on PBS, an article by Ronald Steel (Walter Lippmann's biographer, who ought to know better) in the *New Republic*, and a public forum in New York's Town Hall, featuring Stone, Nora Ephron, and Norman Mailer speaking for the film and Edward Jay Epstein, Max Holland, and Christopher Hitchens speaking against it. The responses of Wicker, Steel, and Valenti seem particularly hysterical. As an aide to Johnson and the current head of the Hollywood trade association, Valenti's annoyance is comprehensible and his attacks on Stone have the tone of a political campaign. Wicker and Steel, however, were less directly involved in the events portrayed, though Wicker was certainly emotionally implicated in the aura of Kennedy. Both express highdecibel outrage at Stone's blending of fact and fiction and were angered by his failure to provide clear, optic-yellow tags to identify each.

The tone and content of this outrage define the problematic cultural legacy of realism as a cultural production. Indeed, the power of propaganda depends upon its audience's viewing such manipulation as veracious. Since the mass media are an industry that employs the devices of realism and are largely controlled by those invested in the persistence of the class relations of corporate liberalism, the means by which "information" may be contextualized and acted upon is largely through the audience's critical perspective. Critical demystification is a necessary device for minimizing such textual and cultural power.

In response to the controversy over the film, the *American Historical Review* published three pieces to address this public outcry. The very fact that such attention was necessary strikes me as problematic, yet the pieces themselves were well conceived and illuminating. In particular, the essay by Roger Rosenstone defines history not as that which has the status of a fact or a body of facts about the past, but as that which "engage[s] the issues, data, and arguments of that discourse" (510). He concludes, "If it is part of the burden of the historical work to make us rethink how we got to where we are, and to make us question values that we and our leaders and nation live by, then, whatever its flaws, *JFK* has to be among the most important works of American history ever to appear on the screen" (511). Rosenstone's assertions restate the project of this study: he reconstrues the idea of history as the informing concept of an "historical work." In doing so he questions the positivist notion of the ideologically neutral, factual text. By questioning this construct within his discipline, he expresses a critical perspective that demystifies the tropes of the realist aesthetic in media such as the novel and cinema, where the status of "fact" is inherently more problematic than in narratives of history. By locating the historical circumstances of the rise of realism in America and considering its cultural legacy, we may cease to accept its embedded notions of a world already made. We thereby open a world of "unrealistic" possibility.

NOTES

Chapter 1: Introduction

1. Everett Carter, *Howells and the Age of Realism;* Edwin Cady, *The Light of Common Day: Realism in American Fiction;* Warner Berthoff, *The Ferment of American Realism: American Literature, 1884–1919;* Donald Pizer, *Realism and Naturalism in Nineteenth-Century American Literature;* Larzer Ziff, *The American 1890s: The Life and Times of a Lost Generation.*

2. Daniel Aaron, *Men of Good Hope: A Story of American Progressives;* Richard Hofstadter, *The Age of Reform: From Bryan to F. D. R.;* George E. Mowry, *The Era of Theodore Roosevelt and the Birth of Modern America;* John Morton Blum, *The Republican Roosevelt.*

3. I have not discussed the studies of this era by Mark Seltzer, *Bodies and Machines,* and Howard Horwitz, *By the Law of Nature: Form and Value in Nineteenth-Century America.* Both studies concern themselves provocatively with literary works of the period under consideration. My reason for this exclusion is that they are so methodologically different from the project I have undertaken that to categorize these distinctions belabors the obvious. Each work is, in its way, brilliantly argued. But if the idealist presuppositions of the five works I do discuss distinguish them significantly from my own study, then both Horwitz and Seltzer compose studies that are significantly more idealist than those considered.

4. Gabriel Kolko, *The Triumph of Conservatism;* James Weinstein, *The Corporate Ideal of the Liberal State;* Martin Sklar, *The Corporate Reconstruction of American Capitalism, 1890–1916;* James Livingston, *Origins of the Federal Reserve System: Money, Class, and Corporate Capitalism, 1890–1913.* I recognize that there are those who reject this analysis. See for example, Barbara Ehrenreich and John Ehrenreich, "The Professional-Managerial Class," for a breakdown of the category of "manager" into a number of classes with various social and economic roles. Also, Steven Fraser, in *Labor Will Rule: Sidney Hillman and the Rise of American Labor,* notes the ways in which managerial methods were distinct within certain types of industry. Both pieces provide a welcome caution against excessive generalization. Fraser points out how particular industries, such as the urban garment trade, did not adopt the model of professional management discussed here and thus exhibited significantly different relations of production from those I discuss. The Ehrenreichs discuss how the lumping together of all managerial personnel into one class is far too general as a description of both function and status. This position echoes the arguments

put forth by C. Wright Mills in his *White Collar*, published in the fifties. Fraser's discussion suggests the necessity of looking at broad cultural movements as other than monolithic. The Ehrenreichs' analysis suggests the degree to which the categories we employ to consider social life may always be refined. I do, however, feel that such microanalysis always requires, for balance, a larger vision, such as that provided by Sklar and the others.

5. I am not proposing a naive historicism. While recognizing the impossibility of answering these questions with certainty, I am convinced that this in no way limits the value of such an inquiry, a value that develops from the plausibility of my discussion. I assert the distinction between plausibility and certainty to remind readers that, though my narrative of history is asserted with force, it is not posited as a totality. It comprises some things but not all things.

6. Well known and accomplished historians of American literature include, for example, Vernon Parrington, F. O. Mathiessen, and Alfred Kazin.

7. Michael Davitt Bell's *The Problem of American Realism: Studies in the Cultural History of a Literary Idea* also explores this period in a literary-historical method. However, his discussion is more in keeping with older approaches to this field and is therefore less involved in broader historical issues than Borus and Wilson.

8. By now, Michaels's oft-quoted assertion that writers cannot be for or against a dominant element of their historical context—capitalism, in this case—because they are in it has raised the eyebrows of many in literary and historical studies. I also disagree with this idea of history as a singular and total formation. Yet, I can say that the result of this problematic formulation is in ways more "historical" than the analyses of other critics who profess to a less problematic view of history. Michaels ends up with a well-defined take, not on an era as a totality, but on a dominant strain as it occurred in a strata of intellectual life.

9. See for example, Henry Nash Smith, *Virgin Land: The American West as Symbol and Myth;* Leo Marx, *The Machine in the Garden: Technology and the Pastoral Ideal in America;* R. W. B. Lewis, *The American Adam: Innocence, Tragedy and Tradition in the Nineteenth Century.* I do not intend to impugn their politics. I am merely noting the broader historical function of the American Studies movement.

10. See Ian Tyrell, *The Absent Marx: Class Analysis and Liberal History in Twentieth-Century America*, for a discussion of the dominance and impact of liberal historiography.

Chapter 2: William Dean Howells and the Order of Progress

1. Burton Bledstein has called this transition "the culture of professionalism." "The professional person released nature's potential and rearranged reality on grounds that were neither artificial, arbitrary, faddish, convenient, nor at the mercy

of popular whim. Such was the august basis for the authority of the professional." *The Culture of Professionalism,* 90.

2. As others have noted, one could look at the anxiety inherent in such repeated assertions. I choose to focus on the affirmative aspect of his position.

3. For a thorough discussion of the novel's prominence in the century since its publication, see Donald Pease's introduction to *New Essays on "The Rise of Silas Lapham."* Pease traces responses from Vernon Parrington's 1928 treatment through Lionel Trilling's in *The Liberal Imagination* (1951) to more recent discussions by Robert Weimann and Michael Spindler. All of this shows the centrality of this novel in the way in which we think about the realist movement in America.

4. Frederick Douglass's *Narrative of the Life of Frederick Douglass an American Slave* was published in 1845. Its emphasis on physical description strongly evokes the realist aesthetic characterized by Howells. However, Douglass's powerful sense of self makes this work other than an objective, and objectifying, account. Its conclusion also drifts into romance, as Douglass discusses the Christian imperatives of emancipation. Elizabeth Barstow Stoddard's 1862 novel, *The Morgesons,* begins as an examination of how realist tropes may assist a young woman in combatting the social constraints of her age, but by the middle of the work it fully accommodates many of the conventions of the romance. Rebecca Harding Davis's *Life in the Iron Mills* (1861) employs much of the aesthetic described by Howells but also offers a romantic conclusion, as Deborah's redemption is spiritual and not physical. These works' focus on extreme conditions suggests that the result of Howells's critical realism was to coopt an aesthetic with radical implications and contain it as a force of dissent. See Sharon M. Harris, *Rebecca Harding Davis and American Realism.*

5. Montgomery cautions, "The Liberal Republican Party of 1872 was *not* the political embodiment of the Liberal reform impulse," since it included all strains of anti-Grant Republicans (385), but Howells aligned himself with its reform elements.

6. This list of best sellers comes from Karol L. Kelly, *Models for the Multitudes: Social Values in the American Popular Novel, 1850–1920,* and Frank Luther Mott, *Golden Multitudes: The Story of Best Sellers in the United States.*

7. In "The Sin of Art and the Problem of American Realism," Michael Davitt Bell argues that Howells used the idea of realism as the *opposite* of aesthetics. That is, for Howells realism was that which was not artificially arrived at. I agree with this analysis of Howells's intentions but find that this in no way alters the philosophical and literary implications of his critical statements or his novels. Howells's denial of his "art" further asserts the positivist assumptions of his writings.

8. James's early vision of the novel as a dramatized narrative suggests Howells's realism. Indeed, his early critical vexation with Anthony Trollope's frequent intrusions into his novels echoes Howells's aesthetic standard (*The Future of the Novel,* 6), a standard they discussed at length in Howells's first years in Boston. However, James left such relatively mundane matters of craft behind and went on to evolve

a sense of internal process, known as psychological realism, which emphasized thought in the way that Howells focused on action. Clemens relied on Howells's editorial advice, particularly concerning matters of taste and propriety. Novels by Mark Twain reveal a relative fidelity to Howells's precepts, even as his subject matter became more and more fanciful as the years passed.

9. A recent collection edited by Donald Pease, *New Essays on "The Rise of Silas Lapham,"* includes a number of essays that approach the political implications of Howells's novel in related terms but finally in ways that diverge from my own. Most helpful were Wai-Chee Dimock, "The Economy of Pain: Capitalism, Humanitarianism and the Realistic Novel," and James M. Cox, *"The Rise of Silas Lapham:* The Business of Morals and Manners."

10. These insights and judgments come from Stephen Thernstrom, *The Other Bostonians,* particularly 228–32; and the collection edited by Ronald Formisano and Constance K. Burns, *Boston 1700–1980: The Evolution of Urban Politics,* particularly Geoffrey Blodgett, "Yankee Leadership in a Divided City, 1860–1910" (87–110).

11. Amy Kaplan, in *The Social Construction of American Realism,* writes, "Howells cannot totally differentiate his own writings from Hubbard's, and exposes realism to be complicit in the same network of cultural practices that makes the interview a necessary mode of communication" (39). While this is to a degree true, Howells's effort to separate himself from Hubbard and the method he chooses to accomplish this estrangement provide insight into the goals and aesthetics of realism.

12. A number of critics have associated Sewell's sentiments with those of Howells. "R. P.," a critic in *Catholic World* at the time of the novel's publication, makes this connection (Edwin H. Cady and Norma W. Cady, eds., *Critical Essays on W. D. Howells, 1866–1920,* 40–46), as do various subsequent critics. See Everett Carter, *The American Idea,* 234; Michaels, *Gold Standard,* 41; Edwin H. Cady, *The Road to Realism,* 234; William Alexander, *William Dean Howells: The Realist as Humanist,* 39.

13. In *Resisting Novels: Ideology and Fiction,* Lennard Davis discusses the novel's role in blurring "the distinction between the inner and outer world," defining the realistic novel as "a cultural phenomenon with certain overt aims and a hidden agenda" (4–5). It would seem that the idealization of the building in this novel well fits Davis's description. See also Philip Fisher, "Appearing and Disappearing in Public: Social Space in Late-Nineteenth-Century Literature and Culture," for a treatment of the redefinition of public and private life that took place in the America of this novel. Fisher well considers the role of the aesthetic object in this reordering.

In *Private Novels, Public Films,* Judith Mayne describes this fetishizing of display as a blurring of public and private space, in which the institution of marriage serves both "personal and economic" interests (40–43). See also her discussion of how this occurs and recurs in a consumerist culture (68–72).

14. Thorstein Veblen's *The Theory of the Leisure Class* critiques in scathing detail

the matter of gaudy display in late nineteenth-century American urban society; see particularly 65–66 and 154.

15. Walter Benn Michaels argues that "nothing is more remarkable in *The Rise of Silas Lapham* than the identification of realism with a morality and an economy that are themselves represented in principle as anticapitalist" (*Gold Standard*, 38). I disagree with this conclusion, though I find Michaels's economic analysis of the work valuable. Howells is not anticapitalist, he merely resists the burgeoning model's excessive dynamism, which so disrupts his desire for continuity. Michaels interprets the novel's conclusion in a way that opposes my own view: "Thus the novel ends with a vindication of realism and domesticity both, at the expense of speculation. Lapham goes bankrupt, but his bankruptcy is not a sign of ruin and disgrace; it becomes instead the vehicle of his final redemption and return to the precapitalist (and in most respects the anticapitalist) ideals of his beginnings" (40). This analysis makes Lapham's failure redemptive rather than a banishment by market forces. It also assumes that Lapham remains the novel's protagonist. I find his move to Vermont a sweeping of him from the American future. Michaels also neglects the fact that Lapham is still a minor figure in the paint business, and therefore is neither a precapitalist nor an anticapitalist; he is only a failed capitalist.

Chapter 3: Thomas Edison and the Machine That Sees

1. Habermas employs this term in "Technology and Science as Ideology," in *Towards a Rational Society*.

2. For discussions of the emergence of cinema in extraordinary detail and notable historical scope, see the writings of Charles Musser, particularly *The Emergence of Cinema: The American Screen to 1907; Before the Nickelodeon;* and with Carol Nelson, *High-Class Moving Pictures: Lyman H. Howe and the Forgotten Era of Travelling Exhibition.* For specific cultural analyses, see Robert Sklar, *Movie-Made America,* 3–18; Garth Jowett, *Film: The Democratic Art,* 23–34. Robert Allen, *Vaudeville and the Film,* 77–79, discusses with detail and insight the attempt to perfect a reliable large-screen projecting device.

3. In *Images and Enterprise,* 262–65, Reese Jenkins discusses the "broadening of interest in the application of photography to the study of motion" (264) in the 1880s. See also Noel Burch's discussion of the phenomenon of reducing animals to motion, and its political and economic implications, in his *Life to Those Shadows,* particularly 8–14.

4. See Noel Burch, *To the Distant Observer,* 61–66, for a synopsis of this technological ideal of representation.

5. See William Dennis Marks, Harrison Allen, and Francis Dercum, *Animal Locomotion: The Muybridge Work at the University of Pennsylvania.*

6. *New York Times,* April 14, 1896.

7. Kemp Niver shows in his *The First Twenty Years* (9) that such tricks often employed an early form of editing, rather than simply stopping and restarting the camera. Tom Gunning explains that the emphasis of such editing is to maintain the integrity and thus the continuity of the frame. See " 'Primitive' Cinema—A Frame Up? Or the Trick's on Us."

8. Tom Gunning makes this point in his "The Cinema of Attraction: Early Film, Its Spectator and the Avant-Garde."

9. Miriam Hansen, *Babel and Babylon*, 60–89; and Mayne, *Private Novels, Public Films*, 68–94; Kathy Peiss, *Cheap Amusements*, 146–62.

10. For an example of this tendency, see Gordon Hendricks, *Origins of the American Film*. See Burch's *Life to Those Shadows*, 27–29, for a critique of this practice.

11. In his introduction to the first volume of *The Papers of Thomas Edison*, Reese Jenkins details Edison's early and ongoing interest in *both* commerce and technology (16–19).

12. For a discussion of how Edison developed his vertical hold on the early cinema, see Charles Musser, "The American Vitagraph, 1897–1901."

13. Films such as *New Bathing Scene at Rockaway* (1896) or the somewhat later *What Happened on 23rd Street, NYC* (1901) seem to have no other reason to exist but their possible titillation of male viewers with objectified women. Also, a film like *Fatima* (1899) offers a more explicit exhibition of a woman, as the named figure whirls in a belly dance.

14. See Lucy Fisher, *Shot/Countershot*, and Teresa DeLauretis, *Alice Doesn't: Feminism, Semiotics, Cinema*, for focused considerations of the normative maleness of the camera's gaze.

15. See Raymond Fielding, *The American Newsreel, 1911–1967*, 9–12.

16. *New York Times* February 22, 1898; April 5, 1898.

17. See Fielding, *American Newsreel*, 29–45. Fielding discusses the propensity of early film producers to create fake news films, and he counts Edison as the most subtle of the counterfeitors (41). He also notes the enthusiastic responses of audiences to these fakes.

Chapter 4: Sister Carrie *and the Natural Power of Things*

1. Many historians of the Progressive period note this equation. See, for example, Samuel Hays, *Conservation and the Gospel of Efficiency*, 122–27; and Robert Wiebe, *The Search for Order: 1877–1920*, 164–195.

2. Michael Hoffman distinguishes realism as "a literary method" from naturalism as "a way of interpreting the world"; see *The Subversive Vision*, 129. Edwin Cady distinguishes them in a similar way, noting naturalism's "ultimate, hard Darwinism" (*Light of Common Day* 49). For examples of other distinctions of realism from naturalism that minimize their great similarities, see Pizer, *Realism and Naturalism,*

and Carter, *Howells and the Age of Realism*. These distinctions remain implicit in the works of many contemporary critics, as I argue in my preface.

3. For discussions of this transition from which I draw, see Mike Davis, *Prisoners of the American Dream*, 29–54; Leon Fink, "The Uses of Political Power: Toward a Theory of Labor Movement in the Era of the Knights of Labor," in Michael H. Frisch and Daniel J. Walkowitz, eds., *Working-Class America*, 104–23; Nell Irvin Painter, *Standing at Armageddon: The United States, 1877–1919*, 85–90.

4. David Montgomery describes the manner in which workers resisted these hegemonic practices and cautions against overarching assumptions of their dominance. See *Workers' Control in America*, particularly 1–8 and 91–112.

5. For discussions of the emphases in content, style, and philosophy of Dreiser's early journalism, see Shelley Fisher Fishkin, *From Fact to Fiction*, 87–111, and Ellen Moers, *Two Dreisers*, 142–45.

6. See Herbert Spencer, *First Principles*.

7. Dreiser was hardly a doctrinaire follower of any system of thought, veering among all varieties of political belief, including populism, Progressivism, Stalinism, and a range of mysticisms. See his *Tragic America* as a document of his peculiar leftism in the thirties.

8. Michaels's critical approach has assisted me in forming my own. Indeed, his analysis of this work strikes me as essential to any reader who seeks to address it in cultural terms. Similarly, Rachel Bowlby's *Just Looking* aptly describes Carrie's place in the burgeoning American system of exchange, but she finds Dreiser's intent more generally critical.

9. Dreiser's representation of this process of commodification of being asserts as fact the economic state discussed by Marx in his 1844 manuscripts. Marx's section entitled "Estranged Labor" (106–19) carefully analyzes the relations of production in the industrial workplace, in terms that provide a foreground for understanding the self-perception of modern economic man. He writes of the increasing objectification of self and the elevation of the object world in this system of production. This process has been eloquently noted by others, as well. In *Eros and Civilization*, for example, Herbert Marcuse writes that "[i]n exchange for the commodities that enrich their life, the individuals sell not only their labor, but their free time. . . . The ideology of today lies in that production and consumption reproduce and justify domination" (100). More recently, Christopher Lasch, in *The Culture of Narcissism* (135–40), writes, "In the period of primitive accumulation, capitalism subordinated being to having, the use value of commodities to their exchange value. Now it subordinates possession itself to appearance and measures exchange value as a commodity's capacity to confer prestige—the illusion of prosperity and well-being" (137). Dreiser's novel projects this condition as it reproduces Marx's conditions of production. He thereby valorizes a reduction of humanity and an elevation of objects as "reality."

10. See Jack Salzman, ed., *Theodore Dreiser: The Critical Reception*, 1–55 for examples of these reviews. See Donald Pizer, *Sister Carrie* 433–54 for a recapitulation of its publication history.

11. For discussion of this effort to rationalize consumption see Alfred D. Chandler, *The Visible Hand: The Managerial Revolution in American Business*, 377–414; and James D. Norris, *Advertising and the Transformation of American Society, 1865–1920*.

12. For a related consideration of the joining of the terms *individuality* and *class* in the early twentieth century, see Walter Benn Michaels, "An American Tragedy, or the Promise of American Life." I would argue that the former term is subsumed under the latter, but I find Michaels's use of the fact of the standardization and mass production of clothes according to size a related occurrence in the last years of the nineteenth century.

13. June Howard distinguishes Carrie's difference as a lesser "sexual desire" (45). This strikes me as an observation that is possibly true but insufficiently explanatory in this novel about consumption.

14. For example, Richard Lehan, *Theodore Dreiser: His World and His Ideas*, 45–53; Sheldon Grebstein, "Dreiser's Victorian Vamp," in Donald Pizer, ed., *Sister Carrie*, 541–51; Sandy Petrey, "The Language of Realism, The Language of False Consciousness: A Reading of *Sister Carrie*."

Chapter 5: Edwin S. Porter and the Facts of Intelligible Narrative

1. For some examples of this approach see David Cook, *A History of Narrative Film*, 19–29, and Lewis Jacobs, *The Rise of the American Film* (35–51). Charles Musser, through his voluminous research and careful discussion, shows the limits of such a conception in *The Emergence of Cinema: The American Screen to 1907*. It is difficult to overemphasize the debt that scholars of this period of American cinema owe to Musser's painstaking research and interpretive clarity. For a more pointed rebuttal and an intriguing argument that disputes the simplification of this organic model, see Noel Burch, "Porter or Ambivalence."

2. See Musser, *The Emergence of Cinema*, 298–336, for a detailed recounting of this process by which American cinema adopted modern industrial practices.

3. See Richard Koszarski, *An Evening's Entertainment: The Age of the Silent Picture, 1915–1928*, 63–94, for detailed consideration of the changing shape of the film industry's corporate methods.

4. Noel Burch discusses the incidence of these lecturers in American and European film as a means of comparing them to the Japanese cinema's *benshi*; see *To the Distant Observer*, 75–82. Musser also considers this practice in *The Emergence*, 368–69. See also Musser, with Carol Nelson, *High-Class Moving Pictures: Lyman H. Howe and the Forgotten Era of Traveling Exhibition*.

5. See Charles Musser, "Before the Nickelodeon," 254 and 310.

6. Films structured like Porter's, that is, films using scenes as units of action to create a narrative, proliferated by 1904. Indeed, the relationship between each scene and the larger whole was the basis for a lawsuit in 1904 (see n. 8 below). For further discussion of the development of cinema narrative, see John Fell, *A History of Films,* 28–53; and Barry Salt, "Film Form, 1900–1906." Also, Noel Burch's vision of the relationship between the form of film narrative and the producer's conception of audience is trenchant; see *Life to Those Shadows,* 109–42.

7. Jon Gartenberg discusses the incidence of camera movement in "Camera Movement in Edison and Biograph Films, 1900–1906." He finds that movement is extensive, as a full pan occurs in films as early as 1900, and is often a film's reason for being, for example in *Circular Panorama of Electric Tower* (1901) or *Panorama of Gorge Railway* (1900). Clearly, then, with great movement possible, this relative lack of movement suggests a reluctance to disrupt excessively the stability of the camera's eye.

8. The Edison Company's disposition to consider their longer narrative films as the sum of a number of discrete units is revealed by their legal strategy in a 1904 copyright suit against Biograph. Edison claimed that each portion of a film was an independent whole, and that copying any single scene was therefore plagiarism. The Edison Company marketed these narratives both as wholes *and* as individual scenes—though the former strategy was demonstrably more effective. See David Levy, "Edison Sales Policy and the Continuous Action Film."

9. I am aware that the Edison catalogue has scenes 3 and 4 occurring simultaneously, and that scenes 10 and 11, according to the same source, take place during the action of scenes 2 through 9. However, within the film itself, no aspect of the presentation asserts this prominently or clearly. Indeed, if this simultaneity is supposed to in fact occur, the reluctance of Porter and the Edison Company to assert it with strength suggests their investment in the trope of realism.

10. For discussion of the film's dramatic precursor, see Nicholas Vardac, *Stage to Screen,* 63.

11. There has been considerable controversy over which version of Porter's film is in fact the one released in 1903. The two versions at issue are a film in the Museum of Modern Art collection and a paper print in the Library of Congress. The latter version was filed for copyright by the Edison Company, while the former seems to have been compiled by the museum staff in 1944. Based on the convincing arguments of Charles Musser, in "The Early Cinema of Edwin Porter," and Andre Gaudreault, in "Detours in Film Narrative: The Development of Cross-Cutting," I have decided to treat the paper print version as the original.

12. In transcribing my notes, I found that my knowledge of other accurate and concise scene-by-scene recountings of these films got in the way. My own summation draws on those accomplished with precision by Cook, *History of Narrative Film,* 22–23, and Gaudreault, "Detours in Film Narrative," 40–41.

13. See Cook, *History of Narrative Film,* 24–25, for a shot-by-shot description.

14. This shot apparently refers to a scene in the stage play by Marble, but it remains mystifying within this generally intelligible narrative. See Vardac, *Stage to Screen*, 63–64.

15. See n. 9 above.

16. For extensive and illuminating discussion of the way the concept of the frontier, and Westerns as resonant narratives, figured in the development of an appropriate cultural mythos of the twentieth-century United States, see Richard Slotkin, *The Fatal Environment* and *Gunfighter Nation*.

17. See A. R. Fulton, *Motion Pictures: The Development of an Art*, 39, and Gerald Mast, *A Short History of the Movies*, 43.

18. See Charles Musser, *Before the Nickelodeon*, 273–326, for a detailed discussion of this transitional year.

Chapter 6: D. W. Griffith's The Birth of a Nation

1. For discussion that focuses on Griffith's career at Biograph, see Robert M. Henderson, *D. W. Griffith: The Years at Biograph;* for a filmography of this period, see Cooper C. Graham, Steven Higgins, Elaine Mancini, Joño Luiz Vieira, *D. W. Griffith and the Biograph Company*. The most illuminating treatment of this period is Tom Gunning's *D. W. Griffith and the Origins of American Narrative Film*. Not only is Gunning's work rigorously based on his own intelligent viewing of countless films, but his sense of context, including cinema and cultural history, makes this an exemplary work.

2. Theodore Huff's *A Shot Analysis of D. W. Griffith's "The Birth of a Nation"* lists the number of shots as 1,368. In " 'The Sword Became a Flashing Vision': D. W. Griffith's *The Birth of a Nation*," 174, Michael Paul Rogin reveals that among those scenes deleted from the final circulating print were those of the castration of the black character Gus.

3. Remarkably, a version of this film televised by the Arts and Entertainment cable television network in the mid–1980s has an introduction by Philip Bosco that reproduces this same split. Says Bosco: "Though it was criticized for its many racist elements, there is no denying that the film's artistry and technical achievement paved the way for modern cinema."

4. In her treatment of the reception of *The Birth of a Nation* in *Interpreting Films*, 142–43, Janet Staiger notes that this splitting of form and content was common in film reviews of 1915.

5. For a discussion of Shaler's views and influence see Joel Williamson, *The Crucible of Race*, 119–21. For a broader discussion of Shaler's theories regarding the raciality of various nationalities, see John Higham, *Strangers in the Land*, 140–41. For a discussion of the role of anthropology in race thinking, see Thomas F. Gossett, *Race: The History of an Idea in America*, 54–83.

6. See Jack Temple Kirby, *Darkness at the Dawning: Race and Reform in the Progressive South*, 44–56, and Williamson, *The Crucible of Race*, 354–95.

7. See David Levy, "Reconstituted Newsreels, Re-Enactments and the American Narrative Film," 243–60. Levy discusses the "joining together of separate strips of action footage to construct fluid if relatively brief *actuality* narrative[s]" (245; my emphasis).

8. Griffith repeatedly asserted that *Birth* was nothing more than a faithful enactment of the facts of history. Writes Richard Schickel in his biography of Griffith: "The guise of objective historian was one Griffith liked. By being as authentic as possible in details of decor and costume, by stressing to the point of exaggeration in his publicity the amount of historical research that underlay the film . . . he was attempting to wrap his inventions in a cloak of fact"; *D. W. Griffith*, 237.

9. Wilson and Dixon had known each other since their days as graduate students at Johns Hopkins University. Perhaps not coincidentally, both were students of Herbert Baxter Adams, who was one of the leading advocates in the United States of the German model of historiography. See Williamson, *Crucible of Race*, 153–54; also n. 11 below.

10. Foner further discusses this historiographical disposition and its various degrees of influence on subsequent treatments of the period; *Reconstruction*, xxi–xxvii. It would be remiss not to mention the noted Southern historian Ulrich B. Phillips as another figure who put forth a Dunning-like analysis, though not simply of Reconstruction. Rather, Phillips's work *American Negro Slavery* (1918) provided a source for those many historians who wished to explain slavery as a civilizing institution. See Kirby, *Darkness at the Dawning*, 91–93, and Eugene Genovese, *The Political Economy of Slavery*, 71–81.

11. Though Ranke stressed the spirituality of the historian and of history, he also devoted himself to the cause of rigorously unearthing primary materials. It is the empirical aspect of his method that has proliferated. Says Stuart Hughes: "Ranke had long outlived his own epoch, and his own pupils and the pupils of his pupils had maintained only a part of his inheritance. . . . Indeed, in a pedestrian and unphilosophic sense, a number of latter-day Rankeans behaved much like positivists" (*Consciousness and Society* 189). See also Dorothy Ross, "On the Misunderstanding of Ranke and the Origins of the Historical Profession in America."

12. The best treatment of the history of the discipline of history is Peter Novick, *That Noble Dream*, particularly 1–108 for the Progressive period. See also Thomas Haskell, *The Emergence of Professional Social Science: The American Social Science Association and the Nineteenth-Century Crisis of Authority*, for a discussion of the role of the social sciences; and Clyde W. Barrow, *Universities and the Capitalist State: Corporate Liberalism and the Reconstruction of American Higher Education*, particularly 186–220 for a recounting of the limits of academic freedom in this same period.

13. Burgess's *Foundations of Political Science* (1933) maps out his theory of race and political culture in a manner that elevates those of Teutonic origins to mastery, and which includes England and the United States as Teutonic nations.

14. In *Gunfighter Nation*, 237–42, Richard Slotkin elaborates the manner in which Griffith refers to various icons of popular culture to provide his work with its full

resonance. In "The Souls of White Folks," Walter Benn Michaels provocatively traces the process in the early twentieth century whereby "race" ceases to be a biological category, since whiteness or blackness is not necessarily apparent, and becomes transcendent as an ideological term, differentiating "real" Americans from others.

15. This response has been well documented. See "Fighting a Vicious Film: Protest against *The Birth of a Nation*," a pamphlet put together by the Boston chapter of the NAACP in 1915 in Harry Geduld, ed., *Focus on D. W. Griffith*, 94–102. See also Thomas Cripps, *Slow Fade to Black*, 41–69; Lary May, *Screening Out the Past*, 82–83, David Nasaw, *Going Out*, 202–4.

16. For a discussion of the "free speech argument" that has focused around this film since its release, see Staiger, *Interpreting Films*, 144–46.

17. Huff uses the term "circle vignette" to describe the framing device often known as the iris. I accept his term for its avoidance of the eye metaphor.

18. The psychobiographer Fawn M. Brodie strongly believes that, indeed, Stevens was sexually involved with Smith; *Thaddeus Stevens: Scourge of the South*, 86–93.

19. The ideal of the lost cause and the waving of the bloody shirt were a deep part of the mythology of the region and rooted in the antebellum aristocratic pretensions of the planters. See the excellent collection edited by Patrick Gerster and Nicholas Cords, *Myth and Southern History*. See also Daniel Joseph Singal, *The War Within*.

20. Racist theories with scientistic bases have abounded in American culture throughout the century. For example, in association with the Harlem Renaissance in the twenties, a movement largely composed of individuals of visibly mixed racial lines, there emerged a popular definition of the "new negro" as a new racial type. See Williamson, *New People*, 141–77.

21. Though I find Gunning's discussion generally illuminating, I disagree with his assertion that these cuts are in any significant way "psychologically motivated" (*D. W. Griffith* 177). Rather, I cannot help but read them as extrinsically and not intrinsically logical.

22. See Eric Foner's discussion of Tourgee and the Klan, *Reconstruction*, 430–31.

23. In Michael Rogin's treatment of the film and its metaphors within an historical frame, he quotes Griffith as noting that "the birth of a nation began with the Klan"; " 'The Sword Became a Fleshing Vision,' " 151.

24. While Griffith does not actually misrepresent Lincoln's call, within the logic of the film it seems to create the need for Southern troops. In fact, on March 6, 1861, some five weeks before Lincoln's order, the Confederate Congress authorized a hundred thousand volunteers. See James McPherson, *Ordeal By Fire*, 162–69.

Chapter 7: *Ernest Hemingway's* In Our Time *and the Objectification of Experience*

1. For provocative discussions of Stein's aesthetic, see Marianne DeKoven, *A Different Language: Gertrude Stein's Experimental Language,* and Lisa Ruddick, *Gertrude Stein and the Burial of Sense.*

2. Illuminating treatments of Pound's Imagism include James Longenbach, *Stone Cottage,* particularly 31–33; and Ronald Bush, "The Rising Metaphor: Yeats, Pound, Eliot and the Unity of Image in Postsymbolist Poetry."

3. For discussions of the politics of modernism and particularly of Stein, Pound, and Eliot, see Peter Nicholls, *Ezra Pound: Politics, Poetics, and Writing;* Michael North, "Eliot, Lukacs and the Politics of Modernism"; Louis Menand, *Discovering Modernism;* and Marcus Klein, *Foreigners: The Making of American Literature,* 7–16.

4. Hemingway actively sought this role of popularizer, never being content to remain the object of a cult of aesthetes. To an extent, this explains his tireless self-promotion. See John Raeburn, *Fame Became of Him.* Writes Raeburn, "Although [Hemingway] occasionally spoke of being willing to wait for the judgment of history, his actions belied his words. He wanted immediate public recognition and approbation and he labored to get them" (9).

5. For examples of this approach, see Linda Wagner Martin, "Introduction," *New Essays on "The Sun Also Rises,"* 5; Philip Young, *Ernest Hemingway: A Reconsideration;* Edmund Wilson, "Ernest Hemingway: Bourdon Gauge of Morale," in *The Portable Edmund Wilson,* 399; Malcolm Cowley, "Introduction," *The Portable Hemingway.* My argument is that the antecedents for this aesthetic precede the war by decades.

6. For extended discussions of Hemingway's nonfiction works see Robert O. Stephens, *Hemingway's Nonfiction: The Public Voice,* and Ronald Weber, *Hemingway's Art of Non-Fiction.* In her *The Politics and Poetics of Journalistic Narrative: The Timely and the Timeless,* Phyllis Frus lucidly shows the devices Hemingway employed to define some writing as specifically "literary" and some as nonfiction. Elaborating on these distinctions, she shows that they are not based on transcendent criteria of goodness and badness but are strictly conventional and historically recoverable (53–89).

7. See Millicent Bell's discussion of his "realist effect," his addition of facts not necessary to his plot and not provided with an explanation of their significance, in "*A Farewell to Arms:* Pseudoautobiography and Personal Metaphor." See also Frus, *Politics and Poetics of Journalistic Narrative,* 61–63, 72–73.

8. While others resort to biographical knowledge to critique Hemingway's aesthetic, I am showing why this is not sufficient. These critics do not appreciate the degree to which this image is not simply a matter of his public swagger or his relations with women but is embodied in his prose.

9. Kenneth Lynn notes in his excellent biography of Hemingway that he did see *The Birth of a Nation* (74) and met Watson. Lynn is uncertain whether Hemingway

read Watson's work, but says that, in any case, "Watsonianism was very much 'in the air' in the twenties" (227n).

10. James had many reservations regarding the behaviorist reduction, and it was this ambivalence toward the emerging scientific bias of psychology that estranged him from the mainstream of the discipline in the early twentieth century. See Daniel Bjork, *The Compromised Scientist: William James in the Development of American Psychology*.

11. My history of psychology comes largely from John M. O'Donnell, *The Origins of Behaviorism: American Psychology, 1870–1920*. See also Bruce Kuklick, *The Rise of American Philosophy: Cambridge, Massachusetts, 1860–1930*.

12. Others who note the relationship between modernism and Taylorism include Lisa Steinman, *Made in America: Science, Technology, and American Modernist Poets*; and James F. Knapp, *Literary Modernism and the Transformation of Work*. Martha Banta in her *Taylorized Lives* considers Taylor's cultural effect: she terms him both "the narratologist who formulates principles and the narrator who practices his art" (4). See also Michael Munley's review of her book, "Stories of Work for the American Century." For a consideration of the aesthetics of history in this period, see Cecelia Tichi, *Shifting Gears: Technology, Literature, Culture in Modernist America*.

13. See Donald A. Mankin, Russell E. Ames, Milton A. Grodsy, "Introduction: The Origins of Industrial and Organization Psychology," ed. Donald Mankin, et. al., *Classics in Industrial and Organizational Psychology*, 1–3; Matthew Hale Jr., *Human Science and Social Order: Hugo Munsterberg and the Origins of Applied Psychology*; Ross Stagner, "Past and Future of Industrial Psychology."

14. This total counts the two sections of "Big Two-Hearted River" as separate stories since they are individually named and are divided by chapter 15. The publication history of these various components is worth noting for what it reveals of Hemingway's intentions. All of the chapters appeared in the volume *in our time* that was published by William Bird's Three Mountain Press in the spring of 1924. This thirty-two-page collection also included two pieces that were elevated to stories in the subsequent edition of *In Our Time*. These were "A Very Short Story" and "The Revolutionist." In October of 1925, *In Our Time* was published by Boni and Liveright. It included these vignettes, altered in sequence as noted above, as well as nine stories that had appeared in various reviews, and four new compositions. The nine included "Indian Camp," "The Doctor and the Doctor's Wife," "Soldier's Home," "Mr. and Mrs. Elliot," "Big Two-Hearted River, Part One," and "Big Two-Hearted River, Part Two." The four new stories were "The End of Something," "The Three Day Blow," "The Battler," and "Cat in the Rain." In 1930 Scribner's reissued the Boni and Liveright edition with the addition of an unitalicized miniature, titled "On the Quai at Smyrna," which begins the book. Also, the Scribner's volume included a critical essay by Edmund Wilson. For various versions of the publication history of *In Our Time* see Michael S. Reynolds, ed., *Critical Essays on Ernest Hemingway's "In Our Time."*

15. For discussion of Anderson's influence on Hemingway and particularly the connection between *Winesburg, Ohio* and *In Our Time,* see Hemingway's various biographers; for example, Carlos Baker, *Ernest Hemingway: A Life Story,* 78–84; and Jeffrey Meyers, *Hemingway: A Biography,* 56, 61, 72–76. Charles Fenton, in *The Apprenticeship of Ernest Hemingway: The Early Years,* notes that "Hemingway told Fitzgerald that his first pattern had been Anderson's *Winesburg, Ohio*" (149).

16. E. R. Hagemann, " 'Only Let the Story End as Soon as Possible': Time and History in Hemingway's *In Our Time,*" Reynolds, ed., *Critical Essays on "In Our Time,"* 52–59. Hagemann makes a convincing case for Mons as the setting of both chapters.

17. See Joseph M. Flora, *Hemingway's Nick Adams,* 12–15, for a discussion of this tendency and the relative logic of it. Flora also devises an overall reading strategy for this book that is similar to my own, though I had not read Flora when, long ago, I devised mine. Since I am primarily interested in the ramifications of Hemingway's strategies, my discussion employs this reading as a point of departure. Nevertheless, I find Flora's treatment astute and valuable: see particularly 105–7.

18. Richard Godden in his *Fictions of Capital,* 39–77, ably considers the economic implications of the Hemingway phenomenon.

19. Hagemann and Robert M. Slabey, "The Structure of *In Our Time,*" in Reynolds, 76–87. Both of these essays added to my understanding of the book's chronology.

20. Robert Scholes discusses Hemingway's devices for calling upon cultural assumptions in his *Textual Power,* 25–38.

21. See Susan Beegel, *Hemingway's Craft of Omission,* for a consideration of what Hemingway deleted from his various works, though her perspective is largely to see these deletions as enhancing the art of his writing.

22. See Thomas Gossett's discussion of this practice in *Race: The History of an Idea in America;* see also George Frederickson, *The Black Image in the White Mind,* 228–55.

23. See Neil Larsen, *Modernism and Hegemony,* 35–40, for a discussion of Edouard Manet's painting *The Execution of Maximilian* (1867) and its reception in terms that illuminate the early practices of this privileging of the aesthetic. Adorno's theories of art and culture were distilled over a lifetime of writing: for an example of his theories of modernism see *The Philosophy of Modern Music,* 3–133. Lukacs's career was similarly long and prolific, and his view of art and society was continuously in transition. For his views on modernism see, for example, *Essays on Realism,* 43–113. This seems a reasonable moment to note that my use of *realism* is quite distinct from Lukacs's. His is a kind of literary ideal that allows an author to represent a totality of social relations. My term tracks a period in the cultural history of the United States and is meant to elucidate the qualities and effects of that method at that time.

24. Among those who argue for the persisting influence of Taylorism in the late

twentieth century are Dan Clawson, *Bureaucracy and the Labor Process,* and Harry Braverman, *Labor and Monopoly Capital.*

25. See Hugh Kenner, *A Homemade World,* 150, for a discussion of this reading.

26. See Malcolm Cowley's introduction to *The Portable Hemingway.*

Chapter 8: Epilogue

1. Both Gardner and Wolfe published portions of these treatises well before their noted form publication. Wolfe's dates back to the late sixties and early seventies and is to a degree a rehash of his introduction to the 1973 anthology, *The New Journalism.* Gardner's *On Moral Fiction* incorporates essays that date back to the mid-sixties.

2. Most critics of Gardner tried to find something to like about his extended essay, but almost all have found its broader assertions unacceptable. For example, Joseph Epstein, in *Commentary,* notes that Gardner aptly restates the admirable project of Tolstoy to employ "art to make us better," to contribute to "deepening our understanding of the world" (57), but he also finds that Gardner's specific judgments deriving from his theory "are easily the most disappointing parts of the book" (59). Epstein's response is typical of more conservative critics, such as Henrietta Buckmaster in the *Christian Science Monitor* and Martin Green in *Commonweal,* in accepting Gardner's general intention but finding his more particular assertions problematic. Roger Sale in the New York *Times Book Review* and Max Apple in *The Nation* were typical of liberal reviewers in their broader dismissal of Gardner's assertions, though Apple does find him "honest and wholesome" (462).

3. Wolfe's essay triggered letter after letter of annoyance in the four subsequent issues of *Harper's,* with writers as prominent as Philip Roth, T. Coraghessan Boyle, and Frederick Barthelme taking issue with Wolfe's diagnoses and prescriptions.

4. Stone's conception of the events around the assassination apparently relies on Garrison's own *On the Trail of the Assassins,* John Newman's *JFK and Vietnam,* Mark Lane's *Rush to Judgment,* and David Scheim's *Contract on America.* These antecedents are noted in Marcus Raskin, "*JFK* and the Culture of Violence," and Alexander Cockburn, "*JFK* and J.F.K."

WORKS CITED

Aaron, Daniel. *Men of Good Hope: A Story of American Progressives*. New York: Oxford University Press, 1951.

Adamson, Walter. *Hegemony and Revolution*. Berkeley and Los Angeles: University of California Press, 1980.

Adorno, Theodor. *The Philosophy of Modern Music*. Trans. Anna G. Mitchell and Wesley V. Blomster. New York: Seabury Press, 1973.

Alexander, William. *William Dean Howells: The Realist as Humanist*. New York: Burt Franklin, 1981.

Allen, Robert. *Vaudeville and the Film*. New York: Arno Press, 1980.

Ansen, David. "Interview with Oliver Stone." *Newsweek,* December 23, 1991, 49.

————. Review of *JFK*. *Newsweek,* December 23, 1991, 50.

Apple, Max. Review of *On Moral Fiction*, by John Gardner. *Nation,* April 22, 1978, 462–63.

Aronowitz, Stanley. *Science as Power: Discourse and Ideology in Modern Society*. Minneapolis: University of Minnesota Press, 1988.

Axeen, David. " 'Heroes of the Engine Room': American 'Civilization' and the War With Spain." *American Quarterly* 36 (Fall 1984): 481–502.

Baker, Carlos. *Ernest Hemingway: A Life Story*. New York: Charles Scribner's Sons, 1969.

Banta, Martha. *Taylorized Lives*. Chicago: University of Chicago Press, 1993.

Barnouw, Erik. *The Magician and the Cinema*. New York: Oxford University Press, 1982.

Barrow, Clyde W. *Universities and the Capitalist State: Corporate Liberalism and the Reconstruction of American Higher Education*. Madison: University of Wisconsin Press, 1990.

Baudry, Jean-Louis. "Ideological Effects of the Basic Cinematic Apparatus." In *Apparatus,* ed. Theresa Hak Kyung Cha. New York: Tanam Press, 1980.

Beegel, Susan. *Hemingway's Craft of Omission*. Ann Arbor: University of Michigan Press, 1988.

Bell, Michael Davitt. *The Problem of American Realism: Studies in the Cultural History of a Literary Idea*. Chicago: University of Chicago Press, 1993.

————. "The Sin of Art and the Problem of American Realism." *Prospects* 9 (1984): 115–42.

Bell, Millicent. "*A Farewell to Arms:* Pseudoautobiography and Personal Metaphor."

In *Ernest Hemingway: The Writer in Context,* ed. James Nagel. Madison: University of Wisconsin Press, 1984.

Bersani, Leo. *A Future for Astyanax: Character and Desire in Literature.* Boston: Little, Brown, 1976.

Berthoff, Warner. *The Ferment of Realism: American Literature, 1884–1919.* New York: Free Press, 1965.

Bethell, Tom. "Conspiracy to End All Conspiracies." *National Review,* December 16, 1991, 48–50.

Bjork, Daniel. *The Compromised Scientist: William James in the Development of American Psychology.* New York: Columbia University Press, 1983.

Bledstein, Burton. *The Culture of Professionalism.* New York: W. W. Norton, 1976.

Blum, John Morton. *The Republican Roosevelt.* New York: Atheneum, 1966.

Boorstin, Daniel. *The Americans: The Democratic Experience.* New York: Random House, 1973.

Borus, Daniel H. *Writing Realism.* Chapel Hill: University of North Carolina Press, 1989.

Bowlby, Rachel. *Just Looking.* New York: Methuen, 1985.

Bowser, Eileen. "Preparation for Brighton: The American Contribution." In *Cinema, 1900–1906: An Analytical Study,* ed. Roger Holman, 1–16. London: FIAF, 1982.

Braverman, Harry. *Labor and Monopoly Capital.* New York: Monthly Review Press, 1974.

Brodie, Fawn M. *Thaddeus Stevens: Scourge of the South.* New York: W. W. Norton, 1959.

Buckmaster, Henrietta. Review of *On Moral Fiction,* by John Gardner. *Christian Science Monitor,* May 8, 1978, 26.

Burch, Noel. *Life to Those Shadows.* Trans. and ed. Ben Brewster. London: British Film Institute Publishing, 1990.

———. "Porter or Ambivalence." In *Cinema, 1900–1906: An Analytical Study,* ed. Roger Holman, 101–14. London: FIAF, 1982.

———. *To the Distant Observer.* Berkeley and Los Angeles: University of California Press, 1979.

Burgess, John C. *The Foundations of Political Science.* New York: Columbia University Press, 1933.

———. "On Methods of Historical Study and Research at Columbia University." In *Methods of Teaching History,* ed. G. Stanley Hall, 215–22. Boston: D.C. Heath, 1898.

———. *Reconstruction and the Constitution.* New York: Charles Scribner's Sons, 1911.

Bush, Ronald. "The Rising Metaphor: Yeats, Pound, Eliot and the Unity of Image in Postsymbolist Poetry." In *Allegory, Myth, and Symbol,* ed. Morton Bloomfield, 371–88. Cambridge: Harvard University Press, 1981.

Bush, W. Steven. Review of *The Birth of a Nation*. In *Focus on "The Birth of a Nation,"* ed. Fred Silva, 25–28. Englewood Cliffs, N.J.: Prentice-Hall, 1971.

Cady, Edwin H. *The Light of Common Day: Realism in American Fiction*. Bloomington: Indiana University Press, 1971.

———. *The Road to Realism*. Syracuse: Syracuse University Press, 1956.

Cady, Edwin H., and Norma W. Cady, eds. *Critical Essays on W. D. Howells, 1866–1920*. Boston: G. K. Hall, 1983.

Carter, Everett. *The American Idea*. Chapel Hill: University of North Carolina Press, 1977.

———. *Howells and the Age of Realism*. Philadelphia: Lippincott, 1956.

Chafe, William H. *The American Woman*. New York: Oxford University Press, 1972.

Chandler, Alfred D. *The Visible Hand: The Managerial Revolution in American Business*. Cambridge: Belknap Press of Harvard University Press, 1977.

Chandler, Alfred D., Stuart Bruchey, and Louis Galambos, eds. *The Changing Economic Order*. New York: Harcourt, Brace and World, 1968.

Clark, Ronald. *Edison: The Man Who Made the Future*. New York: G. P. Putnam's Sons, 1977.

Clawson, Dan. *Bureaucracy and the Labor Process*. New York: Monthly Review Press, 1980.

Cockburn, Alexander. "Beat the Devil: *JFK* and J.F.K." *Nation*, January 6/13, 1992, 6–7.

Cook, David. *A History of Narrative Film*. New York: W. W. Norton, 1981.

Cowley, Malcolm. "Introduction." *The Portable Hemingway*. New York: Viking, 1944.

Cox, James M. "*The Rise of Silas Lapham:* The Business of Morals and Manners." In *New Essays on "The Rise of Silas Lapham,* ed. Donald Peese, 107–28. New York: Cambridge University Press, 1988.

Cripps, Thomas. *Slow Fade to Black*. New York: Oxford University Press, 1977.

Curti, Merle. "The Changing Concept of 'Human Nature' in the Literature of American Advertising." *Business History Review* 4 (Winter 1987): 335–57.

Darnton, Robert. *The Kiss of Lamourette: Reflections in Cultural History*. New York: W. W. Norton, 1990.

Davis, Lennard. *Resisting Novels: Ideology and Fiction*. New York: Methuen, 1987.

Davis, Mike. *Prisoners of the American Dream*. London: Verso, 1986.

DeKoven, Marianne. *A Different Language: Gertrude Stein's Experimental Language*. Madison: University of Wisconsin Press, 1983.

DeLauretis, Teresa. *Alice Doesn't: Feminism, Semiotics, Cinema*. Bloomington: Indiana University Press, 1984.

Denning, Michael. *Mechanic Accents*. London: Verso, 1987.

Dimock, Wai-Chee. "The Economy of Pain: Capitalism, Humanitarianism, and the Realistic Novel." In *New Essays on "The Rise of Silas Lapham,"* ed. Donald Pease, 67–90. New York: Cambridge University Press, 1988.

Dixon, Thomas. "Reply to the *New York Globe.*" In *Focus on "The Birth of a Nation,"* ed. Fred Silva, 75–77. Englewood Cliffs, New Jersey: Prentice-Hall, 1971.

Dreiser, Theodore. *An Amateur Laborer.* Ed. Richard Dowell. Philadelphia: University of Pennsylvania Press, 1983.

————. *American Diaries, 1902–1926.* Ed. Thomas Riggio. Philadelphia: University of Pennsylvania Press, 1982.

————. *A Selection of Uncollected Prose.* Ed. Donald Pizer. Detroit: Wayne State University Press, 1977.

————. *Sister Carrie.* Ed. Donald Pizer. New York: W. W. Norton, 1970.

————. *Tragic America.* New York: Liveright, 1931.

Dubofsky, Melvin. *Industrialism and the American Worker, 1865–1920.* 2d ed. Arlington Heights, Ill.: Harlan Davidson, 1985.

Dunning, William A. *Essays on the Civil War and Reconstruction.* New York: Macmillan, 1910.

————. *Truth in History.* New York: Columbia University Press, 1937.

Eble, Kenneth. *Old Clemens and W.D.H.* Baton Rouge: Louisiana State University Press, 1985.

————, ed. *Howells: A Century of Criticism.* Dallas: Southern Methodist University Press, 1962.

Edison, Thomas. *The Diary and Sundry Observations of Thomas Alva Edison.* Ed. Dagobert Runes. New York: Greenwood Press, 1968.

Ehrenreich, Barbara, and John Ehrenreich. "The Professional-Managerial Class." In *Between Labor and Capital,* ed. Pat Walker, 5–45. Boston: South End Press, 1979.

Eliot, T. S. *Selected Essays.* New York: Harcourt, Brace and World, 1950.

Epstein, Joseph. "Observations." *Commentary,* July 1978, 57–60.

Ewen, Elizabeth. "City Lights: Immigrant Women and the Rise of the Movies." *Signs* 5, supplement (1980): S45–S65.

Ewen, Stuart. *Captains of Consciousness.* New York: McGraw-Hill, 1976.

Fell, John. *A History of Films.* New York: Holt, Rinehart and Winston, 1979.

————, ed. *Film Before Griffith.* Berkeley and Los Angeles: University of California Press, 1983.

Fenton, Charles. *The Apprenticeship of Ernest Hemingway: The Early Years.* New York: Compass, 1958.

Fielding, Raymond. *The American Newsreel, 1911–1967.* Norman: University of Oklahoma Press, 1967.

————. "Hale's Tours: Ultrarealism in the Pre-1910 Motion Picture." In *Film before Griffith,* ed. John Fell, 116–30. Berkeley and Los Angeles: University of California Press, 1983.

Fischer, Lucy. "The Lady Vanishes: Women, Magic and the Movies." In *Film Before Griffith,* ed. John Fell, 339–54. Berkeley and Los Angeles: University of California Press, 1983.

————. *Shot/Countershot.* Princeton: Princeton University Press, 1989.

Fisher, Philip. "Appearing and Disappearing in Public: Social Space in Late-

Nineteenth-Century Literature and Culture." In *Reconstructing American Literary History*, ed. Sacvan Bercovitch, 155–88. Cambridge: Harvard University Press, 1986.

——— . *Hard Facts*. New York: Oxford University Press, 1985.

Fishkin, Shelley Fisher. *From Fact to Fiction*. Baltimore: Johns Hopkins University Press, 1985.

Flora, Joseph M. *Hemingway's Nick Adams*. Baton Rouge: Louisiana State University Press, 1982.

Foner, Eric. *Reconstruction*. New York: Harper and Row, 1988.

——— , ed. *The New American History*. Philadelphia: Temple University Press, 1990.

Formisano, Ronald P., and Constance K. Burns, eds. *Boston 1700–1980: The Evolution of Urban Politics*. Westport, Conn.: Greenwood Press, 1984.

Fraser, Steven. *Labor Will Rule: Sidney Hillman and the Rise of American Labor*. New York: Free Press, 1991.

Frederickson, George. *The Black Image in the White Mind*. New York: Harper and Row, 1972.

Frisch, Michael H., and Daniel J. Walkowitz, eds. *Working-Class America*. Urbana: University of Illinois Press, 1983.

Frus, Phyllis. *The Politics and Poetics of Journalistic Narrative: The Timely and The Timeless*. New York: Cambridge University Press, 1994.

Fulton, A. R. *Motion Pictures: The Development of an Art*. Norman: University of Oklahoma Press, 1980.

Gardner, John. *On Moral Fiction*. New York: Basic Books, 1978.

Garrison, Jim. *On the Trail of the Assassins*. New York: Warner Books, 1992.

Gartenberg, Jon. "Camera Movement in Edison and Biograph Films, 1900–1906." In *Cinema, 1900–1906: An Analytical Study*, ed. Roger Holman, 169–81. London: FIAF, 1982.

Gaudreault, André. "Detours in Film Narrative: The Development of Cross-Cutting." *Cinema Journal* 19 (Fall 1979): 39–59.

Genovese, Eugene. *The Political Economy of Slavery*. New York: Vintage, 1967.

Gerster, Patrick, and Nicholas Cords, eds. *Myth and Southern History*. Urbana: University of Illinois Press, 1989.

Gibson, William. *William Dean Howells*. Minneapolis: University of Minnesota Press, 1967.

Godden, Richard. *Fictions of Capital*. Cambridge: Cambridge University Press, 1990.

Gossett, Thomas F. *Race: The History of an Idea in America*. New York: Schocken Books, 1965.

Graham, Cooper C., Steven Higgins, Elaine Mancini, and João Luiz Vieira. *D. W. Griffith and the Biograph Company*. Metuchen, N.J.: Scarecrow Press, 1985.

Gramsci, Antonio. *Selections from the Prison Notebooks*. Ed. and trans. Quentin Hoare and Geoffrey Nowell Smith. New York: International Publishers, 1971.

Green, Martin. "Tromping on Babies." *Commonweal*, August 18, 1978, 535–36.

Griffith, D. W. "Reply to the *New York Globe.*" In *Focus on "The Birth of a Nation,"* ed. Fred Silva, 77–79. Englewood Cliffs, N.J.: Prentice-Hall, 1971.

———. "Some Prophecies: Film and Theatre, Screenwriting, Education." In *Focus on D. W. Griffith,* ed. Harry Geduld, 34–35. Englewood Cliffs, N.J.: Prentice-Hall, 1971.

Gunning, Tom. "The Cinema of Attraction: Early Film, Its Spectator and the Avant-Garde." *Wide-Angle* 8, nos. 3–4 (1986): 63–71.

———. *D. W. Griffith and the Origins of American Narrative Film.* Urbana: University of Illinois Press, 1990.

———. " 'Primitive' Cinema—A Frame Up? or The Trick's on Us." *Cinema Journal* 28 (Winter 1989): 3–12.

Haber, Samuel. *Efficiency and Uplift: Scientific Management in the Progressive Era.* Chicago: University of Chicago Press, 1964.

Habermas, Jürgen. *Towards a Rational Society.* Trans. Jeremy Shapiro. Boston: Beacon Press, 1970.

Hale, Matthew, Jr. *Human Science and Social Order: Hugo Munsterberg and the Origins of Applied Psychology.* Philadelphia: Temple University Press, 1980.

Handlin, David. *American Architecture.* London: Thames and Hudson, 1985.

Hansen, Miriam. *Babel and Babylon.* Cambridge: Harvard University Press, 1991.

———. "Early Silent Cinema: Whose Public Sphere?" *New German Critique* 29 (Winter 1983): 147–94.

Harris, Sharon M. *Rebecca Harding Davis and American Realism.* Philadelphia: University of Pennsylvania Press, 1991.

Hartsock, Nancy C. M. *Money, Sex, and Power.* New York: Longman, 1983.

Haskell, Thomas. *The Emergence of Professional Social Science: The American Social Science Association and the Nineteenth-Century Crisis of Authority.* Urbana: University of Illinois Press, 1977.

Hays, Samuel. *Conservation and the Gospel of Efficiency.* New York: Atheneum, 1974.

———. *The Response to Industrialism.* Chicago: University of Chicago Press, 1957.

Hemingway, Ernest. *Death in the Afternoon.* New York: Charles Scribner's Sons, 1960.

———. *Green Hills of Africa.* New York: Charles Scribner's Sons, 1935.

———. *In Our Time.* New York: Charles Scribner's Sons, 1958.

———. "A Letter to Bernard Kalb." *Saturday Review,* September 6, 1952, 11.

———. *Men at War.* New York: Charles Scribner's Sons, 1942.

———. "Monologue to the Maestro: A High Seas Letter." In *By-Line Ernest Hemingway,* ed. William White, 213–20. New York: Charles Scribner's Sons, 1967.

———. *A Moveable Feast.* New York: Charles Scribner's Sons, 1964.

———. "Old Newsman Writes." *Esquire,* December 1934, 26–34.

———. *Selected Letters.* Ed. Carlos Baker. New York: Charles Scribner's Sons, 1981.

Henderson, Robert M. *D. W. Griffith: The Years at Biograph.* New York: Farrar, Straus and Giroux, 1970.

Hendricks, Gordon. *Origins of the American Film.* New York: Arno Press, 1972.

Higham, John. *Strangers in the Land.* New York: Atheneum, 1966.

Hoffman, Michael. *The Subversive Vision.* Port Washington, N.Y.: Kennikat Press, 1972.

Hofstadter, Richard. *The Age of Reform: From Bryan to F.D.R.* New York: Alfred A. Knopf, 1955.

Horwitz, Howard. *By the Law of Nature: Form and Value in Nineteenth-Century America.* New York: Oxford University Press, 1991.

Howard, June. *Form and History in American Literary Naturalism.* Chapel Hill: University of North Carolina Press, 1985.

Howells, William Dean. "Certain Dangerous Tendencies in American Life." *Atlantic Monthly* 42 (October 1878): 385–402.

———. *Criticism and Fiction and Other Essays.* Ed. Clara Marburg Kirk and Rudolf Kirk. New York: New York University Press, 1959.

———. *Editor's Study.* Ed. James W. Simpson. Troy, N.Y.: Whitston, 1983.

———. *The Rise of Silas Lapham.* New York: Penguin, 1971.

———. *Selected Letters.* Vol. 3. Ed. Robert C. Leitz, with Richard H. Ballinger and Christoph K. Lohmann. Boston: Twayne, 1980.

———. *Selected Letters.* Vol. 4. Ed. Thomas Wortham with Christoph K. Lohmann and David J. Nordloh. Boston: Twayne, 1981.

———. *William Dean Howells as Critic.* Ed. Edwin Cady. Boston: Routledge and Kegan Paul, 1973.

Huff, Theodore. *A Shot Analysis of D. W. Griffith's "The Birth of a Nation."* New York: Museum of Modern Art Film Library, 1961.

Hughes, H. Stuart. *Consciousness and Society.* New York: Vintage, 1961.

Hughes, Thomas. *American Genesis.* New York: Viking, 1989.

Jacobs, Lewis. *The Rise of the American Film, a Critical History.* New York: Teacher's College Press, 1968.

James, Henry. *The Art of the Novel.* Ed. R. P. Blackmur. Boston: Northeastern University Press, 1984.

———. *The Future of the Novel.* Ed. Leon Edel. New York: Vintage, 1956.

James, William. *The Principles of Psychology.* Vol. 2. New York: Dover, 1950.

Jenkins, Reese. "Elements of Style: Continuities in Edison's Thinking." *Annals of the New York Academy of Sciences* 20 (January 1987): 149–62.

———. *Images and Enterprise.* Baltimore: Johns Hopkins University Press, 1975.

———, ed. *The Papers of Thomas Edison.* Vol. 1. Baltimore: Johns Hopkins University Press, 1989.

Jowett, Garth. *Film: The Democratic Art.* Boston: Little, Brown, 1976.

Kaplan, Amy. *The Social Construction of American Realism.* Chicago: University of Chicago Press, 1988.

Kauffmann, Stanley. Review of *JFK. New Republic,* January 27, 1992, 26–28.

———. "Yes, *JFK* Again." *New Republic,* April 6, 1992, 26–27.

Kelly, Karol L. *Models for the Multitudes: Social Values in the American Popular Novel, 1850–1920.* Westport, Conn.: Greenwood Press, 1987.

Kenner, Hugh. *A Homemade World*. New York: Alfred A. Knopf, 1975.

Kirby, Jack Temple. *Darkness at the Dawning: Race and Reform in the Progressive South*. Philadelphia: Lippincott, 1972.

Klawans, Stewart. Review of *JFK*. *Nation*, January 20, 1992, 62–63.

Klein, Marcus. *Foreigners: The Making of American Literature*. Chicago: University of Chicago Press, 1981.

Knapp, James F. *Literary Modernism and the Transformation of Work*. Evanston, Ill.: Northwestern University Press, 1988.

Kolko, Gabriel. *The Triumph of Conservatism*. Chicago: Quadrangle Books, 1967.

Kopkind, Andrew. Review of *JFK*. *Nation*, January 20, 1992, 40–41.

Koszarski, Richard. *An Evening's Entertainment: The Age of the Silent Picture, 1915–1928*. New York: Charles Scribner's Sons, 1990.

Kuklick, Bruce. *The Rise of American Philosophy: Cambridge, Massachusetts, 1860–1930*. New Haven: Yale University Press, 1977.

Lane, Mark. *Rush to Judgment*. New York: Dell, 1976.

Larsen, Neil. *Modernism and Hegemony*. Minneapolis: University of Minnesota Press, 1990.

Lasch, Christopher. *The Culture of Narcissism: American Life in an Age of Diminishing Expectations*. New York: Norton, 1978.

Lathrop, George. "Edison's Kinetograph." In *The Movies in Our Midst*, ed. Gerald Mast, 8–12. Chicago: University of Chicago Press, 1982.

Leach, William R. "Transformation in a Culture of Consumption: Women and Department Stores, 1890–1925." *Journal of American History* 71 (September 1984): 319–42.

Lears, T. J. Jackson. *No Place of Grace: Antimodernism and the Transformation of American Culture*. New York: Pantheon, 1981.

———. "Reality in America, Cont'd." *New Republic*, December 4, 1989, 34–38.

Lehan, Richard. *Theodore Dreiser: His World and His Ideas*. Carbondale: Southern Illinois University Press, 1969.

Lentricchia, Frank. "Lyric in the Culture of Capital." In *Subject to History*, ed. David Simpson, 191–216. Ithaca: Cornell University Press, 1991.

Levine, Lawrence. *Highbrow/Lowbrow*. Cambridge: Harvard University Press, 1988.

Levy, David. "Edison Sales Policy and the Continuous Action Film." In *Film Before Griffith*, ed. John Fell, 207–22. Berkeley and Los Angeles: University of California Press, 1983.

———. "Edwin S. Porter and the Origins of American Narrative Film, 1894–1907." Ph.D. diss., McGill University, 1983.

———. "Reconstituted Newsreels, Re-enactments and the American Narrative Film." In *Cinema, 1900–1906: An Analytical Study*, ed. Roger Holman, 243–60. London: FIAF, 1982.

Lewis, R. W. B. *The American Adam: Innocence, Tragedy and Tradition in the Nineteenth Century*. Chicago: University of Chicago Press, 1955.

Lingeman, Richard. *Theodore Dreiser*. New York: G. P. Putnam's, 1986.

Link, Arthur, and Richard McCormick. *Progressivism*. Arlington Heights, Ill.: Harlan Davidson, 1983.

Livingston, James. *The Origins of the Federal Reserve System: Money, Class, and Corporate Capitalism, 1890–1913*. Ithaca: Cornell University Press, 1989.

Longenbach, James. *Stone Cottage*. New York: Oxford University Press, 1988.

Lukács, Georg. *Essays on Realism*. Ed. Rodney Livingstone. Trans. David Fernbach. Cambridge: MIT Press, 1981.

Lynn, Kenneth S. *Hemingway*. New York: Simon and Schuster, 1987.

———. *William Dean Howells: An American Life*. New York: Harcourt Brace Jovanovich, 1971.

Mankin, Donald A., Russell E. Ames, Milton A. Grodsy, eds. *Classics in Industrial and Organizational Psychology*. Oak Park, Ill.: Moore Publishing, 1980.

Marcuse, Herbert. *Eros and Civilization*. Boston: Beacon Press, 1966.

Marey, Etienne Jules. *Movement*. New York: Arno Press, 1972.

Marks, William Dennis, Harrison Allen, and Francis Dercum. *Animal Locomotion: The Muybridge Work at the University of Pennsylvania*. New York: Arno Press, 1973.

Martin, Linda Wagner. "Introduction." *New Essays on "The Sun Also Rises,"* ed. Linda Wagner Martin. New York: Cambridge University Press, 1987.

Marx, Karl. *The Economic and Philosophic Manuscripts of 1844*. Ed. Dirk J. Struik. New York: International Publishers, 1964.

Marx, Leo. *The Machine in the Garden: Technology and the Pastoral Idea in America*. New York: Oxford University Press, 1966.

Mast, Gerald. *A Short History of the Movies*. Indianapolis: Bobbs-Merrill, 1975.

May, Lary. *Screening Out the Past*. New York: Oxford University Press, 1980.

Mayne, Judith. *Private Novels, Public Films*. Athens: University of Georgia Press, 1985.

McCormick, Richard. *The Party Period and Public Policy*. New York: Oxford University Press, 1986.

———. "Public Life in Industrial America, 1877–1919." In *The New American History*, ed. Eric Foner, 93–118. Philadelphia: Temple University Press, 1990.

McIntosh, Ned. Review of *The Birth of a Nation*. In *Focus on "The Birth of a Nation,"* ed. Fred Silva, 33–36. Englewood Cliff, N.J.: Prentice-Hall, 1971.

McPherson, James. *Ordeal By Fire*. New York: Alfred A. Knopf, 1982.

Mellow, James. *Hemingway*. Boston: Houghton Mifflin, 1992.

Menand, Louis. *Discovering Modernism*. New York: Oxford University Press, 1987.

Meyer, Donald. *The Protestant Search for Political Realism*. Middletown, Conn.: Wesleyan University Press, 1988.

Meyers, Jeffrey. *Hemingway: A Biography*. New York: Harper and Row, 1985.

Michaels, Walter Benn. "An American Tragedy, or the Promise of American Life." *Representations* 21 (Winter 1988): 71–98.

———. *The Gold Standard and the Logic of Capitalism: American Literature at the Turn of the Century.* Berkeley and Los Angeles: University of California Press, 1987.

————. "The Souls of White Folk." In *Literature and the Body,* ed. Elaine Scarry, 185–209. Baltimore: Johns Hopkins University Press, 1988.

Millard, André. *Edison and the Business of Innovation.* Baltimore: Johns Hopkins University Press, 1990.

Mills, C. Wright. *White Collar.* New York: Oxford University Press, 1951.

Moers, Ellen. *Two Dreisers.* New York: Viking, 1969.

Monteiro, George, and Brenda Murphy, eds. *John Hay-Howells Letters.* Boston: Twayne, 1980.

Montgomery, David. *Beyond Equality: Labor and the Radical Republicans, 1862–1872.* Urbana: University of Illinois Press, 1981.

————. *The Fall of the House of Labor: The Workplace, the State, and American Labor Activism, 1865–1925.* New York: Cambridge University Press, 1987.

————. *Workers' Control in America.* New York: Cambridge University Press, 1979.

Mott, Frank Luther. *Golden Multitudes: The Story of Best Sellers in the United States.* New York: R. R. Bowker, 1947.

Mowry, George. *The Era of Theodore Roosevelt and the Birth of Modern America.* New York: Harper and Row, 1962.

Munley, Michael. "Stories of Work for the American Century." *American Quarterly* 46, no. 3 (1994): 462–70.

Musser, Charles. "The American Vitagraph, 1897–1901." In *Film before Griffith,* ed. John Fell, 22–66. Berkeley and Los Angeles: University of California Press, 1983.

————. *Before the Nickelodeon.* Berkeley and Los Angeles: University of California Press, 1991.

————. "Before the Nickelodeon." Ph.D. diss., New York University, 1987.

————. "The Early Cinema of Edwin Porter." *Cinema Journal* 19 (Fall 1979): 1–38.

————. *The Emergence of Cinema: The American Screen to 1907.* New York: Charles Scribner's Sons, 1991.

————. *Guide to Motion Picture Catalogues by American Producers and Distributors, 1894–1908.* Frederick, Md.: University Publications of America, 1985.

Musser, Charles, with Carol Nelson. *High-Class Moving Pictures: Lyman H. Howe and the Forgotten Era of Travelling Exhibition.* Princeton: Princeton University Press, 1990.

Nasaw, David. *Going Out.* New York: Basic Books, 1993.

Nelson, Daniel. *Frederick W. Taylor and the Rise of Scientific Management.* Madison: University of Wisconsin Press, 1980.

Newman, John. *JFK and Vietnam.* New York: Warner, 1992.

Nicholls, Peter. *Ezra Pound: Politics, Poetics, and Writing.* London: Macmillan, 1984.

Nichols, Bill. *Ideology and the Image.* Bloomington: Indiana University Press, 1981.

Niver, Kemp. *The First Twenty Years.* Los Angeles: Locare Research Group, 1968.

Noble, David F. *America By Design: Science Technology and the Rise of Corporate Capitalism.* New York: Oxford University Press, 1977.

Norris, James D. *Advertising and the Transformation of American Society, 1865–1920.* New York: Greenwood Press, 1990.

North, Michael. "Eliot, Lukacs and the Politics of Modernism." In *T. S. Eliot: The Modernist in History,* ed. Ronald Bush, 169–90. New York: Cambridge University Press, 1991.

Novick, Peter. *That Noble Dream.* New York: Cambridge University Press, 1988.

Oakes, Jeannie. *Keeping Track.* New Haven: Yale University Press, 1985.

O'Donnell, John M. *The Origins of Behaviorism: American Psychology, 1870–1920.* New York: New York University Press, 1985.

Ohmann, Richard. *Politics of Letters.* Middletown, Conn.: Wesleyan University Press, 1987.

Orvell, Miles. *The Real Thing: Imitation and Authenticity in American Culture, 1880–1940.* Chapel Hill: University of North Carolina Press, 1989.

Painter, Nell Irvin. "'Social Equality,' Miscegenation, Labor and Power." In *The Evolution of Southern Culture,* ed. Numan Bartley, 47–67. Athens: University of Georgia Press, 1988.

————. *Standing at Armageddon: The United States, 1877–1919.* New York: W. W. Norton, 1977.

Pease, Donald, ed. *New Essays on "The Rise of Silas Lapham."* New York: Cambridge University Press, 1991.

Peiss, Kathy. *Cheap Amusements.* Philadelphia: Temple University Press, 1986.

Petrey, Sandy. "The Language of Realism, The Language of False Consciousness: A Reading of *Sister Carrie.*" *Novel* 10 (Winter 1977): 101–13.

Phillips, Ulrich Bonnell. *American Negro Slavery.* New York: Appleton, 1918.

Pizer, Donald. *Realism and Naturalism in Nineteenth-Century American Literature.* Carbondale: Southern Illinois University Press, 1966.

————, ed. *New Essays on "Sister Carrie."* New York: Cambridge, 1991.

Pratt, George. "No Magic, No Mystery, No Sleight of Hand." In *The American Film Industry,* ed. Tino Balio, 46–58. Madison: University of Wisconsin Press, 1976.

Price, Brian. "Frank and Lillian Gilbreth and the Motion Study Controversy, 1907–1930." In *A Mental Revolution,* ed. Daniel Nelson, 58–76. Columbus: Ohio State University Press, 1992.

Raeburn, John. *Fame Became of Him.* Bloomington: Indiana University Press, 1984.

Raskin, Marcus. "*JFK* and the Culture of Violence." *American Historical Review* 97 (April 1992): 487–99.

Reynolds, Michael S., ed. *Critical Essays on Ernest Hemingway's "In Our Time."* Boston: G. K. Hall, 1983.

Rogin, Michael Paul. "'The Sword Became a Flashing Vision': D. W. Griffith's *The Birth of a Nation.*" *Representations* 9 (Winter 1985): 150–95.

Rosenstone, Robert. "Historical Fact/Historical Film." *American Historical Review* 97 (April 1992): 506–11.

Rosensweig, Roy. *Eight Hours for What We Will: Workers and Leisure in an Industrial City, 1870–1920.* New York: Cambridge University Press, 1983.

Ross, Dorothy. "On the Misunderstanding of Ranke and the Origins of the Historical Profession in America." In *Leopold von Ranke and the Shaping of the Historical Discipline,* eds. Georg G. Iggers and James W. Powell, 154–69. Syracuse: Syracuse University Press, 1990.

Ruddick, Lisa. *Gertrude Stein and the Burial of Sense.* Ithaca: Cornell University Press, 1992.

Sale, Roger. Review of *On Moral Fiction,* by John Gardner. *New York Times Book Review,* April 16, 1978, 10.

Salt, Barry. "Film Form, 1900–1906." *Sight and Sound* 47 (Summer 1978): 148–53.

Salzman, Jack, ed. *Theodore Dreiser: The Critical Reception.* New York: David Lewis, 1973.

Scheim, David. *Contract on America.* New York: Zebra, 1989.

Schickel, Richard. *D. W. Griffith.* New York: Simon and Schuster, 1984.

Scholes, Robert. *Textual Power.* New Haven: Yale University Press, 1985.

Seltzer, Mark. *Bodies and Machines.* New York: Routledge, 1992.

Shannon, David A. *Between the Wars, 1919–1941.* Boston: Houghton Mifflin, 1979.

Singal, Daniel Joseph. *The War Within.* Chapel Hill: University of North Carolina Press, 1982.

Sklar, Martin. *The Corporate Reconstruction of American Capitalism, 1890–1916.* New York: Cambridge University Press, 1988.

Sklar, Robert. *Movie-Made America.* New York: Vintage, 1976.

Slotkin, Richard. *The Fatal Environment.* New York: Atheneum, 1985.

———. *Gunfighter Nation.* New York: Atheneum, 1992.

Smith, Henry Nash. *Virgin Land: The American West as Symbol and Myth.* Cambridge: Harvard University Press, 1950.

Spencer, Herbert. *First Principles.* New York: Appleton, 1898.

Stagner, Ross. "Past and Future of Industrial Psychology," *Professional Psychology* 13 (December 1982): 892–903.

Staiger, Janet. *Interpreting Films.* Princeton: Princeton University Press, 1992.

Steel, Ronald. "Mr. Smith Goes to the Twilight Zone." *New Republic,* February 3, 1992, 30–32.

Steinman, Lisa. *Made in America: Science, Technology, and American Modernist Poets.* New Haven: Yale University Press, 1987.

Stephens, Robert O. *Ernest Hemingway: The Critical Reception.* New York: Burt Franklin, 1977.

———. *Hemingway's Nonfiction: The Public Voice.* Chapel Hill: University of North Carolina Press, 1968.

Story, Ronald. *The Forging of an Aristocracy: Harvard and the Boston Upper Class, 1800–1870.* Middletown, Conn.: Wesleyan University Press, 1980.

Susman, Warren I. *Culture as History.* New York: Pantheon, 1984.

Teaford, Jon C. *The Unheralded Triumph: City Government in America, 1870–1900.* Baltimore: Johns Hopkins University Press, 1984.

Tebbel, John. *A History of Book Publishing in the United States.* Vol. 2. New York: R. R. Bowker, 1975.

Thernstrom, Stephen. *The Other Bostonians.* Cambridge: Harvard University Press, 1973.

Tichi, Cecelia. *Shifting Gears: Technology, Literature, Culture in Modernist America.* Chapel Hill: University of North Carolina Press, 1987.

Trachtenberg, Alan. *The Incorporation of America.* New York: Hill and Wang, 1982.

———. "Who Narrates? Dreiser's Presence in *Sister Carrie.*" In *New Essays on "Sister Carrie,"* ed. Donald Pizer, 87–122. New York: Cambridge University Press, 1991.

Trelease, Allen W. *White Terror: The Ku Klux Klan Conspiracy and Southern Reconstruction.* New York: Harper and Row, 1971.

Turner, Frederick Jackson. *The Turner Thesis.* Ed. George Rogers Taylor. Lexington, Mass.: D. C. Heath, 1972.

Tyrell, Ian. *The Absent Marx: Class Analysis and Liberal History in Twentieth-Century America.* New York: Greenwood Press, 1986.

Updike, John. "Howells as an Anti-Novelist." *New Yorker,* July 13, 1987, 78–88.

Vance, Mark. Review of *The Birth of a Nation.* In *Focus on "The Birth of a Nation,"* ed. Fred Silva, 22–25. Englewood Cliff, N.J.: Prentice-Hall, 1971.

Vardac, Nicholas. *Stage to Screen.* Cambridge: Harvard University Press, 1949.

Veblen, Thorstein. *The Theory of the Leisure Class.* New York: New American Library, 1954.

Wachhorst, Wyn. *Thomas Alva Edison: An American Myth.* Cambridge: MIT Press, 1982.

Warner, Sam Bass, Jr. *Streetcar Suburbs: The Process of Growth in Boston, 1870–1900.* Cambridge: Harvard University Press, 1962.

Watson, J. B. *Psychology from the Standpoint of a Behaviorist.* Dover, N.H.: Frances Pinter, 1983.

Watts, Steven. "The Idiocy of American Studies: Poststructuralism, Language, and the Politics of Self-Fulfillment." *American Quarterly* 43, no. 4 (1991): 625–60.

Weber, Ronald. *Hemingway's Art of Non-Fiction.* New York: St. Martin's, 1990.

Weinstein, James. *The Corporate Ideal of the Liberal State.* Boston: Beacon Press, 1968.

White, Hayden. *Tropics of Discourse.* Baltimore: Johns Hopkins University Press, 1978.

Wicker, Tom. "*JFK* and History." *New York Times,* December 15, 1991, sec. 2, 1.

Wiebe, Robert. *The Search for Order, 1877–1920.* New York: Hill and Wang, 1967.

Williams, Martin. *D. W. Griffith.* New York: Oxford University Press, 1980.

Williams, Raymond. *The Sociology of Culture*. New York: Schocken Books, 1982.

Williamson, Joel. *After Slavery*. Chapel Hill: University of North Carolina Press, 1965.

———. *The Crucible of Race*. New York: Oxford University Press, 1984.

———. *New People*. New York: Free Press, 1980.

Wilson, Christopher. *The Labor of Words: Literary Professionalism in The Progressive Era*. Athens: University of Georgia Press, 1985.

Wilson, Edmund. "Ernest Hemingway: Bourdon Gauge of Morale." In *The Portable Edmund Wilson*, ed. Lewis Dabney. New York: Viking, 1983.

Wolfe, Tom. *The New Journalism*. New York: Harper and Row, 1973.

———. "Stalking the Billion-Footed Beast." *Harper's*, March 1990, 4–6.

Young, Philip. *Ernest Hemingway: A Reconsideration*. University Park: Pennsylvania State University Press, 1966.

Ziff, Larzer. *The American 1890s: The Life and Times of a Lost Generation*. New York: Viking, 1966.

INDEX